AstroPaws

AstroPaws

Matthew Petchinsky

CONTENTS

AstroPaws: The Celestial Guide to Your Dog's Zodiac Destiny
By: Matthew Petchinsky

Introduction: Welcome to AstroPaws

Dogs have long been known as loyal companions, but what if I told you that there's more to your furry friend than meets the eye? Just like humans, dogs have personalities shaped by the stars. Their behaviors, quirks, and unique characteristics can be linked to the zodiac, offering a deeper understanding of their nature and how they interact with the world. Welcome to *AstroPaws*, a journey into the fascinating world of dog astrology.

The Purpose of This Book

At its core, *AstroPaws* seeks to bridge the connection between the ancient wisdom of astrology and the loving bond we share with our dogs. This book is not just a guide to understanding how your dog's zodiac sign influences their behavior, but also a tool to help strengthen your relationship through the cosmos' guidance. Whether you're looking for insight into your dog's personality, how they communicate, or even ways to improve training and care, astrology offers a new perspective on the unique connection you share with your four-legged companion.

Dogs, like humans, are influenced by the planets, stars, and celestial events. Each zodiac sign carries its own set of traits, strengths, and challenges, and by understanding your dog's astrological sign, you can tailor your approach to better meet their needs. This isn't just about fun or novelty—it's about fostering a deeper, more harmonious relationship with your pet by tapping into the cosmic forces that influence them.

How to Use This Book

AstroPaws is designed to be accessible to both astrology enthusiasts and newcomers alike. You don't need to be an expert in star charts or horoscopes to use this book effectively. Here's how you can make the most of it:

1. **Identify Your Dog's Zodiac Sign:** Each dog, like each person, is born under a particular zodiac sign based on their birth date.

If you know your dog's birthday, you can easily find their sign. If you don't, try estimating their personality based on the descriptions provided for each sign.

2. **Explore the Traits of Your Dog's Zodiac Sign:** Once you know your dog's sign, dive into the chapters dedicated to each zodiac. Each chapter provides a detailed overview of your dog's general personality, strengths, quirks, and how they interact with their environment. From playful Aries pups to the steadfast loyalty of Taurus dogs, you'll find in-depth descriptions of their core nature.

3. **Understanding Behavioral Patterns:** Have you ever wondered why your dog is particularly independent or especially clingy? Why do they prefer certain toys, routines, or even have unique responses to commands? Understanding your dog's astrological traits can help explain these tendencies. For example, Gemini dogs are known for their adaptability and love of learning new tricks, while Cancers might need more emotional support and a stable environment.

4. **Practical Tips for Training and Care:** Astrology doesn't just help us understand personality—it also gives us insight into how best to train and care for our dogs. Each zodiac chapter includes tips on what motivates each sign, how to approach training, and the types of environments they thrive in. For instance, an active Sagittarius dog might need more outdoor time and adventure, while a Virgo dog might respond better to structured training and routines.

5. **Compatibility Between Dog and Owner:** Not only can astrology help you understand your dog better, but it can also reveal how your astrological sign interacts with theirs. We've included sections on owner-dog compatibility, offering insight into how your zodiac sign shapes your relationship with your dog. Are you a Capricorn who enjoys structure and discipline, paired with a

free-spirited Aquarius dog? This book will provide guidance on balancing those differences and creating a harmonious dynamic.

6. **Astrological Events and Your Dog:** Beyond zodiac signs, this book also touches on how larger celestial events—such as lunar phases, eclipses, and planetary transits—can affect your dog's mood and behavior. You'll learn how to tune into these cosmic cycles to understand why your dog might be more excitable during a full moon or more restless during certain planetary alignments.

A Cosmic Approach to Canine Companionship

Dogs are creatures of instinct and emotion, yet they are also deeply connected to the energies of the cosmos. *AstroPaws* gives you the tools to tap into these astrological insights, allowing you to better care for and bond with your dog. Whether you're curious about your dog's sun sign or simply looking for new ways to understand their behavior, this book is your guide to a more enlightened and compassionate relationship with your canine companion.

Through the lens of astrology, *AstroPaws* helps you see your dog in a new light—as a being influenced by the stars, with a unique personality shaped by celestial forces. Let the stars guide you as you embark on this journey, strengthening the bond you share with your dog and discovering the cosmic connections that make them who they are.

Welcome to *AstroPaws*—where the wisdom of the cosmos meets the love of your pet!

Chapter 1: History of Astrology and Canines

Astrology is an ancient practice, rooted in humanity's desire to understand the universe and its influence on life on Earth. For millennia, people have looked to the stars and planets to find meaning, predict events, and explain the mysteries of existence. But while astrology has often been associated with human fate, it has also held a special place for animals—creatures with whom we share our lives, including our most loyal companions: dogs. In this chapter, we will explore the rich history of astrology, its ancient connections to animals, and the evolution of dog astrology as a modern interpretation of this celestial art.

The Origins of Astrology

Astrology is believed to have originated in ancient Mesopotamia, where the Sumerians, Babylonians, and Assyrians closely observed the movement of the stars and planets. They saw these celestial bodies as deities or cosmic forces that influenced everything from seasonal changes to human destinies. Around 3,000 BCE, the Babylonians began developing the zodiac, a system that divided the sky into twelve equal sections, each associated with a constellation.

As astrology evolved, these zodiac constellations came to represent archetypal energies or characteristics that influenced individuals born under their sign. The ancient Greeks later adopted this system, blending it with their own philosophical and astronomical beliefs. The Greeks, particularly through the works of scholars like Ptolemy, formalized astrology into a sophisticated system that connected celestial movements to events on Earth.

Though astrology was initially focused on human affairs—predicting the outcomes of battles, the success of crops, or the fortunes of rulers—it didn't take long for its scope to expand. Ancient cultures believed that animals, too, were influenced by the stars, and their behavior could be understood through astrological principles.

Astrology and the Animal Kingdom

In many ancient societies, animals were considered sacred or symbolic representations of gods and cosmic forces. In Egypt, for example, the god Anubis, often depicted as a jackal or a dog, was associated with protection, mummification, and the afterlife. Similarly, the zodiac sign of Leo, symbolized by the lion, and Taurus, represented by the bull, show how animals became woven into the astrological narrative.

Astrologers began to recognize that animals, just like humans, could be influenced by celestial bodies. Certain animals were associated with specific zodiac signs due to their characteristics. For example, the dog, with its loyalty and protective nature, became associated with signs like Cancer, which represents nurturing and care, or Aries, which is known for courage and protectiveness.

In ancient Rome, astrologers would often cast horoscopes not just for people, but also for animals, especially those with significant roles, such as warhorses, hunting dogs, and even livestock. The Romans believed that the fate of these animals, particularly dogs, could be read in the stars, as their well-being was crucial to the success of human endeavors, especially in war and survival.

The Evolution of Dog Astrology

While astrology's connection to animals has ancient roots, the specific study of dog astrology is a more recent phenomenon. As dogs became domesticated and their role in human society evolved from hunters and protectors to companions and family members, interest in understanding their behavior grew. By the modern era, particularly in the 20th century, astrology had become a widespread tool for self-reflection and understanding relationships. Naturally, this extended to the relationships humans have with their pets, particularly dogs.

The idea of using astrology to better understand dogs gained popularity as pet ownership rose, and people sought deeper connections with their canine companions. Just as astrology had long been used to explain human personalities and predict behavior, dog astrology emerged as a way to comprehend why some dogs are more independent, playful, or protective, and how their birth date and star sign could reveal hidden truths about their nature.

The Astrological Connection to Dog Breeds

As dog astrology developed, astrologers began to associate specific dog breeds with zodiac signs based on their inherent traits. Just as certain signs are known for being fiery, intellectual, or emotional, dog breeds came to be categorized in similar ways. For instance, a bold and courageous breed like the German Shepherd might be linked to Aries, while a gentle and nurturing breed like the Golden Retriever could be associated with Cancer.

These associations helped dog owners make sense of their pets' personalities and tendencies. Astrologers posited that, much like humans, dogs are influenced by their astrological sign and that these celestial forces can shape their temperament, behavior, and even their health. For example, a dog born under the sign of Sagittarius might have an adventurous spirit, always eager to explore and roam, while a Virgo dog might be more disciplined and prefer a structured routine.

The Role of Celestial Events in Dog Astrology

Dog astrology also takes into account larger celestial events that influence all living beings on Earth. The phases of the moon, planetary transits, and eclipses are all believed to affect not just human behavior but also that of animals, including dogs. Full moons, for example, are often associated with heightened emotions and restless energy, and many dog owners report that their pets become more excitable or anxious during these periods.

In the same way, retrogrades—particularly Mercury retrograde, known for its disruptive energy—are said to influence dogs' moods and behaviors. Owners may notice their dogs acting out of character, becoming more nervous or unsettled during these times, which dog astrologers attribute to the cosmic shifts occurring in the heavens.

Modern-Day Dog Astrology

Today, dog astrology has become an increasingly popular way for pet owners to connect with their furry friends on a deeper level. In a world where dogs are considered part of the family, many people are turning to astrology to better understand their dogs' needs, personalities, and behavior patterns. Dog horoscopes, astrological birth charts for pets, and compatibility readings between pets and owners have become common tools used by astrologers and dog enthusiasts alike.

With the rise of holistic pet care and a growing emphasis on the emotional and psychological well-being of dogs, astrology offers a unique approach to understanding and caring for our canine companions. By recognizing how cosmic forces influence our pets, we can become more attuned to their needs and create a more harmonious living environment for them.

Conclusion: The Stars and Your Dog

The practice of astrology has evolved over thousands of years, from its origins in ancient Mesopotamia to its modern-day applications. While its connection to animals has always been present, the focus on dogs as astrological beings has grown as our relationship with them deepened. By understanding the historical roots of astrology and its connection to animals, we can appreciate the significance of this cosmic bond.

In the chapters to come, we'll delve deeper into each zodiac sign, exploring how the stars shape your dog's personality, behavior, and preferences. Whether your dog is an adventurous Aries or a gentle Pisces, *AstroPaws* will guide you through the celestial map of your dog's unique traits, helping you forge an even stronger connection with your loyal companion.

Through the wisdom of astrology, we can unlock a greater understanding of the dogs we cherish so much, gaining insights that help us care for them better, strengthen our bond, and appreciate their place in the cosmic order. Welcome to the world of dog astrology, where the stars shine brightly for all, including our beloved canine companions.

Part 1: Zodiac Signs and Your Dog

Chapter 2: Aries Dogs (March 21 - April 19)

Bold, energetic, and fiercely independent, Aries dogs are natural leaders in the canine world. Born under the fire sign ruled by Mars, Aries dogs embody the spirit of the ram, charging forward with enthusiasm, confidence, and a fearless attitude. This chapter delves deep into the traits, behavior, and care tips for Aries dogs, helping you understand their unique needs and how to nurture their fiery temperament.

Traits of Aries Dogs

Aries dogs are the trailblazers of the zodiac. They are known for their bold, courageous personalities and their love of adventure. Here are some key traits that define an Aries dog:

1. **Fearless and Brave:** Aries dogs rarely shy away from challenges. Whether it's defending their territory or standing their ground in front of larger animals, they are fearless in nature. This boldness often makes them excellent watchdogs, always alert and ready to spring into action when they sense danger.

2. **Energetic and Playful:** These dogs are bundles of energy. They thrive on physical activity and are happiest when they're engaged in play, exploration, or high-intensity activities like running or agility training. If not given enough outlets for their energy, they can become restless or destructive.

3. **Independent Thinkers:** Aries dogs like to do things their way. They have a strong sense of independence and can sometimes be stubborn. This means they might not always follow commands right away, especially if they feel like doing something else. However, their intelligence is undeniable, and with proper training, they can be highly capable companions.

4. **Curious and Adventurous:** Always eager to explore, Aries dogs have an insatiable curiosity. They love new experiences and can be quite the little adventurers, whether it's chasing squirrels, investigating new scents, or trying to figure out how to escape the yard for another adventure.

5. **Confident and Assertive:** Confidence radiates from Aries dogs. They know what they want and aren't afraid to go after it. This assertiveness can sometimes come across as bossy, especially if they feel they aren't getting the attention or control they desire.

6. **Impatient and Impulsive:** While Aries dogs are confident, their impulsiveness can sometimes get them into trouble. They may act before thinking, leading to situations where they dive into danger without hesitation. Additionally, they can be quite impatient, which means they may struggle with long waiting periods or activities that require calm and focus.

Behavior of Aries Dogs

Understanding the behavior patterns of Aries dogs is key to managing their strong personalities and ensuring they're happy and well-balanced. Here are some common behavioral tendencies:

1. **Natural Leaders:** Aries dogs tend to take charge in social settings. Whether they're interacting with other dogs or asserting dominance in the household, they want to be seen as leaders. While this can be beneficial in certain situations, it can also lead to power struggles if not properly managed.

2. **Attention Seekers:** Aries dogs love being the center of attention. They crave affection and acknowledgment from their owners and will often perform tricks or act out to get noticed. If they feel ignored, they might resort to barking or other attention-seeking behaviors.

3. **Fast Learners, But Easily Bored:** Aries dogs are intelligent and quick learners, but they can get bored with repetitive tasks. They

need mental stimulation alongside physical activity, so training should be varied and engaging to keep their interest.

4. **Protective of Their Space:** These dogs are territorial and protective of their homes and families. While this can make them excellent guard dogs, it's important to ensure their protective instincts don't translate into aggression toward strangers or other animals.

5. **Competitive:** Aries dogs love to win. Whether it's a game of fetch or a friendly competition with other dogs, they have a natural competitive streak. They want to come out on top, which can sometimes make them a bit pushy during play.

6. **High Energy and Restlessness:** Without enough exercise and stimulation, Aries dogs can become restless and even destructive. They may chew on furniture, dig in the yard, or bark excessively if they're not given enough outlets for their energy.

Care Tips for Aries Dogs

Caring for an Aries dog requires patience, creativity, and a commitment to meeting their high energy needs. Here are some essential care tips to keep your Aries dog happy and healthy:

1. **Daily Exercise is a Must:** Aries dogs need plenty of physical activity to burn off their abundant energy. Aim for at least an hour of vigorous exercise each day, whether it's a run, a hike, or a game of fetch in the park. Incorporating agility training or obstacle courses can also keep them engaged and mentally stimulated.

2. **Mental Stimulation is Key:** In addition to physical exercise, Aries dogs thrive on mental challenges. Puzzle toys, interactive games, and training sessions that require them to think and problem-solve will help keep their minds sharp and prevent boredom.

3. **Firm, Consistent Training:** Aries dogs need clear boundaries and consistent training to manage their independent and sometimes stubborn streak. Positive reinforcement works best with

this sign, but be firm and persistent. Avoid harsh punishments, as Aries dogs respond better to encouragement and rewards.

4. **Socialization:** Start socializing your Aries dog early to ensure they are well-adjusted around other animals and people. Due to their strong personalities, it's essential they learn how to interact appropriately in various situations. Taking them to dog parks, puppy classes, and on regular walks in different environments will help them develop good social skills.

5. **Structured Routines:** While Aries dogs love adventure, they also benefit from having a structured routine. This helps to curb their impulsiveness and provides a sense of stability. Regular feeding times, walks, and play sessions can create a balanced environment for your Aries dog.

6. **Safe Space for Relaxation:** Aries dogs may seem like they're always on the go, but even they need downtime. Provide a quiet, cozy space where your dog can relax and recharge. This can help them calm down after a day of high energy activities and prevent overstimulation.

7. **Be Prepared for Boldness:** Don't be surprised if your Aries dog exhibits bold behavior, like trying to take control of situations or asserting their dominance. It's important to manage this by reinforcing training, showing them who's in charge (in a kind but firm way), and redirecting their leadership tendencies into positive activities, such as advanced obedience or agility training.

8. **Watch Out for Impulsive Behavior:** Given their impulsive nature, Aries dogs can sometimes find themselves in risky situations—whether it's bolting after a squirrel or jumping into unfamiliar water. Be cautious and aware of their environment to prevent accidents, and work on recall training to help manage their impulsive tendencies.

Building a Strong Relationship with Your Aries Dog

Building a relationship with an Aries dog requires patience, understanding, and a willingness to embrace their bold and energetic nature. Here's how you can create a strong bond:

- **Be a Confident Leader:** Aries dogs respect strength and confidence. Be assertive and clear in your commands, but always use positive reinforcement. They need a leader they can look up to and trust, so consistency and fairness are key.

- **Celebrate Their Achievements:** Aries dogs love to be praised and rewarded for their accomplishments. Whether it's mastering a new trick or being well-behaved in social settings, make sure you give them plenty of praise and attention for a job well done.

- **Embrace Adventure Together:** Aries dogs love to explore, so take them on adventures—whether that's hiking through the woods, visiting new parks, or engaging in sports like flyball or agility. The more active and varied their experiences, the happier and more bonded they will be with you.

- **Respect Their Independence:** While Aries dogs love attention, they also value their independence. Give them space to explore and make decisions on their own, but be there to guide and support them when necessary. This balance of freedom and structure will foster a strong and respectful bond.

Conclusion

Aries dogs are truly one-of-a-kind companions, full of life, energy, and an undeniable zest for adventure. With their fearless nature and independent spirit, they bring excitement and passion into their owners' lives. By understanding their traits, behavior, and care needs, you can ensure that your Aries dog thrives both physically and emotionally. Embrace their fiery personality, and you'll find yourself with a loyal, loving, and endlessly entertaining companion who will keep you on your toes and your heart full of joy.

Chapter 3: Taurus Dogs (April 20 - May 20)

Grounded, patient, and deeply loyal, Taurus dogs bring stability and comfort to those around them. Born under the earth sign ruled by Venus, the planet of love and beauty, Taurus dogs are known for their affectionate and steady nature. This chapter explores the unique traits, behavior, and care tips for Taurus dogs, helping you to understand and nurture your canine companion's serene, yet determined, personality.

Traits of Taurus Dogs

Taurus dogs embody the classic characteristics of their zodiac sign: they are calm, reliable, and enjoy the finer things in life. Here are some defining traits that mark a Taurus dog:

1. **Loyal and Devoted:** Taurus dogs are incredibly loyal to their families. They form deep bonds with their owners and tend to be unwaveringly faithful. Once you've earned their trust, you can expect a lifelong companion who will always be by your side.

2. **Calm and Relaxed:** These dogs have a serene nature, often content to lounge around the house, enjoying the quiet and comfort of their home environment. They are not easily rattled by chaos or change, preferring a peaceful, stable atmosphere where they can feel secure.

3. **Stubborn Yet Determined:** Taurus dogs are known for their stubbornness. When they set their minds to something, it can be difficult to persuade them otherwise. However, this determination can be a double-edged sword; it means they are persistent in learning new tasks but may also resist change or commands if they're not in the mood.

4. **Appreciators of Comfort:** Ruled by Venus, Taurus dogs have a special love for comfort. They seek out the coziest spots in the house, the softest blankets, and the most luxurious beds. They

also enjoy being pampered, whether that's through gentle grooming, massages, or belly rubs.

5. **Food-Motivated:** One of the most common traits among Taurus dogs is their love of food. They are highly food-motivated, making treats an excellent incentive for training. However, their love for food also means they can be prone to overeating, so it's important to monitor their diet closely.

6. **Reliable and Steady:** Taurus dogs thrive on routine and consistency. They are dependable and do well in homes where there is a structured daily schedule. You can count on them to follow their routine, whether it's knowing exactly when it's time for a walk or expecting dinner at the same time every evening.

Behavior of Taurus Dogs

Taurus dogs' behaviors are closely linked to their steady, grounded nature. Understanding these behaviors will help you better cater to their needs and create a harmonious environment for them:

1. **Routine-Oriented:** Taurus dogs love routine and may become agitated or stressed when their regular schedules are disrupted. They enjoy predictability, from meal times to walks and even playtime. Keeping a consistent routine is essential for their emotional well-being.

2. **Slow to Warm Up:** These dogs tend to take their time when forming relationships, both with humans and other animals. They aren't the type to jump into a new situation or bond immediately with strangers. However, once they trust someone, that bond is unshakeable.

3. **Homebodies at Heart:** Taurus dogs are most comfortable in their familiar environment. While they enjoy the occasional adventure or trip to the park, they are happiest lounging at home. They thrive in calm, quiet spaces where they can relax and feel safe.

4. **Selective Playfulness:** While Taurus dogs aren't typically high-energy, they do enjoy playtime—on their own terms. They prefer low-key activities like fetch or tug-of-war, and they are unlikely to chase after every ball thrown their way unless it interests them. They will only engage in activities that they feel are worth their time.

5. **Guardians of Their Domain:** Despite their calm demeanor, Taurus dogs can be protective of their homes and families. They are not as aggressive as some other signs, but if they sense a threat, they will stand their ground and defend their space. Their protective instincts, combined with their loyalty, make them excellent watchdogs.

6. **Stubborn at Times:** A Taurus dog's stubborn streak can manifest in ways that are both charming and challenging. While they may resist commands or refuse to move from their favorite napping spot, they are also deeply persistent when they want something, whether that's food or attention.

Care Tips for Taurus Dogs

Caring for a Taurus dog means providing a lifestyle that caters to their need for comfort, consistency, and indulgence. Here are some essential care tips for ensuring your Taurus dog is happy and healthy:

1. **Stick to a Routine:** Establish a daily routine and stick to it as much as possible. Taurus dogs feel secure when they know what to expect throughout the day. Set regular times for meals, walks, and play sessions. Disrupting their routine can lead to stress, so consistency is key.

2. **Create a Comfortable Environment:** Taurus dogs thrive in cozy, luxurious environments. Invest in a soft, supportive dog bed, and provide them with plenty of blankets and cushy areas to rest. They love to feel pampered, so make sure their resting spaces are inviting and comfortable.

3. **Watch Their Diet:** Given their love of food, it's important to monitor your Taurus dog's diet closely. Avoid overfeeding and be cautious about giving too many treats, as they can easily gain weight. Stick to a balanced diet and ensure they're getting enough exercise to burn off any excess calories.

4. **Exercise in Moderation:** While Taurus dogs aren't naturally high-energy, they still need regular exercise to stay healthy. A daily walk and some light playtime will suffice. Don't push them too hard, though—they prefer leisurely strolls over intense runs. Taurus dogs also enjoy sniffing and exploring their surroundings at their own pace.

5. **Provide Mental Stimulation:** While they enjoy their downtime, Taurus dogs also benefit from mental challenges. Puzzle toys and interactive games that involve food rewards are excellent ways to engage their minds without requiring too much physical exertion.

6. **Patience in Training:** Training a Taurus dog requires patience, especially when dealing with their stubbornness. Use positive reinforcement and plenty of treats, as they respond well to food-based rewards. Avoid harsh or overly strict training methods, as they can cause your dog to shut down. Instead, gently encourage them with praise and patience.

7. **Grooming as Pampering:** Taurus dogs often enjoy the pampering that comes with grooming. Make grooming sessions relaxing and enjoyable for them—gentle brushing, ear cleaning, and massages can help them feel calm and cared for. Taurus dogs with thick or longer coats will appreciate regular grooming, as it adds to their sense of comfort and well-being.

8. **Socialization on Their Terms:** Taurus dogs may take longer to warm up to new people or pets, but regular socialization is important to keep them balanced. Take things slow and allow your Taurus dog to approach new situations at their own pace. They

may not be the most social dogs, but with time and patience, they can become comfortable in a variety of settings.

Building a Strong Relationship with Your Taurus Dog

Building a bond with a Taurus dog requires understanding their need for stability, comfort, and affection. Here are some ways to create a deep connection with your Taurus dog:

- **Show Them Affection:** Taurus dogs love being close to their owners. Physical touch, such as cuddles, belly rubs, and gentle petting, is essential for them to feel secure and loved. Make time each day for one-on-one bonding moments.
- **Respect Their Space:** While Taurus dogs are affectionate, they also appreciate their alone time. They may retreat to their favorite spot in the house to nap or relax. Give them space when they need it, and they'll come to you when they're ready for attention.
- **Be Patient and Calm:** Taurus dogs don't respond well to forceful or hurried interactions. Approach them with calm energy and patience, especially during training or new experiences. They'll respond positively to your steady demeanor and will trust you more as a result.
- **Reward Them with Comfort:** Treat your Taurus dog to the comforts they crave. Soft toys, comfortable beds, and their favorite treats will go a long way in showing them that they are cherished. They'll reward your care with unwavering loyalty.

Conclusion

Taurus dogs are the embodiment of calm, steady companionship. With their loyal hearts and love of comfort, they make excellent companions for those who enjoy a peaceful, stable home life. By understanding their traits, behaviors, and needs, you can ensure that your Taurus dog thrives in an environment filled with love, routine, and comfort.

Embrace their steady nature, and you'll find yourself with a devoted, reliable companion who brings warmth, loyalty, and unwavering love into your life. Taurus dogs may move at their own pace, but their bond with you will be unbreakable—steadfast and enduring, just like the earth element they are born under.

Chapter 4: Gemini Dogs (May 21 - June 20)

Playful, curious, and full of energy, Gemini dogs are the social butterflies of the canine zodiac. Ruled by Mercury, the planet of communication and intellect, Gemini dogs are known for their lively personalities, quick learning ability, and dual nature. This chapter explores the traits, behaviors, and care tips for Gemini dogs, providing insights into how to nurture their dynamic, ever-changing personalities.

Traits of Gemini Dogs

Gemini dogs, like their human counterparts, are defined by their versatility and love of mental stimulation. Their personality can seem as though it has two distinct sides—one moment they are playful and mischievous, and the next they are calm and observant. Here are the key traits that define Gemini dogs:

1. **Highly Curious:** Gemini dogs are inquisitive by nature. They love exploring their surroundings, discovering new places, and investigating any new scents or objects they encounter. Their curiosity can often lead them into mischief, so it's important to keep a watchful eye on them during their explorations.

2. **Playful and Energetic:** These dogs are full of energy and always ready for playtime. Whether it's chasing a ball, engaging in a game of tug-of-war, or simply running around the yard, Gemini dogs need regular physical activity to keep them entertained and balanced. They're likely to try to engage both humans and other animals in play, making them a joy to be around.

3. **Intelligent and Quick Learners:** Gemini dogs are naturally smart and love mental challenges. They pick up new commands and tricks quickly, making them excellent candidates for advanced training or even dog sports. Their sharp intellect, however, can sometimes make them a little manipulative—using their charm and wit to get what they want.

4. **Social and Friendly:** Ruled by Mercury, the planet of communication, Gemini dogs are highly social and love interacting with

people and other animals. They enjoy being part of the action, whether it's at home, the park, or in a group of dogs. They thrive on attention and can quickly become the center of any gathering with their lively antics.

5. **Adaptable and Versatile:** Gemini dogs are highly adaptable and can easily adjust to new situations, environments, and people. They're not easily phased by changes in routine or environment, which makes them excellent travel companions and great in social settings. This adaptability also means they can shift from playful to calm, depending on the situation.

6. **Restless and Easily Bored:** With their quick minds and energetic spirits, Gemini dogs can become easily bored if not properly stimulated. They require variety and mental engagement to stay happy. Without enough stimulation, they may resort to destructive behaviors, such as chewing on furniture or getting into things they shouldn't.

7. **Dual Natured:** Gemini is the sign of the twins, which means these dogs can sometimes seem to have two sides to their personality. One moment they may be outgoing and playful, and the next they may retreat to a quiet spot, becoming introspective and observant. This duality makes them fascinating companions, though it may also confuse owners who are unfamiliar with their shifting moods.

Behavior of Gemini Dogs

The behavior of Gemini dogs is often driven by their need for stimulation and social interaction. Understanding their behavior can help you manage their energy and ensure they are happy, well-adjusted pets:

1. **Highly Communicative:** Gemini dogs are talkers. They tend to vocalize more than other signs, whether through barking, whining, or even howling. They use these vocalizations to communicate their needs, emotions, or to engage in play. Owners of

Gemini dogs often find their pets trying to "talk" to them with expressive sounds and body language.

2. **Loves Variety:** These dogs thrive on change and variety. They enjoy learning new tricks, playing different games, and exploring unfamiliar environments. Repetitive routines can bore them quickly, so it's important to keep things fresh and interesting.

3. **Attention Seekers:** Gemini dogs crave attention and will go out of their way to get it. They might perform a new trick, bring you a toy, or even nudge you for pets if they feel they aren't receiving enough attention. Without regular engagement, they may turn to attention-seeking behaviors, such as barking or misbehaving, just to get you to notice them.

4. **Mischievous Streak:** With their sharp minds and adventurous spirit, Gemini dogs can sometimes get into trouble. Their curiosity often leads them to explore areas they shouldn't, and their playful side means they may push boundaries just to see what they can get away with. It's essential to set clear boundaries early on to prevent this behavior from becoming problematic.

5. **Natural Charmers:** Gemini dogs have an undeniable charm. They know how to win over humans and other dogs with their playful antics and sweet nature. This makes them well-loved by almost everyone they meet, and they tend to form strong social bonds easily.

6. **Restless Energy:** Gemini dogs have a lot of energy to burn, both physically and mentally. Without enough outlets, they can become restless and agitated. They need regular mental stimulation and physical activity to keep their energy in check, otherwise, they may engage in undesirable behaviors like excessive barking or chewing.

Care Tips for Gemini Dogs

Caring for a Gemini dog means understanding their need for stimulation, variety, and social interaction. Here are some essential care tips for keeping your Gemini dog happy and well-balanced:

1. **Regular Mental Stimulation:** Gemini dogs thrive on mental challenges. Incorporate puzzle toys, interactive games, and training exercises into their daily routine to keep their minds sharp. Teaching them new tricks or commands regularly will keep them engaged and prevent boredom.

2. **Engage in Interactive Play:** These dogs love interactive play that allows them to use both their brains and their bodies. Games like fetch, hide-and-seek, and tug-of-war are excellent ways to burn off their energy while keeping them entertained. Keep play sessions varied to prevent them from losing interest.

3. **Socialization is Key:** Gemini dogs are social animals who enjoy interacting with other dogs, humans, and even other pets. Regular socialization is crucial to their happiness. Take them to dog parks, arrange playdates, and introduce them to new environments to satisfy their need for social interaction.

4. **Variety in Exercise:** A simple walk around the block might not be enough to satisfy your Gemini dog. They enjoy variety in their physical activities, so mix up their exercise routine. Alternate between brisk walks, runs, visits to the dog park, or hikes in nature. Engaging in different activities will keep them physically stimulated and mentally engaged.

5. **Training Through Play:** Gemini dogs respond best to training when it feels like a game. Use positive reinforcement and incorporate toys and treats into your training sessions. Their intelligence means they'll pick up new commands quickly, but it's essential to keep the training fun and light to hold their interest.

6. **Preventing Boredom:** Gemini dogs are prone to boredom if left alone for too long or if they don't have enough variety in their

day. Rotate their toys frequently, provide them with interactive puzzle toys when you're away, and ensure they have enough stimulation to avoid boredom-related behaviors, such as chewing or digging.

7. **Communication and Vocalization:** Since Gemini dogs are highly communicative, it's important to acknowledge their vocalizations. Whether they're barking to alert you or trying to engage in play, be responsive to their attempts at communication. However, make sure to train them to understand when excessive barking is not acceptable, as they may overdo it in their quest for attention.

8. **Handling Their Dual Nature:** Gemini dogs can shift between being energetic and calm, social and introspective. Be patient with these changes and adapt to their moods. When they're in an energetic phase, engage them with play and mental challenges. When they're feeling quiet or withdrawn, allow them to have their space to recharge.

Building a Strong Relationship with Your Gemini Dog

Building a bond with a Gemini dog involves embracing their curious, playful, and social nature. Here's how you can foster a strong connection with your Gemini dog:

- **Keep Communication Open:** Gemini dogs thrive on communication. Talk to them regularly, using a variety of vocal tones, and reward them when they respond positively to commands or engage in conversation with you. This back-and-forth communication builds trust and deepens your bond.

- **Engage Their Curiosity:** Feed their need for exploration by introducing them to new environments, toys, and activities. Take them on adventures where they can explore new sights, smells, and experiences. The more you engage their curiosity, the more connected they'll feel to you as their source of new adventures.

- **Make Time for Play:** Play is a huge part of a Gemini dog's life, so make sure to engage in fun, interactive play sessions daily. Incorporate games that challenge both their minds and bodies, and make them feel like they're winning by rewarding their efforts with praise and treats.
- **Respect Their Independence:** While Gemini dogs are social, they also have an independent side. They need moments of solitude to recharge, so respect their space when they need it. Balance playtime and socialization with quiet moments to ensure they feel comfortable and secure.

Conclusion

Gemini dogs are lively, intelligent, and full of charm. With their playful spirit and sharp minds, they make fantastic companions for those who can keep up with their ever-changing moods and endless curiosity. By understanding their traits, behavior, and care needs, you can provide the mental and physical stimulation they crave, fostering a happy and fulfilling relationship.

Embrace their dual nature, and you'll find a loyal, loving companion who brings energy, joy, and endless entertainment into your life. Gemini dogs are never boring, and their zest for life will keep you on your toes, making every day an adventure full of fun and discovery.

Chapter 5: Cancer Dogs (June 21 - July 22)

Nurturing, loyal, and deeply intuitive, Cancer dogs are the caregivers of the canine zodiac. Ruled by the Moon, which governs emotions, these dogs are known for their sensitivity, strong attachment to their families, and protective nature. This chapter delves into the traits, behaviors, and care tips for Cancer dogs, offering insights into how to best support their emotional needs and foster their well-being.

Traits of Cancer Dogs

Cancer dogs are defined by their emotional depth, loyalty, and protective instincts. They are the ultimate companion animals, always seeking to provide comfort and love to their owners. Here are the key traits that define Cancer dogs:

1. **Loyal and Devoted:** Cancer dogs form incredibly deep bonds with their families. They are devoted to their owners and will go to great lengths to protect and care for those they love. Once you've earned their trust, they are likely to be your constant companion, always seeking to be close to you.

2. **Emotional and Sensitive:** Ruled by the Moon, Cancer dogs are highly in tune with their emotions and the emotions of those around them. They can sense when their owners are feeling sad, stressed, or anxious and will often try to comfort them. This sensitivity also means they can be easily affected by changes in the home environment or the mood of their family members.

3. **Protective and Nurturing:** These dogs have a strong protective instinct, especially when it comes to their home and family. Cancer dogs are natural caregivers, often watching over children, other pets, or even their human owners. Their nurturing side makes them excellent companions for families, as they thrive on providing love and care.

4. **Homebodies:** Cancer dogs love the comfort and security of home. They are happiest when surrounded by their family in a familiar, safe environment. While they may enjoy the occasional ad-

venture outside, they tend to prefer the calm and coziness of their home life.

5. **Cautious and Reserved:** Cancer dogs are naturally cautious, especially in new or unfamiliar situations. They take their time to assess people and environments before warming up. This cautious nature can make them a bit shy around strangers, but once they feel comfortable, they reveal their affectionate and playful side.

6. **Emotionally Resilient:** Despite their sensitivity, Cancer dogs have a remarkable emotional resilience. While they may be deeply affected by their environment or the moods of their owners, they quickly recover and adapt, always seeking to bring balance and comfort to their surroundings.

7. **Strong Intuition:** Cancer dogs possess an almost psychic ability to understand their owners' emotions and needs. They seem to know when you need a cuddle, a nudge, or simply their presence to lift your spirits. This strong intuitive connection makes them incredibly empathetic companions.

Behavior of Cancer Dogs

Cancer dogs' behavior is closely tied to their emotional and nurturing nature. Understanding their behavior can help you create a supportive and loving environment that allows them to thrive:

1. **Constant Companionship:** Cancer dogs thrive on close, constant companionship. They may follow you from room to room, always wanting to be near you. This behavior is a reflection of their deep emotional attachment to their family. They find comfort in physical proximity and may become anxious or stressed when left alone for long periods.

2. **Gentle and Patient:** Cancer dogs are known for their gentle demeanor. They are patient with children and other animals, making them excellent family pets. Their nurturing instincts lead

them to be protective yet gentle, especially with those who are vulnerable or in need of care.

3. **Sensitivity to Changes:** Cancer dogs are highly attuned to changes in their environment. Any disruption in routine, such as moving to a new home, the arrival of a new family member, or even a shift in their owner's mood, can deeply affect them. They thrive in stable, predictable environments where they feel safe and secure.

4. **Strong Attachment to Home:** Cancer dogs are homebodies and tend to be territorial. They are protective of their space and may become anxious when strangers enter their home. While they aren't typically aggressive, they will be on alert until they feel the stranger poses no threat to their family.

5. **Moodiness:** Just like the tides ruled by the Moon, Cancer dogs' moods can ebb and flow. They may be playful and affectionate one moment, then retreat to a quiet corner the next. Their moodiness is often a reflection of their deep emotional sensitivity, and they may need time alone to process their feelings before returning to their usual, loving selves.

6. **Separation Anxiety:** Cancer dogs' deep emotional bonds with their families can sometimes lead to separation anxiety. They may become distressed when left alone, exhibiting behaviors like barking, whining, or destructive chewing. It's essential to help Cancer dogs feel secure and to ease their anxiety through training and gradual alone time.

Care Tips for Cancer Dogs

Caring for a Cancer dog requires understanding their emotional sensitivity and need for security. Here are some essential care tips to keep your Cancer dog happy and emotionally balanced:

1. **Provide a Stable Environment:** Cancer dogs thrive in a stable, predictable environment. Try to keep their daily routine as con-

sistent as possible. Regular feeding times, walks, and play sessions will help them feel secure and reduce any anxiety caused by sudden changes.

2. **Create a Safe, Cozy Space:** These dogs love the comfort of home, so make sure they have a dedicated space that feels safe and cozy. A soft bed in a quiet corner, complete with their favorite blankets and toys, can provide a sanctuary where they can retreat when they need some downtime.

3. **Stay Close and Offer Comfort:** Cancer dogs crave closeness with their owners. Spend time cuddling, petting, and talking to your dog to help them feel loved and secure. Their attachment to you is strong, and they will appreciate the emotional support you provide in return.

4. **Socialization in Safe Environments:** While Cancer dogs can be shy around strangers, regular socialization is important to help them feel more comfortable in new situations. Introduce them to new people and environments slowly, ensuring they feel safe and supported. With time, they will warm up and show their affectionate side.

5. **Ease Separation Anxiety:** If your Cancer dog struggles with separation anxiety, it's important to gradually help them become more comfortable with alone time. Start by leaving them for short periods and gradually increase the time away. Providing toys, treats, and a calming environment can help ease their anxiety.

6. **Exercise and Emotional Balance:** Although Cancer dogs love being at home, they still need regular physical exercise to stay healthy and emotionally balanced. Daily walks, playtime, and outdoor adventures are essential for their physical and mental well-being. These activities also provide an outlet for any stress or anxiety they may be feeling.

7. **Emotional Support During Changes:** Cancer dogs are sensitive to changes in their environment or family dynamics. If you're moving, bringing in a new pet, or experiencing changes in your

routine, be sure to provide extra emotional support for your Cancer dog. Comfort them with gentle words, physical affection, and plenty of reassurance.

8. **Nurture Their Protective Instincts:** Cancer dogs have a natural desire to protect their family and home. While they are typically gentle, it's important to reinforce positive protective behaviors. Teach them to alert you to potential dangers without becoming overly defensive or territorial. This balance will help them feel confident in their role as protectors.

Building a Strong Relationship with Your Cancer Dog

Building a bond with a Cancer dog means recognizing their emotional depth and nurturing their sensitive, loving nature. Here's how you can create a strong connection with your Cancer dog:

- **Offer Unconditional Love:** Cancer dogs thrive on love and affection. Make time for cuddles, petting, and one-on-one bonding moments every day. Your emotional connection is essential to their happiness, and they will return your love with deep loyalty.

- **Be Patient and Gentle:** Cancer dogs are sensitive and can easily pick up on harsh tones or negative emotions. Use a gentle, calm approach when training or interacting with them. Patience is key, as they may take longer to adjust to changes or new commands due to their emotional nature.

- **Provide Emotional Stability:** These dogs need to feel emotionally secure. Be consistent in your interactions, and try to maintain a calm, peaceful household. When they sense emotional stability from their owners, they feel more secure and relaxed.

- **Respect Their Need for Space:** While Cancer dogs love being close to their owners, they also need time to themselves. Allow them to retreat to their safe space when they need to recharge emotionally. This balance of closeness and independence will strengthen your bond.

Conclusion

Cancer dogs are the ultimate nurturers, offering love, loyalty, and protection to their families. With their deep emotional sensitivity and strong attachment to home, they bring warmth and comfort to any household. By understanding their traits, behaviors, and care needs, you can ensure that your Cancer dog thrives in an environment filled with love, stability, and security.

Embrace their protective and nurturing nature, and you'll find yourself with a devoted companion who always has your back. Cancer dogs' ability to sense and respond to your emotional needs makes them truly special, creating a bond that is both profound and enduring.

Chapter 6: Leo Dogs (July 23 - August 22)

Regal, confident, and full of life, Leo dogs are the true stars of the canine zodiac. Ruled by the Sun, which symbolizes vitality and leadership, Leo dogs have an undeniable presence. With their charismatic personalities and love for attention, these dogs shine in any setting. This chapter explores the traits, behaviors, and care tips for Leo dogs, offering insight into how to best nurture their leadership qualities and exuberant personalities.

Traits of Leo Dogs

Leo dogs are natural-born leaders, with a flair for the dramatic and a love for being the center of attention. Here are the key traits that define a Leo dog:

1. **Confident and Proud:** Leo dogs exude confidence. They carry themselves with a sense of pride and often have a commanding presence. Whether in a group of dogs or at home, Leo dogs want to be noticed, and they expect to be treated like royalty. They love praise and recognition for their efforts.

2. **Loyal and Protective:** Despite their need for attention, Leo dogs are fiercely loyal to their families. They form deep bonds and are protective of their loved ones. Like a lion guarding its pride, a Leo dog will go to great lengths to ensure the safety and well-being of their human family.

3. **Playful and Enthusiastic:** Leo dogs have an infectious enthusiasm for life. They love to play, whether it's a game of fetch, tug-of-war, or simply running around the yard. Their playful energy often brings joy to their owners and anyone around them. They are also highly sociable and enjoy interacting with other dogs and humans alike.

4. **Dramatic and Expressive:** These dogs are known for their flair for the dramatic. Whether it's through barking, body language, or other forms of communication, Leo dogs have a way of making their presence known. If they feel ignored, they may exaggerate

their behavior to gain attention, whether through a dramatic sigh or an exaggerated reaction.

5. **Leader of the Pack:** Leo dogs have natural leadership qualities. In social settings, they often assume the role of leader, guiding or even dominating interactions with other dogs. They enjoy being in control and may assert their dominance if they feel their position is being challenged.

6. **Generous and Affectionate:** Leo dogs have big hearts and are incredibly affectionate toward their families. They love showering their owners with affection, whether through cuddles, nuzzles, or playful licks. Their generous nature makes them great companions for families, especially those who can match their energy and love of attention.

7. **Attention-Seeking:** Leo dogs thrive on attention and admiration. They enjoy being the focus of their family's affection and will often seek out praise or recognition for their actions. If a Leo dog feels ignored, they may resort to attention-seeking behaviors, such as barking or performing tricks to get the spotlight back on them.

Behavior of Leo Dogs

Leo dogs' behaviors reflect their larger-than-life personalities. Understanding these behaviors will help you manage their need for attention and leadership:

1. **Love of the Spotlight:** Leo dogs are happiest when they are the center of attention. They enjoy showing off, whether through learned tricks, playful antics, or simply basking in the admiration of their owners. If they feel ignored, they may act out in order to regain attention, often with dramatic flair.

2. **Protective Instincts:** Leo dogs are deeply protective of their families. While they are typically friendly and sociable, they will not hesitate to defend their home or loved ones if they sense

a threat. Their strong protective instincts make them excellent guard dogs, though they must be trained to avoid becoming overly territorial.

3. **Social Butterflies:** These dogs love being around others, whether it's humans or other animals. They thrive in social environments and enjoy interacting with a variety of people and pets. Their natural charisma often makes them the life of the party, and they enjoy being admired by those around them.

4. **Dominant in Group Settings:** Leo dogs have a natural desire to lead. In group settings, they may assert themselves as the alpha, especially around other dogs. While they are not typically aggressive, they will not back down if challenged. This assertive behavior can sometimes lead to conflicts with other dominant dogs, so early socialization and training are important.

5. **Playful and Energetic:** Leo dogs have an abundance of energy and a love for play. They enjoy games that challenge them physically and mentally, and they are always eager for a game of fetch or a romp in the park. Their playful nature makes them great companions for active families who can keep up with their energy levels.

6. **Affectionate and Loving:** While they may have a dramatic side, Leo dogs are also incredibly affectionate. They love being close to their owners, whether it's through cuddling on the couch or giving kisses. They are loyal companions who will always seek to provide love and comfort to those they care about.

7. **Strong-Willed and Stubborn:** Leo dogs can be strong-willed, especially when they believe they know best. Their natural confidence sometimes leads them to ignore commands or do things their own way. Training a Leo dog requires patience, consistency, and a firm but loving hand to guide their behavior.

Care Tips for Leo Dogs

Caring for a Leo dog requires understanding their need for attention, leadership, and affection. Here are some essential care tips to keep your Leo dog happy and healthy:

1. **Shower Them with Attention:** Leo dogs crave attention and thrive when they are the focus of their family's love. Make sure to spend quality time with your Leo dog every day, whether through play, training, or simply cuddling. Praise and recognition go a long way in keeping your Leo dog content.

2. **Provide Regular Exercise:** Leo dogs have a lot of energy to burn, so regular physical activity is a must. Daily walks, runs, or playtime in the yard will help them stay physically fit and mentally stimulated. Engage them in activities that challenge them both physically and mentally, such as agility training or puzzle toys.

3. **Training with Positive Reinforcement:** While Leo dogs are natural leaders, they need to learn boundaries and proper behavior. Use positive reinforcement during training, rewarding them with treats and praise when they follow commands. Avoid harsh training methods, as Leo dogs respond best to encouragement and recognition.

4. **Socialization from an Early Age:** Leo dogs are social creatures, but they can become dominant if not properly socialized. Introduce your Leo dog to a variety of people, pets, and environments from an early age to help them develop good social skills. This will also prevent them from becoming overly territorial or dominant in group settings.

5. **Create Opportunities for Play:** Play is essential for a Leo dog's well-being. Provide a variety of toys and games to keep them entertained and mentally stimulated. Interactive toys, tug-of-war,

and fetch are great options for burning off their energy while also keeping them engaged.

6. **Be a Confident Leader:** Leo dogs respect confidence and will follow a leader they trust. Be firm but loving in your interactions with your Leo dog, and establish yourself as the pack leader. Consistency and structure will help them feel secure and reduce any tendencies toward stubborn or dominant behavior.

7. **Balanced Diet and Grooming:** Leo dogs enjoy being pampered, and this extends to their diet and grooming routine. Provide them with a balanced diet that meets their nutritional needs, and ensure they receive regular grooming sessions to keep their coat healthy and shiny. Brushing their coat regularly will not only keep them looking their best but also provide an opportunity for bonding.

8. **Encourage Their Protective Instincts Positively:** While Leo dogs are naturally protective, it's important to guide this behavior in a positive direction. Teach them to alert you to potential dangers without becoming overly aggressive or territorial. Reinforce their protective instincts with praise, but also ensure they understand when it's time to stand down.

Building a Strong Relationship with Your Leo Dog

Building a bond with a Leo dog means recognizing their need for attention, leadership, and affection. Here's how you can create a strong connection with your Leo dog:

- **Give Them the Spotlight:** Leo dogs love being the center of attention. Praise them often, engage them in activities where they can show off their skills, and make them feel special. Their confidence will grow when they feel admired and loved.

- **Be a Calm and Confident Leader:** Leo dogs respect strong leadership. Be calm, confident, and consistent in your interactions with them. Establish clear boundaries, and they will look to you as their trusted leader.

- **Engage in Play and Fun:** Leo dogs are playful by nature, and they thrive on interaction. Spend time playing with them, whether it's through games of fetch, tug-of-war, or simply running around the yard. This playful engagement will deepen your bond and keep them happy.

- **Offer Affection and Praise:** Leo dogs are affectionate and thrive on love and praise. Regularly offer them affection through cuddles, pets, and verbal praise. They will return your love tenfold, always eager to show their loyalty and devotion.

Conclusion

Leo dogs are charismatic, loyal, and full of life. With their playful energy and love of attention, they bring joy and vitality to any home. By understanding their traits, behaviors, and care needs, you can ensure that your Leo dog thrives in an environment filled with love, leadership, and plenty of opportunities to shine.

Embrace their larger-than-life personality, and you'll find a loyal companion who will always stand by your side, offering protection, affection, and a lifetime of unforgettable moments. Leo dogs may crave the spotlight, but their love for their family is what truly makes them shine.

Chapter 7: Virgo Dogs (August 23 - September 22)

Virgo dogs are known for their practical, reliable, and detail-oriented nature. Ruled by Mercury, the planet of communication and intellect, Virgo dogs are meticulous, intelligent, and focused on routine and order. These dogs are often highly attuned to their surroundings, and their thoughtful, methodical approach to life makes them excellent companions. This chapter explores the traits, behaviors, and care tips for Virgo dogs, helping you understand how to best nurture their need for structure and stability.

Traits of Virgo Dogs

Virgo dogs are characterized by their calm demeanor, attention to detail, and strong work ethic. They are the organizers of the canine zodiac, often thriving on routine and order. Here are some key traits that define Virgo dogs:

1. **Practical and Reliable:** Virgo dogs are grounded and dependable. They thrive on structure and predictability, making them highly reliable pets. These dogs tend to be cautious in unfamiliar situations, preferring to assess before diving into something new. Their practicality also makes them excellent problem-solvers.

2. **Attentive and Observant:** These dogs are highly observant, paying close attention to their environment and the people around them. They notice small changes and are quick to react if something is out of place. Virgo dogs are often described as "watchful" and can sense when something isn't right.

3. **Clean and Tidy:** Virgo dogs are known for their love of cleanliness and order. They prefer clean, organized spaces and can be a bit fussy about their environment. They are also particular about

their hygiene, and some Virgo dogs even enjoy being groomed or kept neat.

4. **Health-Conscious:** Ruled by Mercury, Virgo dogs are naturally attuned to their physical well-being. They can be sensitive to changes in their diet or routine and may have a keen awareness of their health. This trait makes them more prone to noticing when they're not feeling well, and they may be more cautious about what they eat or how they behave when unwell.

5. **Modest and Reserved:** Virgo dogs are modest and unassuming. They don't crave the spotlight like some other signs, preferring to remain in the background and observe. Their reserved nature can make them seem a bit shy or introverted, especially in new social settings, but they are deeply loyal to those they trust.

6. **Intelligent and Methodical:** Virgo dogs are highly intelligent and often excel in learning new tasks or commands. They approach training in a methodical, step-by-step way, making them quick learners. They are particularly adept at tasks that require precision, such as agility training or advanced obedience.

7. **Nurturing and Caring:** While they may seem focused on routine and order, Virgo dogs have a deeply nurturing side. They are often protective and caring toward their families, showing their love through small, thoughtful gestures. Their caring nature also extends to other pets, children, or vulnerable individuals in the household.

Behavior of Virgo Dogs

Understanding the behaviors of Virgo dogs can help you create an environment that caters to their need for order and routine. Here are some common behaviors associated with Virgo dogs:

1. **Preference for Routine:** Virgo dogs thrive on routine and structure. They prefer predictable schedules and may become anxious or unsettled when their routine is disrupted. Whether it's meal-

time, walks, or play sessions, they appreciate consistency and tend to stick to their habits.

2. **Detail-Oriented Play:** While Virgo dogs enjoy playtime, they prefer games that involve focus and precision. Activities like puzzle toys, scent work, or obedience training are particularly appealing to them. They are less likely to engage in chaotic or overly energetic play, favoring activities that challenge their minds.

3. **Tendency to Be Perfectionistic:** Virgo dogs can have perfectionist tendencies, which may manifest in their behavior. For example, they might be particular about where they sleep, eat, or play. They may even "organize" their toys or insist on a clean and orderly environment. If something is out of place, they are quick to notice and may try to correct it.

4. **Sensitive to Cleanliness:** Cleanliness is important to Virgo dogs. They may avoid dirty or muddy areas and can be particular about their grooming. If they get dirty, they might seem uncomfortable until they are cleaned up. This sensitivity also extends to their living spaces, as they prefer clean, well-organized areas.

5. **Observant and Analytical:** Virgo dogs are highly observant and will often take their time to analyze new situations before reacting. They may appear cautious or even a bit shy when meeting new people or encountering unfamiliar environments. Once they've assessed the situation, they are more likely to engage, but only after they feel comfortable.

6. **Helpful and Protective:** Virgo dogs have a nurturing side and often look out for their family members. They may try to "help" by keeping watch over the household or ensuring that routines are followed. Their protective nature isn't aggressive, but they are always alert to potential threats or disruptions.

7. **Modest and Low-Key:** These dogs prefer a low-key, quiet environment where they can feel in control. They don't seek attention in loud or flashy ways but rather through their quiet, reliable

presence. They are happiest in homes that offer a sense of calm and order, free from chaos or excessive noise.

Care Tips for Virgo Dogs

Caring for a Virgo dog means creating a stable, structured environment that caters to their practical and health-conscious nature. Here are some essential care tips for keeping your Virgo dog happy and well-balanced:

1. **Stick to a Routine:** Virgo dogs thrive on routine and predictability. Establish a consistent schedule for feeding, walking, playtime, and grooming, and stick to it as closely as possible. Disruptions to their routine can cause anxiety or stress, so maintaining structure is key to their emotional well-being.

2. **Provide Mental Stimulation:** These dogs love to engage their minds, so offer them plenty of mental challenges. Puzzle toys, interactive games, and tasks that require focus, such as scent training or obedience drills, are excellent ways to keep their minds sharp and engaged.

3. **Keep Their Environment Clean:** Virgo dogs are particularly sensitive to their surroundings, especially when it comes to cleanliness. Make sure their living spaces are clean and free of clutter. Regularly clean their bedding, toys, and feeding areas to ensure they remain comfortable in their environment.

4. **Balanced, Nutritious Diet:** Given their health-conscious tendencies, Virgo dogs benefit from a balanced, nutritious diet. Pay close attention to their dietary needs and avoid feeding them unhealthy treats or foods that may upset their sensitive stomachs. High-quality, wholesome foods are ideal for keeping them in optimal health.

5. **Grooming and Hygiene:** Virgo dogs tend to enjoy grooming and being kept neat. Regular brushing, nail trimming, and ear cleaning should be part of their routine. They may be particularly

sensitive to feeling dirty, so keep their coat clean and their paws wiped after walks to ensure they remain comfortable.

6. **Calm and Quiet Spaces:** Virgo dogs prefer calm, orderly environments. Provide them with a quiet, comfortable space where they can retreat when they need some downtime. A cozy bed in a low-traffic area of the home can give them the peace and tranquility they crave.

7. **Training with Precision:** Virgo dogs excel in training, particularly when tasks are broken down into clear, methodical steps. They are quick learners and appreciate precision, so keep training sessions focused and reward them for their attention to detail. Patience and consistency are key to ensuring success in their training.

8. **Health Monitoring:** Virgo dogs are naturally in tune with their bodies and may be more sensitive to changes in their health. Keep an eye on any signs of discomfort or illness, as they are likely to communicate when something isn't right. Regular vet check-ups and a focus on preventative care are essential for keeping them healthy.

Building a Strong Relationship with Your Virgo Dog

Building a bond with a Virgo dog requires understanding their need for order, cleanliness, and routine. Here's how you can create a strong connection with your Virgo dog:

- **Respect Their Need for Routine:** Virgo dogs feel secure when their routine is consistent. Respect their need for predictability and avoid making sudden changes to their daily schedule. They will feel more comfortable and connected to you when they can rely on a steady routine.

- **Engage Their Intelligence:** Virgo dogs love to use their brains, so keep them mentally stimulated through training, problem-solving tasks, and interactive play. They will appreciate the mental challenge and enjoy the opportunity to show off their intelligence.

- **Provide a Clean and Tidy Space:** Virgo dogs are sensitive to their surroundings, so make sure their living area is clean and organized. A tidy, clutter-free space will help them feel more relaxed and content.

- **Be Patient and Gentle:** Virgo dogs can be reserved or shy, especially in new situations. Be patient with them and give them time to adjust to new environments or people. A gentle, understanding approach will help them trust you and feel secure in your care.

Conclusion

Virgo dogs are calm, intelligent, and reliable companions who thrive on routine and structure. With their keen attention to detail and love for cleanliness, they bring a sense of order and stability to their homes. By understanding their traits, behaviors, and care needs, you can create an environment where your Virgo dog feels safe, loved, and valued.

Embrace their methodical nature, and you'll find a loyal, thoughtful companion who is always by your side, quietly supporting you in their own unique way. Virgo dogs may not seek the spotlight, but their steady presence and caring hearts make them irreplaceable members of the family.

Chapter 8: Libra Dogs (September 23 - October 22)

Charming, balanced, and sociable, Libra dogs are the peacekeepers of the canine zodiac. Ruled by Venus, the planet of love and beauty, Libra dogs thrive on harmony, companionship, and aesthetic pleasures. These dogs are known for their gentle nature, their desire for fairness, and their love of social interactions. In this chapter, we explore the traits, behaviors, and care tips for Libra dogs, offering insights on how to nurture their need for balance and connection.

Traits of Libra Dogs

Libra dogs are the epitome of charm and grace. They are natural diplomats, seeking to create harmony in their homes and amongst their pack. Here are the key traits that define Libra dogs:

1. **Sociable and Friendly:** Libra dogs love being around people and other animals. They are naturally friendly and enjoy making new friends, whether at home, the dog park, or on walks. Their easy-going nature makes them popular with both humans and pets alike, and they thrive on social interaction.

2. **Charming and Attractive:** Ruled by Venus, Libra dogs often have an irresistible charm. They know how to win over the hearts of those around them with their affectionate behavior and graceful demeanor. Whether through a well-placed nuzzle or a playful wag of the tail, Libra dogs have a way of making people feel special and loved.

3. **Balanced and Harmonious:** Balance is essential to Libra dogs. They dislike conflict and will do whatever they can to maintain peace in their environment. If there's tension in the household, a Libra dog may try to mediate or offer comfort to defuse the situation. They have a natural sense of fairness and often seek to ensure that everyone around them is treated equally.

4. **Indecisive at Times:** While Libra dogs are thoughtful and considerate, they can also be indecisive. They may struggle to make decisions, such as choosing between two toys or deciding which

path to take on a walk. This indecision is often due to their desire for balance—they want to make the "right" choice and are hesitant to commit until they're sure.

5. **Affectionate and Loving:** These dogs are incredibly affectionate and thrive on love and companionship. They enjoy being close to their owners and will often seek out cuddles or attention. Libra dogs are happiest when they are surrounded by their family, and they have a natural ability to make those around them feel cherished.

6. **Aesthetic Sensibilities:** Ruled by Venus, the planet of beauty, Libra dogs have an appreciation for comfort and aesthetics. They enjoy soft, comfortable surroundings and may even prefer plush bedding or luxurious toys. They are drawn to pleasant environments and may avoid areas that are too loud, chaotic, or unpleasant.

7. **Diplomatic and Fair-Minded:** Libra dogs have a strong sense of justice and fairness. They are not typically aggressive or confrontational, and they prefer to resolve conflicts peacefully. They may even act as mediators between other pets, helping to calm tensions and restore balance to the household.

Behavior of Libra Dogs

Libra dogs' behaviors reflect their need for balance, harmony, and social interaction. Understanding their behavior can help you create a peaceful and loving environment for them:

1. **Craving for Companionship:** Libra dogs are highly social creatures who love spending time with their families. They may follow you from room to room, seeking your company and affection. They do not like being left alone for long periods, as they can become lonely or anxious when separated from their loved ones.

2. **Dislike of Conflict:** These dogs are sensitive to conflict and tension. If there's an argument or disagreement in the household, a Libra dog may become anxious or try to intervene to restore peace. They are natural peacemakers and will often go out of their way to avoid or diffuse conflicts, whether between humans or other pets.

3. **Indecision and Hesitation:** Libra dogs can be indecisive when faced with choices. They may hesitate before choosing a toy or deciding on a path during a walk. This indecision comes from their desire to maintain balance—they want to make the best choice and often take their time before committing.

4. **Gentle and Non-Confrontational:** Libra dogs are gentle by nature and rarely show aggression. They prefer calm, peaceful environments and may become distressed if exposed to loud noises or chaotic situations. Their non-confrontational demeanor makes them excellent companions for families with children or other pets.

5. **Love of Aesthetics and Comfort:** These dogs enjoy being surrounded by beauty and comfort. They are drawn to cozy, well-decorated spaces and may show a preference for soft, plush bedding or toys. If given the choice, they will often gravitate toward the most comfortable spots in the house.

6. **Playful and Sociable:** Libra dogs enjoy socializing and playing with others. They are great at reading social cues and know when to engage in play and when to offer comfort. Their playful side is gentle and balanced, making them well-suited to playing with children, older adults, or other pets.

Care Tips for Libra Dogs

Caring for a Libra dog means creating an environment that nurtures their need for companionship, balance, and comfort. Here are some essential care tips to keep your Libra dog happy and emotionally fulfilled:

1. **Prioritize Social Interaction:** Libra dogs thrive on social interaction and companionship. Make sure they have plenty of opportunities to engage with family members, friends, and other pets. Regular playdates, trips to the dog park, and family bonding time are important for their emotional well-being.

2. **Maintain a Peaceful Environment:** These dogs are sensitive to conflict and chaos, so it's essential to maintain a calm, peaceful environment for them. If there are arguments or tensions in the household, try to keep your Libra dog away from the conflict to prevent them from becoming anxious or stressed.

3. **Comfortable and Aesthetic Living Spaces:** Libra dogs appreciate comfortable, cozy living spaces. Invest in a plush dog bed, soft blankets, and a few aesthetically pleasing toys to create an environment they will love. Keep their living area clean, organized, and free from harsh noises or bright lights.

4. **Balanced Playtime and Rest:** Libra dogs enjoy both playtime and relaxation. Provide them with a balanced routine that includes regular play, exercise, and rest. They enjoy activities that allow them to interact with others, such as fetch, tug-of-war, or gentle play with other dogs. At the same time, ensure they have a quiet, cozy space to relax and recharge.

5. **Gentle Training Techniques:** These dogs respond best to positive reinforcement and gentle training techniques. Harsh methods or punishments may upset their sensitive nature. Focus on rewarding good behavior with praise, treats, or affection, and be patient with their learning process. Libra dogs are eager to please and will respond well to a kind, balanced approach.

6. **Help Them with Decision-Making:** Libra dogs can be indecisive, so offer guidance when they seem unsure. Whether it's choosing a toy or deciding which direction to take on a walk, help them by offering clear choices and gentle encouragement. This will alleviate any stress they feel from having to make decisions.

7. **Regular Grooming and Pampering:** Libra dogs enjoy being pampered, and regular grooming sessions can help keep them looking and feeling their best. Bathing, brushing, and nail trimming should be part of their routine, and they may even enjoy the extra attention that comes with grooming. Consider using soothing, pleasant-smelling grooming products to enhance their experience.

8. **Avoid Long Periods of Isolation:** Libra dogs do not like being left alone for extended periods. If you need to leave them alone, provide them with toys, comfort items, or calming music to keep them company. Consider using a pet sitter or doggy daycare to ensure they have the social interaction they need when you're away.

Building a Strong Relationship with Your Libra Dog

Building a bond with a Libra dog means understanding their need for love, companionship, and harmony. Here's how you can create a strong connection with your Libra dog:

- **Be a Calm and Loving Presence:** Libra dogs thrive in calm, peaceful environments. Approach them with gentleness and kindness, and they will reward you with unwavering loyalty and affection.

- **Spend Quality Time Together:** Libra dogs love being close to their owners, so make time for regular bonding sessions. Whether it's playing, going for walks, or simply sitting together, your Libra dog will feel more connected to you through shared experiences.

- **Create a Balanced Routine:** Libra dogs appreciate balance in all aspects of life. Establish a daily routine that includes a mix of socialization, play, exercise, and relaxation. They will feel more secure and content when their days are predictable and well-balanced.

- **Encourage Socialization:** Libra dogs love being around people and other animals, so give them plenty of opportunities to socialize. Arrange playdates, take them to the dog park, and encourage positive interactions with other pets and humans.

Conclusion

Libra dogs are the embodiment of charm, balance, and affection. With their gentle nature and love of companionship, they bring harmony and peace to any home. By understanding their traits, behaviors, and care needs, you can create an environment that nurtures their sociable and balanced spirit.

Embrace their love for social interaction and peaceful living, and you'll find a loyal companion who fills your life with love, grace, and harmony. Libra dogs may not enjoy conflict, but their presence will always bring a sense of calm and beauty to those lucky enough to share their lives with them.

Chapter 9: Scorpio Dogs (October 23 - November 21)

Scorpio dogs are intense, loyal, and mysterious. Ruled by Pluto, the planet of transformation, and Mars, the planet of energy and action, these dogs are known for their deep emotions, strong instincts, and powerful personalities. They form strong bonds with their owners and often exhibit a protective and sometimes enigmatic nature. In this chapter, we'll explore the traits, behaviors, and care tips for Scorpio dogs, providing insight into how to manage their complex and emotionally charged personalities.

Traits of Scorpio Dogs

Scorpio dogs are complex creatures with a depth of emotion that sets them apart from other dogs. Their loyalty is unwavering, and they often exhibit a mix of passion, protectiveness, and independence. Here are the key traits that define Scorpio dogs:

1. **Intensely Loyal:** Scorpio dogs form deep, almost unbreakable bonds with their owners. Once they have chosen their person or family, their loyalty knows no bounds. They are protective and will stand by your side through thick and thin, often exhibiting a level of devotion that borders on the obsessive.

2. **Emotionally Complex:** Scorpio dogs are highly emotional and sensitive to the moods of those around them. They experience a wide range of feelings and often have a strong sense of empathy for their owners. While they may not always outwardly show it, they feel deeply and are attuned to their environment.

3. **Protective and Courageous:** These dogs have a natural protective instinct. They are not afraid to defend their territory or loved ones, often showing great courage in the face of danger. Scorpio

dogs make excellent guard dogs due to their fearless nature and their intense drive to protect.

4. **Mysterious and Independent:** Scorpio dogs are known for their mysterious aura. They often keep their emotions guarded, and it can be difficult to understand what they are thinking or feeling. Despite their deep bond with their owners, they also enjoy their independence and may seek out time alone to recharge.

5. **Determined and Strong-Willed:** Scorpio dogs are incredibly determined and can be quite stubborn. Once they set their mind on something, it's hard to change their course. This trait can make training a challenge at times, but it also gives them a strong sense of perseverance and focus.

6. **Intuitive and Perceptive:** Scorpio dogs have an uncanny ability to sense things that others may miss. They are highly intuitive, often picking up on subtle cues from their owners or their environment. This makes them excellent companions for people who need emotional support, as they are quick to recognize when something is wrong.

7. **Secretive:** There is an element of secrecy with Scorpio dogs. They may hide their emotions, toys, or even food. This secretive behavior adds to their mysterious nature, making them seem aloof at times. However, once trust is established, they are more likely to share their inner world with those they love.

Behavior of Scorpio Dogs

The behavior of Scorpio dogs is often shaped by their emotional depth and strong sense of loyalty. Understanding these behaviors will help you manage their intense personalities and create a balanced, fulfilling relationship:

1. **Strong Bond with Owners:** Scorpio dogs form deep, almost soul-level connections with their owners. They may follow you around the house, keeping a close watch on your every move.

This loyalty is often accompanied by a level of protectiveness, as they view their family as their responsibility to guard and defend.

2. **Territorial and Protective:** These dogs are highly territorial and will defend their home and loved ones with great intensity. They are vigilant and alert, always on the lookout for potential threats. While they are not necessarily aggressive, they are quick to react if they sense danger or feel that their territory is being encroached upon.

3. **Reserved Around Strangers:** Scorpio dogs are not quick to warm up to strangers. They tend to be cautious and reserved when meeting new people, often taking their time to assess whether or not they can trust someone. Once they decide a person is trustworthy, they will be loyal and affectionate, but it can take time for them to reach this point.

4. **Emotional Sensitivity:** These dogs are highly sensitive to the emotions of those around them. If their owner is feeling stressed, anxious, or upset, a Scorpio dog will pick up on this and may even mirror these emotions. They are deeply empathetic and will often try to comfort their owners during difficult times.

5. **Secretive and Independent:** While they form strong bonds with their owners, Scorpio dogs also value their independence. They may retreat to a quiet space when they need time to themselves, and they often keep certain aspects of their personality or behavior hidden. For example, they may bury toys or food in secret spots around the house or yard.

6. **High Drive and Focus:** Scorpio dogs are incredibly driven and focused when it comes to tasks or goals. Whether it's learning a new trick, guarding their territory, or playing with a favorite toy, they approach everything with intensity. This focus makes them excellent working dogs or companions for activities that require determination and stamina.

7. **Stubborn and Determined:** While their determination can be an asset, it can also make them a bit stubborn at times. If a Scor-

pio dog doesn't want to do something, it may take a lot of convincing to change their mind. Training requires patience and consistency, as they may resist commands that don't align with their desires.

Care Tips for Scorpio Dogs

Caring for a Scorpio dog requires understanding their emotional complexity, loyalty, and need for independence. Here are some essential care tips to keep your Scorpio dog happy and emotionally balanced:

1. **Establish Trust Early:** Trust is the foundation of your relationship with a Scorpio dog. Establishing a strong bond early on is crucial, as they need to feel secure and connected to their owners. Be consistent in your actions and provide them with plenty of affection to build this trust over time.

2. **Provide Mental and Physical Stimulation:** Scorpio dogs are intelligent and driven, so they need plenty of mental and physical stimulation to stay happy. Engage them in activities that challenge their minds, such as puzzle toys, scent work, or advanced training exercises. Regular physical exercise, like long walks, runs, or agility training, will also help burn off their excess energy.

3. **Respect Their Independence:** While Scorpio dogs are deeply bonded to their owners, they also need time to themselves. Provide them with a quiet, comfortable space where they can retreat when they need to recharge. Respect their independence and allow them to have alone time without interruption.

4. **Train with Patience and Consistency:** Scorpio dogs can be strong-willed and stubborn, so training requires patience and consistency. Use positive reinforcement and reward-based training methods to motivate them. Be firm but fair, and avoid harsh punishments, as they can become emotionally withdrawn if treated unfairly.

5. **Offer Emotional Support:** These dogs are highly sensitive and may need extra emotional support during times of stress or change. Provide comfort and reassurance when they seem anxious or upset, and be mindful of how your own emotions may affect them. Their empathetic nature means they are closely attuned to your emotional state.

6. **Protect Their Territory:** Scorpio dogs are naturally territorial, so it's important to create a safe and secure environment for them. They may become anxious or defensive if they feel their territory is being threatened. Establish clear boundaries for visitors and other pets to prevent territorial disputes.

7. **Respect Their Privacy:** Scorpio dogs value their privacy and may be secretive about certain aspects of their behavior. Whether it's hiding toys or retreating to a quiet space, allow them to express their need for privacy without interfering. This respect will help strengthen your bond and create a sense of trust.

Building a Strong Relationship with Your Scorpio Dog

Building a bond with a Scorpio dog requires patience, trust, and a deep understanding of their emotional complexity. Here's how you can create a strong connection with your Scorpio dog:

- **Earn Their Trust:** Scorpio dogs take their time when forming bonds, but once they trust you, their loyalty is unbreakable. Be consistent, caring, and patient in your interactions to earn their trust and deepen your relationship.

- **Be Emotionally Available:** These dogs are highly sensitive to the emotions of their owners, so be mindful of your emotional state. Offer them comfort and reassurance when they sense you're upset, and be present for them when they need emotional support.

- **Respect Their Boundaries:** Scorpio dogs value their independence and privacy, so respect their need for space. Allow them to retreat when they need alone time, and avoid pushing them into social situations if they seem uncomfortable.

- **Engage Their Intelligence:** Scorpio dogs love a challenge. Provide them with mentally stimulating activities, such as puzzle toys, scent work, or advanced obedience training. Engaging their minds will strengthen your bond and keep them mentally sharp.

Conclusion

Scorpio dogs are intense, loyal, and deeply emotional companions. With their strong protective instincts and complex personalities, they bring a sense of mystery and devotion to any household. By understanding their traits, behaviors, and care needs, you can create a harmonious and fulfilling relationship with your Scorpio dog.

Embrace their depth of emotion, respect their independence, and provide them with the mental and physical challenges they crave. In return, you'll find yourself with a fiercely loyal companion who will stand by your side through thick and thin, offering protection, love, and an unwavering bond that is truly special.

Chapter 10: Sagittarius Dogs (November 22 - December 21)

Adventurous, energetic, and free-spirited, Sagittarius dogs are the explorers of the canine zodiac. Ruled by Jupiter, the planet of expansion and optimism, these dogs are always seeking new experiences, love to be active, and have a boundless enthusiasm for life. With their curious nature and desire for freedom, Sagittarius dogs bring excitement and joy to their owners. In this chapter, we explore the traits, behaviors, and care tips for Sagittarius dogs, helping you nurture their adventurous spirit and zest for life.

Traits of Sagittarius Dogs

Sagittarius dogs are known for their love of adventure, their energetic personalities, and their optimistic outlook on life. They are the ultimate canine explorers, always eager to discover new places and meet new people. Here are the key traits that define Sagittarius dogs:

1. **Adventurous and Curious:** Sagittarius dogs are always on the move, eager to explore the world around them. They have a natural curiosity and love to investigate new scents, environments, and experiences. Whether it's a hike in the woods or a new toy at home, they are happiest when they're discovering something new.

2. **Energetic and Playful:** These dogs are full of energy and love to play. They need plenty of physical activity to keep them happy and healthy, and they are always up for a game of fetch, a run in the park, or a hike with their owners. Their playful nature makes them fun and lively companions.

3. **Optimistic and Happy-Go-Lucky:** Sagittarius dogs have an infectious optimism. They are rarely in a bad mood and approach life with a sense of joy and excitement. Their positive energy is contagious, and they have a way of lifting the spirits of everyone around them.

4. **Independent and Free-Spirited:** While they are loving and loyal, Sagittarius dogs also value their independence. They enjoy

their freedom and may sometimes prefer to explore on their own terms. They are not clingy and can be quite self-sufficient, though they still appreciate the company of their human companions.

5. **Bold and Fearless:** Sagittarius dogs are not afraid to take risks or try new things. Their bold nature means they are always ready to dive headfirst into new experiences, whether it's exploring unfamiliar territory or interacting with new dogs and people. They are fearless and love the thrill of adventure.

6. **Restless and Impulsive:** With their love of movement and exploration, Sagittarius dogs can become restless if they're cooped up for too long. They have a tendency to act on impulse, which can sometimes get them into trouble. They may dart off on a walk if they catch an interesting scent or become overly excited when they encounter something new.

7. **Sociable and Friendly:** Sagittarius dogs are naturally friendly and love meeting new people and animals. They are highly sociable and enjoy being in social environments where they can interact with others. Their easy-going nature makes them well-liked by both humans and other pets.

Behavior of Sagittarius Dogs

Sagittarius dogs' behavior is driven by their desire for freedom, adventure, and social interaction. Understanding their behavior will help you create an environment that satisfies their need for exploration and movement:

1. **Constant Need for Activity:** Sagittarius dogs have a seemingly endless supply of energy. They need regular physical exercise to stay happy and balanced. If they don't get enough activity, they may become restless, bored, or even destructive. Long walks, runs, and plenty of playtime are essential for keeping their energy levels in check.

2. **Love of Exploration:** These dogs are natural explorers. They love being outside, whether it's in a park, a forest, or even just the backyard. They are likely to wander off if given the chance, so it's important to keep an eye on them during walks and outdoor activities to prevent them from getting lost.

3. **Restlessness When Confined:** Sagittarius dogs do not do well in confined spaces or sedentary environments. They can become anxious or restless if they are kept indoors for too long without an outlet for their energy. They need space to roam and explore, so it's important to provide them with regular outdoor time and plenty of mental stimulation.

4. **Impulsive Behavior:** With their adventurous spirit comes a certain impulsiveness. Sagittarius dogs may act without thinking, whether it's chasing after a squirrel or jumping into a new situation without hesitation. This impulsive behavior can sometimes lead to accidents or risky situations, so it's important to keep them on a leash in unfamiliar environments and teach them basic recall commands.

5. **Sociable and Friendly in Group Settings:** Sagittarius dogs love being around people and other animals. They are highly sociable and thrive in environments where they can interact with others. They are likely to be the life of the party at the dog park, making friends easily and enjoying the company of both humans and other pets.

6. **Positive Outlook and Playful Demeanor:** These dogs are eternal optimists, always ready for fun and excitement. Their playful nature means they are always up for a game or an adventure, and their happy-go-lucky demeanor makes them a joy to be around. They are rarely moody or irritable and bring a sense of joy to those around them.

Care Tips for Sagittarius Dogs

Caring for a Sagittarius dog requires an understanding of their need for adventure, exercise, and social interaction. Here are some essential care tips to keep your Sagittarius dog happy and well-balanced:

1. **Provide Plenty of Physical Activity:** Sagittarius dogs need a lot of physical exercise to burn off their excess energy. Make sure they get at least an hour of vigorous activity each day, whether it's a long walk, a run, or a play session at the park. Engaging them in activities like hiking, agility training, or even fetch will help keep them physically and mentally stimulated.

2. **Encourage Exploration:** These dogs love to explore new environments, so give them plenty of opportunities to do so. Take them to different parks, hiking trails, or beaches where they can experience new sights, smells, and sounds. Just be sure to keep them on a leash in unfamiliar areas to prevent them from wandering too far.

3. **Offer Mental Stimulation:** In addition to physical exercise, Sagittarius dogs need mental stimulation to stay engaged. Puzzle toys, interactive games, and training exercises are great ways to keep their minds sharp. Activities that challenge their problem-solving skills will help prevent boredom and keep them entertained.

4. **Socialize Them Regularly:** Sagittarius dogs are highly social and enjoy interacting with other dogs and people. Make sure they have plenty of opportunities to socialize by taking them to the dog park, scheduling playdates, or bringing them along on outings where they can meet new people and pets.

5. **Respect Their Independence:** While Sagittarius dogs love being around others, they also value their independence. Give them the freedom to explore and make their own choices, but always keep safety in mind. Allow them some time to roam and sniff dur-

ing walks, and provide them with toys and activities that allow for independent play.

6. **Keep an Eye on Their Impulsiveness:** Sagittarius dogs can be impulsive, so it's important to keep an eye on them in situations where they might act without thinking. Train them with basic commands like "come" and "stay" to help manage their impulsive tendencies, especially when off-leash or in unfamiliar environments.

7. **Create a Safe Outdoor Space:** If you have a yard, make sure it's securely fenced so your Sagittarius dog can explore and play safely without the risk of wandering off. Providing them with a safe outdoor space where they can run and explore freely will satisfy their need for adventure while keeping them safe.

8. **Balanced Diet for Active Dogs:** Sagittarius dogs burn a lot of energy, so it's important to provide them with a balanced diet that supports their active lifestyle. High-quality, nutrient-dense food will help keep them healthy and energized. Make sure they have access to plenty of water, especially after long play sessions or outdoor adventures.

Building a Strong Relationship with Your Sagittarius Dog

Building a bond with a Sagittarius dog requires understanding their adventurous spirit and giving them the freedom they crave. Here's how you can create a strong connection with your Sagittarius dog:

- **Engage in Adventures Together:** Sagittarius dogs love exploring new places, so take them on adventures with you. Whether it's a hike in the woods, a trip to the beach, or a walk in a new park, sharing these experiences will deepen your bond.

- **Provide Freedom with Boundaries:** While Sagittarius dogs enjoy their independence, they still need structure. Give them the freedom to explore within safe boundaries, such as a securely fenced yard or a long leash during walks.

- **Be Playful and Engaging:** Sagittarius dogs love to play, so make time for regular play sessions. Engage them with interactive toys, games of fetch, or agility training to keep them physically and mentally stimulated.
- **Socialize Them Often:** These dogs thrive on social interaction, so make sure they have plenty of opportunities to meet new people and pets. Introduce them to new environments and social settings to keep them happy and well-adjusted.

Conclusion

Sagittarius dogs are adventurous, energetic, and always ready for the next big adventure. With their love of exploration and positive outlook on life, they bring excitement and joy to their owners. By understanding their traits, behaviors, and care needs, you can provide a stimulating and fulfilling environment where your Sagittarius dog can thrive.

Embrace their adventurous spirit, respect their independence, and give them plenty of opportunities to explore the world around them. In return, you'll find yourself with a loyal, playful companion who will always be by your side, ready for the next exciting chapter of life.

Chapter 11: Capricorn Dogs (December 22 - January 19)

Capricorn dogs are disciplined, determined, and incredibly reliable. Ruled by Saturn, the planet of structure and responsibility, these dogs thrive on order and routine. Known for their hardworking nature and steadfast loyalty, Capricorn dogs are the steady rocks of the canine zodiac, bringing a sense of calm and stability to their homes. This chapter explores the traits, behaviors, and care tips for Capricorn dogs, helping you understand their need for structure and how to nurture their responsible and loyal personalities.

Traits of Capricorn Dogs

Capricorn dogs are characterized by their sense of duty, patience, and quiet strength. They approach life with a mature attitude, often displaying a wisdom beyond their years. Here are the key traits that define Capricorn dogs:

1. **Disciplined and Hardworking:** Capricorn dogs have a strong work ethic. They take their "jobs" seriously, whether that means guarding the house, learning new commands, or helping around the farm. They enjoy being given responsibilities and will work diligently to fulfill their tasks.

2. **Loyal and Devoted:** Capricorn dogs form deep, unwavering bonds with their families. They are incredibly loyal and will remain devoted to their owners for life. Their loyalty extends to protecting their home, ensuring that their family and environment remain safe and secure.

3. **Patient and Steady:** These dogs have a calm, patient nature and do not easily get flustered. They approach challenges with a steady mindset, taking their time to think things through before reacting. This makes them excellent problem-solvers and companions who can handle stressful situations with ease.

4. **Mature and Responsible:** Capricorn dogs are often described as old souls. Even at a young age, they display a sense of maturity and responsibility that is rare in other dogs. They are not prone

to impulsive behavior and prefer a structured environment where they know what is expected of them.

5. **Reserved and Independent:** While they are deeply loyal, Capricorn dogs tend to be more reserved than some other signs. They are independent by nature and may not seek out constant affection or attention. Instead, they are content to spend time on their own, quietly observing their surroundings.

6. **Goal-Oriented and Determined:** Capricorn dogs are incredibly determined and goal-oriented. Once they set their mind on something, they will pursue it with unwavering focus. Whether it's learning a new command or protecting their home, they will work hard to achieve their objectives.

7. **Practical and Grounded:** These dogs have a practical, no-nonsense approach to life. They prefer routine and structure and thrive in environments that provide clear expectations. Capricorn dogs are not easily swayed by distractions or frivolity—they are focused and grounded in their actions.

Behavior of Capricorn Dogs

The behavior of Capricorn dogs is often shaped by their desire for structure, responsibility, and routine. Understanding their behavior can help you create an environment where they feel secure and fulfilled:

1. **Thrives on Routine and Structure:** Capricorn dogs are happiest when they have a clear routine to follow. They appreciate consistency in their daily schedule, including feeding times, walks, and play sessions. Disruptions to their routine may cause them to become unsettled or anxious, so it's important to maintain a structured environment.

2. **Loyal to a Fault:** These dogs are fiercely loyal and will do whatever it takes to protect their family. They form deep emotional bonds with their owners and are always on alert to ensure the safety and security of their home. This protective nature can

sometimes manifest as wariness around strangers or new environments.

3. **Independent but Close:** Capricorn dogs enjoy their independence and may not be as needy as some other signs. They are content to spend time alone or quietly observing from a distance. However, this doesn't mean they don't love their family—they just show their affection in more subtle ways, such as staying close by or offering quiet companionship.

4. **Serious and Focused:** Capricorn dogs are not the type to engage in frivolous or overly playful behavior. While they can enjoy playtime, they are more focused on tasks and responsibilities. They approach life with a serious, focused mindset and may prefer activities that engage their mind and challenge them.

5. **Protective and Cautious:** These dogs are naturally protective and cautious, especially when it comes to their home and family. They are not overly aggressive, but they will not hesitate to defend their territory if they sense a threat. Their cautious nature also means they may take time to warm up to new people or environments.

6. **Problem-Solving Skills:** Capricorn dogs are excellent problem solvers. They are methodical in their approach to challenges and enjoy tasks that require them to think critically. Whether it's figuring out how to open a door or completing an agility course, these dogs excel at finding solutions to problems.

7. **Takes Time to Warm Up:** Capricorn dogs can be slow to warm up to new people or situations. They are naturally cautious and prefer to assess their surroundings before engaging. Once they feel comfortable and safe, they will open up and become loyal, affectionate companions.

Care Tips for Capricorn Dogs

Caring for a Capricorn dog means creating a structured, stable environment that supports their hardworking and responsible nature. Here are some essential care tips for keeping your Capricorn dog happy and fulfilled:

1. **Establish a Consistent Routine:** Capricorn dogs thrive on routine and structure. Establish a daily schedule for feeding, walks, and playtime, and stick to it as closely as possible. They will feel more secure and content when they know what to expect each day.

2. **Give Them Responsibilities:** Capricorn dogs love having tasks to complete. Whether it's carrying a small bag on a hike, helping with farm chores, or learning new tricks, they enjoy being given responsibilities. These tasks give them a sense of purpose and help them feel useful and fulfilled.

3. **Provide Mental Stimulation:** In addition to physical exercise, Capricorn dogs need mental challenges to stay engaged. Puzzle toys, obedience training, and problem-solving activities are great ways to keep their minds sharp. They enjoy tasks that require focus and concentration, so be sure to provide them with activities that challenge their intelligence.

4. **Create a Safe, Quiet Space:** Capricorn dogs appreciate having a quiet, secure space where they can retreat when they need to relax or recharge. Provide them with a comfortable bed or crate in a low-traffic area of the house where they can have some alone time when needed.

5. **Encourage Independence:** These dogs value their independence, so allow them the freedom to explore their environment and spend time alone when they want to. Don't overwhelm them with too much affection or attention—Capricorn dogs are content to be close by without being constantly doted on.

6. **Be Patient in Social Settings:** Capricorn dogs can be reserved or cautious around new people or situations, so it's important to be patient when introducing them to new environments. Give them time to assess and feel comfortable before encouraging so-

cial interaction. Gradual introductions to new people and pets will help them feel more at ease.

7. **Exercise with Purpose:** Capricorn dogs prefer activities that have a purpose or goal. Rather than just running around aimlessly, they enjoy structured exercises like agility training, scent work, or hiking. These activities engage their mind and body, providing them with the sense of accomplishment they crave.

8. **Balanced Diet for Steady Energy:** Given their hardworking nature, Capricorn dogs need a balanced, nutrient-rich diet to maintain their energy levels. Make sure they have high-quality food that supports their active lifestyle and helps them stay strong and healthy. Avoid overfeeding, as Capricorn dogs can be prone to weight gain if they aren't getting enough exercise.

Building a Strong Relationship with Your Capricorn Dog

Building a bond with a Capricorn dog requires understanding their need for structure, responsibility, and independence. Here's how you can create a strong connection with your Capricorn dog:

- **Respect Their Independence:** Capricorn dogs appreciate their alone time, so respect their need for space when they seek it. Allow them to retreat to their quiet area when they need to recharge, and avoid overwhelming them with constant attention.
- **Provide Mental and Physical Challenges:** Capricorn dogs enjoy tasks that challenge their mind and body. Engage them in activities like training, problem-solving games, or structured play that allows them to use their intelligence and energy in productive ways.
- **Be Consistent in Your Actions:** Capricorn dogs value consistency and reliability. Be steady and predictable in your interactions with them, and they will trust you more deeply. They appreciate knowing what to expect from their owners and will respond positively to a calm, structured environment.

- **Show Affection in Subtle Ways:** While Capricorn dogs may not seek out affection constantly, they still appreciate your love and attention. Offer them gentle affection in quiet moments, such as a pet or a cuddle after a long day. They may not be as outwardly affectionate as other signs, but they will show their loyalty through their calm presence and reliable companionship.

Conclusion

Capricorn dogs are the epitome of loyalty, responsibility, and discipline. With their mature approach to life and their strong work ethic, they bring a sense of calm and stability to their homes. By understanding their traits, behaviors, and care needs, you can create a structured environment that allows your Capricorn dog to thrive.

Embrace their need for routine, provide them with meaningful tasks, and offer them the mental and physical challenges they crave. In return, you'll find yourself with a reliable, hardworking companion who will stand by your side with unwavering loyalty and quiet strength, offering you a lifelong partnership built on trust and mutual respect.

Chapter 12: Aquarius Dogs (January 20 - February 18)

Aquarius dogs are unique, quirky, and highly independent. Ruled by Uranus, the planet of innovation and change, these dogs often march to the beat of their own drum. Known for their originality and love of freedom, Aquarius dogs bring a sense of unpredictability and excitement to any home. They are both intellectual and emotionally detached, making them fascinating companions with a personality all their own. This chapter explores the traits, behaviors, and care tips for Aquarius dogs, helping you understand their individuality and how to nurture their need for stimulation and independence.

Traits of Aquarius Dogs

Aquarius dogs are known for their eccentric personalities, intelligence, and love of freedom. They are the innovators of the canine zodiac, always seeking new experiences and thinking outside the box. Here are the key traits that define Aquarius dogs:

1. **Quirky and Unpredictable:** Aquarius dogs are known for their quirks and unpredictable nature. They may exhibit behaviors that seem odd or unusual, such as developing unique routines or fixating on certain toys. Their quirkiness is part of their charm, making them stand out in any crowd.

2. **Independent and Free-Spirited:** These dogs value their independence and often prefer to make their own decisions. They enjoy exploring their surroundings on their own terms and may not always follow commands right away. While they love their family, they also need personal space and the freedom to roam and explore.

3. **Intelligent and Innovative:** Aquarius dogs are highly intelligent and have a natural curiosity about the world around them. They enjoy solving puzzles, learning new tricks, and figuring out how things work. Their problem-solving abilities are impressive,

and they often come up with creative ways to entertain themselves.

4. **Sociable but Detached:** While Aquarius dogs enjoy socializing with people and other animals, they often maintain an emotional distance. They are not overly affectionate or clingy and may seem aloof at times. However, they do enjoy being around others and can be very friendly when in the right mood.

5. **Open-Minded and Tolerant:** Aquarius dogs are open-minded and tend to be accepting of new experiences, people, and other animals. They are usually tolerant of differences and enjoy meeting new friends. Their easy-going nature makes them great companions in diverse social settings.

6. **Rebellious and Non-Conformist:** These dogs have a rebellious streak and may resist traditional training methods or routines. They don't like to be told what to do and prefer to find their own way. This non-conformist attitude can make them challenging to train but also adds to their unique personality.

7. **Humanitarian and Caring:** Despite their emotional detachment, Aquarius dogs have a caring side. They may show concern for other animals or try to help in their own way. They are often drawn to those who are vulnerable and may become protective or nurturing in unexpected ways.

Behavior of Aquarius Dogs

The behavior of Aquarius dogs is often driven by their need for independence, mental stimulation, and freedom. Understanding their behavior can help you create an environment that allows them to thrive while respecting their need for individuality:

1. **Curiosity and Exploration:** Aquarius dogs are natural explorers. They love to investigate new environments, scents, and experiences. They may wander off during walks if not kept on a leash, driven by their curiosity to see what's around the next corner.

It's important to provide them with safe opportunities to explore while keeping an eye on them to prevent them from getting into trouble.

2. **Inconsistent Obedience:** Due to their independent nature, Aquarius dogs may not always follow commands immediately. They are not disobedient but prefer to think for themselves. They may respond when they feel like it rather than when you ask them to. Patience and creativity in training are key to managing their unpredictable responses.

3. **Aloof but Friendly:** While Aquarius dogs enjoy the company of people and other pets, they are not overly clingy or dependent. They may seem aloof or distant at times, preferring to observe from afar rather than actively seek out affection. However, they are generally friendly and approachable when they choose to engage.

4. **Playful and Inventive:** These dogs love to play, but they often approach playtime in unique ways. They may create their own games or find unconventional uses for toys. Aquarius dogs enjoy interactive and mentally stimulating activities, such as puzzle toys, and they excel in problem-solving challenges.

5. **Rebellious Streak:** Aquarius dogs are known for their rebellious tendencies. They may test boundaries or ignore rules if they feel constrained. This rebelliousness is part of their personality, and it's important to approach training with flexibility and patience. Harsh or strict methods will only make them more resistant.

6. **Social, But on Their Terms:** Aquarius dogs enjoy being around others, but they also value their personal space. They may happily join in social activities or play with other dogs, but when they've had enough, they will retreat to a quiet spot to recharge. They are not the type to demand constant attention or affection.

7. **Emotionally Detached:** Unlike some other signs, Aquarius dogs are not overly emotional or clingy. They can be loving, but they don't need constant reassurance or physical contact to feel secure.

They are more likely to show their affection through subtle gestures, such as sitting near you or following you around the house.

Care Tips for Aquarius Dogs

Caring for an Aquarius dog requires understanding their need for independence, mental stimulation, and personal space. Here are some essential care tips to keep your Aquarius dog happy and well-balanced:

1. **Provide Mental Stimulation:** Aquarius dogs are highly intelligent and need regular mental challenges to stay engaged. Provide them with puzzle toys, interactive games, and tasks that require problem-solving. Keep their environment interesting by introducing new toys or changing up their routine to keep them mentally stimulated.

2. **Encourage Exploration:** These dogs love to explore, so give them opportunities to safely roam and investigate. Take them on walks in different environments, such as parks, beaches, or forests, where they can experience new sights and smells. Just be sure to keep them on a leash or in a secure area to prevent them from wandering off.

3. **Respect Their Independence:** Aquarius dogs value their independence, so it's important to respect their need for personal space. Avoid being overly clingy or demanding of their attention. Allow them to come to you when they're ready for affection, and give them the freedom to explore their surroundings.

4. **Be Flexible with Training:** Traditional training methods may not work as effectively with Aquarius dogs due to their independent and rebellious nature. Instead, use creative and flexible training techniques that engage their intelligence and allow them to think for themselves. Positive reinforcement and patience will go a long way in helping them learn.

5. **Socialization on Their Terms:** While Aquarius dogs are social, they may not always want to interact with others. Be mindful of

their social cues and allow them to engage with people and pets on their own terms. Regular socialization is important, but don't force them into situations where they feel uncomfortable or overwhelmed.

6. **Keep Their Environment Interesting:** Aquarius dogs get bored easily, so it's important to keep their environment stimulating. Rotate their toys, introduce new activities, and provide plenty of opportunities for mental and physical exercise. They thrive in environments that challenge their curiosity and intellect.

7. **Offer Personal Space:** These dogs enjoy having a quiet space to retreat to when they need alone time. Provide them with a comfortable bed or crate in a low-traffic area where they can relax without being disturbed. Respect their need for solitude, and they will come to you when they're ready for interaction.

Building a Strong Relationship with Your Aquarius Dog

Building a bond with an Aquarius dog requires understanding their unique personality and giving them the freedom to express themselves. Here's how you can create a strong connection with your Aquarius dog:

- **Give Them Space to Be Themselves:** Aquarius dogs are independent by nature, so give them the freedom to explore and make their own decisions. Allow them to be quirky and embrace their unique personality without trying to mold them into something they're not.

- **Engage Their Mind:** These dogs love mental challenges, so keep their minds sharp with interactive games and puzzle toys. Engage them in activities that require problem-solving and creativity, and they will appreciate the intellectual stimulation.

- **Be Flexible and Open-Minded:** Aquarius dogs are non-conformists, so be flexible in your approach to training and care. Don't be rigid in your expectations, and allow them to explore different ways of doing things. They will respond positively to a creative and open-minded approach.

- **Respect Their Boundaries:** While Aquarius dogs enjoy socializing, they also value their personal space. Respect their need for independence and don't force them into constant interaction. Allow them to come to you when they're ready for affection or playtime.

Conclusion

Aquarius dogs are unique, intelligent, and full of personality. With their love of freedom and curiosity about the world, they bring excitement and unpredictability to any home. By understanding their traits, behaviors, and care needs, you can provide a stimulating and supportive environment where your Aquarius dog can thrive.

Embrace their quirks, respect their independence, and provide them with plenty of mental and physical challenges. In return, you'll find yourself with a fascinating and loyal companion who will keep you on your toes, always ready for the next adventure.

Chapter 13: Pisces Dogs (February 19 - March 20)

Pisces dogs are gentle, empathetic, and deeply intuitive. Ruled by Neptune, the planet of dreams and spirituality, these dogs are highly sensitive to their surroundings and the emotions of those around them. Pisces dogs are often seen as the dreamers of the canine zodiac, possessing a soft, nurturing nature combined with a mystical, almost otherworldly charm. In this chapter, we explore the traits, behaviors, and care tips for Pisces dogs, helping you create a loving and emotionally supportive environment for these sensitive and compassionate companions.

Traits of Pisces Dogs

Pisces dogs are defined by their sensitivity, emotional intelligence, and creativity. They are the caregivers of the zodiac, always ready to provide comfort and support to their family members. Here are the key traits that define Pisces dogs:

1. **Empathetic and Intuitive:** Pisces dogs are highly attuned to the emotions of those around them. They can sense when their owners are upset or stressed and will often respond with comforting behavior. Their intuition allows them to understand unspoken feelings, making them natural emotional support animals.

2. **Gentle and Compassionate:** These dogs have a soft, caring nature and are always willing to offer comfort to those in need. They are especially good with children and other pets, often acting as protectors or caregivers. Pisces dogs dislike conflict and will go out of their way to create harmony in their environment.

3. **Dreamy and Imaginative:** Ruled by Neptune, Pisces dogs are dreamers. They have an active imagination and often exhibit behaviors that suggest they are lost in thought or fantasy. This dreamy nature can make them appear aloof at times, but it also contributes to their unique charm.

4. **Adaptable and Flexible:** Pisces dogs are highly adaptable and can adjust to a wide range of environments and situations. They are not rigid in their routines and are often content to go with the flow. This flexibility makes them easy to care for and good companions for families with varying schedules.

5. **Loyal and Devoted:** These dogs form deep emotional bonds with their owners. Their loyalty is unwavering, and they will go to great lengths to ensure the happiness and well-being of their loved ones. Pisces dogs are happiest when they feel emotionally connected to their family, and they thrive in homes where they are treated with kindness and care.

6. **Artistic and Expressive:** Pisces dogs have a creative and artistic side that may manifest in playful or expressive behavior. They enjoy engaging in imaginative play and often come up with unique ways to entertain themselves. Whether it's inventing a game or showing off their creativity through play, these dogs bring an artistic flair to everyday life.

7. **Sensitive and Emotional:** Pisces dogs are incredibly sensitive and can be easily affected by changes in their environment or the emotions of their family members. They need a calm, nurturing atmosphere to feel secure. Loud noises, tension, or conflict can cause them stress, so it's important to create a peaceful, stable environment for them.

Behavior of Pisces Dogs

Pisces dogs' behavior is closely linked to their emotional depth and sensitivity. Understanding their behavior will help you create a harmonious environment where they feel safe and loved:

1. **Comforting Presence:** Pisces dogs are natural caregivers. They have a calming presence and will often stay close to their owners when they sense that something is wrong. They may cuddle, nuzzle, or simply sit by your side to offer emotional support. Their

ability to comfort and soothe makes them excellent therapy or emotional support animals.

2. **Avoidance of Conflict:** These dogs dislike conflict and will avoid it whenever possible. If there is tension in the household, a Pisces dog may retreat to a quiet corner or try to diffuse the situation by offering affection. They are peacekeepers by nature and strive to create a calm, harmonious environment.

3. **Daydreaming and Imagination:** Pisces dogs are often lost in their own world. They may stare off into space or appear to be daydreaming, especially when they are in a relaxed state. This behavior is a reflection of their imaginative nature, and they may even seem to "drift away" during playtime or rest.

4. **Gentle and Patient:** These dogs are incredibly gentle, especially around children or smaller animals. They have a naturally patient demeanor and are unlikely to become aggressive or frustrated. Their gentle nature makes them ideal companions for families, especially those with young children or other pets.

5. **Emotional Sensitivity:** Pisces dogs are highly sensitive to the emotions of others. They can pick up on subtle cues, such as changes in tone of voice or body language, and will often respond with concern if they sense sadness or distress. This sensitivity makes them highly empathetic companions, but it also means they can become stressed or anxious if their environment is chaotic or emotionally charged.

6. **Adaptive and Easygoing:** These dogs are very adaptable and can adjust to new environments or changes in routine with ease. They are not demanding and are generally content to go along with whatever their owners are doing. However, they do need emotional stability to feel secure, so sudden, disruptive changes should be minimized.

7. **Strong Emotional Bonds:** Pisces dogs form deep emotional connections with their owners and may experience separation anxiety if left alone for long periods. They are happiest when they

are close to their loved ones, and they thrive in homes where they receive plenty of affection and emotional support.

Care Tips for Pisces Dogs

Caring for a Pisces dog requires understanding their emotional sensitivity and providing a peaceful, nurturing environment. Here are some essential care tips to keep your Pisces dog happy and well-balanced:

1. **Create a Calm Environment:** Pisces dogs are highly sensitive to their surroundings, so it's important to create a calm, peaceful home for them. Avoid loud noises, sudden changes, or high-stress situations that could upset them. A serene, loving environment will help them feel secure and relaxed.

2. **Offer Emotional Support:** These dogs thrive on emotional connection and need plenty of affection and reassurance. Spend time cuddling, petting, and talking to your Pisces dog to strengthen your bond. They are highly attuned to your emotions, so offering them emotional support will help them feel secure and loved.

3. **Provide Quiet Time:** Pisces dogs need downtime to recharge, especially if they've been in a busy or noisy environment. Make sure they have a quiet, comfortable space where they can retreat when they need to relax. A cozy bed in a quiet corner of the house is ideal for them to unwind and feel safe.

4. **Engage Their Imagination:** These dogs have a creative side and enjoy activities that engage their imagination. Provide them with toys that encourage creative play, such as interactive toys, soft plushies, or puzzle toys. They will enjoy coming up with their own ways to play and will appreciate toys that stimulate their creative instincts.

5. **Be Gentle in Training:** Pisces dogs respond best to gentle, positive reinforcement. They are sensitive to harsh tones or punishment, so it's important to use a calm, encouraging approach

when training them. Patience and kindness will help them learn without feeling stressed or anxious.

6. **Offer Emotional Stability:** Pisces dogs need emotional stability to feel secure. Try to maintain a consistent routine and avoid sudden changes that could cause them stress. They are very in tune with the emotions of their owners, so providing them with a stable, loving home will help them thrive.

7. **Nurture Their Social Side:** While Pisces dogs are gentle and sensitive, they also enjoy socializing with other pets and people. Regular interaction with other dogs and social experiences in a calm, controlled environment will help them develop confidence and maintain their emotional balance.

Building a Strong Relationship with Your Pisces Dog

Building a bond with a Pisces dog requires understanding their emotional depth and need for connection. Here's how you can create a strong connection with your Pisces dog:

- **Be Emotionally Available:** Pisces dogs thrive on emotional connection, so be present and available for them when they need comfort or affection. Offering them love and support will strengthen your bond and help them feel secure.

- **Provide Consistent Affection:** These dogs need regular displays of affection to feel loved and valued. Spend time cuddling, petting, and talking to your Pisces dog every day to show them how much you care.

- **Be Patient and Gentle:** Pisces dogs are sensitive souls, so approach them with kindness and patience. Avoid harsh training methods or sudden changes in routine, as these can upset them. Instead, use positive reinforcement and gentle guidance to help them learn and grow.

- **Respect Their Sensitivity:** Understand that Pisces dogs are emotionally sensitive and may need extra care during stressful situations. Be mindful of their emotional needs and provide them with a safe space to retreat to when they feel overwhelmed.

Conclusion

Pisces dogs are gentle, loving, and deeply empathetic companions. With their emotional sensitivity and intuitive nature, they bring a sense of peace and comfort to their families. By understanding their traits, behaviors, and care needs, you can create an environment where your Pisces dog feels secure, loved, and emotionally fulfilled.

Embrace their nurturing spirit, provide them with a calm and supportive environment, and offer them the emotional connection they crave. In return, you'll find yourself with a loyal and compassionate companion who will always be by your side, offering comfort, love, and emotional support whenever you need it most.

Part 2: Planetary Influences

Chapter 14: The Sun and Your Dog: How the Sun Sign Influences Your Dog's Core Personality

In astrology, the Sun sign is one of the most influential factors in shaping a being's personality. Just as it plays a critical role in determining the core traits of humans, the Sun sign similarly defines the essence of your dog's character. The Sun represents vitality, identity, and the innate qualities that shine through in everyday behaviors. It governs your dog's natural instincts, strengths, and how they interact with the world. In this chapter, we explore how the Sun sign influences your dog's core personality and how understanding this can help you better connect with and care for your canine companion.

What is the Sun Sign?

The Sun sign is determined by the position of the Sun at the time of birth, and it reflects your dog's essential self. It is the foundation of their personality, influencing how they respond to different situations, how they interact with others, and what motivates them. The Sun sign reveals your dog's core traits—their temperament, energy levels, and overall disposition. While other planetary influences, such as the Moon or rising sign, also play a role in shaping their character, the Sun sign is the most powerful force behind your dog's general behavior and life outlook.

How the Sun Influences Your Dog's Personality

The Sun's energy is vital in astrology because it represents life force and identity. For dogs, the Sun sign helps explain why one dog might be more energetic, while another is calmer or more cautious. The Sun sign influences how your dog approaches life, whether they are adventurous and bold or thoughtful and reserved. By understanding your dog's Sun sign, you gain insight into their natural preferences, tendencies, and overall temperament.

Understanding Your Dog's Core Personality Based on Their Sun Sign

Below is a general overview of how each Sun sign affects a dog's core personality. Each sign brings distinct traits that make your dog unique, and recognizing these qualities can help you cater to their needs and strengthen your bond.

Aries (March 21 - April 19): The Trailblazer

- **Core Traits:** Bold, energetic, adventurous
- **Influence of the Sun:** Aries dogs are natural leaders. Ruled by Mars, the planet of action, they are filled with vitality and enthusiasm. Aries dogs are confident and love to explore, often leading the pack or eagerly jumping into new adventures. They have an impulsive nature and may act without thinking, driven by the excitement of the moment. Their fiery energy makes them fearless, but they can also be impatient or headstrong at times. As their owner, it's important to provide Aries dogs with plenty of physical activities to satisfy their energetic personalities.

Taurus (April 20 - May 20): The Steadfast Companion

- **Core Traits:** Loyal, patient, and comfort-seeking
- **Influence of the Sun:** Taurus dogs are ruled by Venus, the planet of beauty and pleasure, which makes them calm and loving companions. These dogs are incredibly loyal and thrive on routine and comfort. They are slow to anger, preferring stability and relaxation over chaos. However, once they form a bond, it's deep and unshakable. Taurus dogs love indulging in the finer things, whether that's a cozy bed or their favorite treat. They prefer a structured environment and dislike sudden changes in their routine.

Gemini (May 21 - June 20): The Communicator

- **Core Traits:** Curious, lively, and playful
- **Influence of the Sun:** Ruled by Mercury, the planet of communication, Gemini dogs are highly intelligent and always curious. They love to learn and are often quick to pick up on commands and tricks. Gemini dogs have a dual nature—one moment they're calm and observant, and the next they're bursting with energy and excitement. Their playful and social nature makes them great companions in a busy household where they can interact with both people and other animals. They need constant mental stimulation and variety to stay happy.

Cancer (June 21 - July 22): The Nurturer

- **Core Traits:** Caring, protective, and intuitive
- **Influence of the Sun:** Cancer dogs are ruled by the Moon, which governs emotions, making them deeply intuitive and protective of their family. These dogs are nurturing by nature and are happiest when they feel secure in their environment. Cancer dogs are sensitive to the emotions of their owners and often act as emotional support animals, offering comfort when they sense someone is upset. They thrive on closeness and loyalty and may become anxious when left alone for long periods.

Leo (July 23 - August 22): The Performer

- **Core Traits:** Confident, playful, and affectionate
- **Influence of the Sun:** Leo is ruled by the Sun itself, giving these dogs a naturally radiant and confident personality. Leo dogs love being the center of attention and enjoy entertaining their family and friends with their playful antics. They are affectionate

and loyal, often forming strong bonds with their owners. These dogs are natural leaders and thrive in environments where they are treated like the star of the show. Leo dogs enjoy praise and recognition and can become bored or restless if they are not given enough attention.

Virgo (August 23 - September 22): The Perfectionist

- **Core Traits:** Practical, intelligent, and detail-oriented
- **Influence of the Sun:** Virgo dogs, ruled by Mercury, are known for their intelligence and practical nature. These dogs thrive on routine and enjoy being helpful. Virgo dogs are highly observant and meticulous, often paying close attention to their surroundings and learning quickly from their experiences. They have a calm and composed demeanor and prefer a clean, orderly environment. Virgo dogs enjoy tasks that challenge their minds, such as puzzle toys or agility training, and they appreciate being part of a structured household.

Libra (September 23 - October 22): The Diplomat

- **Core Traits:** Social, balanced, and charming
- **Influence of the Sun:** Ruled by Venus, Libra dogs are naturally sociable and charming. They thrive in harmonious environments and are skilled at maintaining balance in social settings. Libra dogs are affectionate and love being around people and other animals. Their easy-going nature makes them excellent companions for families, and they often act as mediators in situations of tension. They enjoy environments filled with beauty and comfort and may become stressed if they are exposed to conflict or disorder.

Scorpio (October 23 - November 21): The Intense Guardian

- **Core Traits:** Loyal, intense, and protective
- **Influence of the Sun:** Ruled by Pluto, Scorpio dogs have a depth of emotion and intensity that sets them apart from other dogs. These dogs are fiercely loyal and protective, often forming strong bonds with their family members. Scorpio dogs have a mysterious and independent side, preferring to keep their emotions hidden unless they fully trust their owner. While they can be reserved around strangers, they are extremely loving and devoted to those they care about.

Sagittarius (November 22 - December 21): The Explorer

- **Core Traits:** Adventurous, optimistic, and free-spirited
- **Influence of the Sun:** Sagittarius dogs are ruled by Jupiter, the planet of expansion and adventure, giving them an insatiable curiosity and a love for exploration. These dogs are always ready for the next adventure, whether it's a trip to the park or a hike in the mountains. Sagittarius dogs are energetic and playful, often displaying a carefree attitude that brings joy to their owners. They dislike being confined and need plenty of space to roam and explore.

Capricorn (December 22 - January 19): The Responsible Leader

- **Core Traits:** Disciplined, responsible, and patient
- **Influence of the Sun:** Capricorn dogs, ruled by Saturn, are natural-born leaders who thrive on structure and routine. These dogs are disciplined, hardworking, and often prefer a quiet, organized environment. Capricorn dogs are loyal and devoted, form-

ing deep bonds with their family members. They take their responsibilities seriously and enjoy having a clear role within the household, whether that's guarding the home or helping with tasks.

Aquarius (January 20 - February 18): The Innovator

- **Core Traits:** Quirky, independent, and intelligent
- **Influence of the Sun:** Ruled by Uranus, Aquarius dogs are known for their originality and independent nature. These dogs enjoy thinking outside the box and often exhibit unique behaviors that set them apart from others. Aquarius dogs are highly intelligent and need plenty of mental stimulation to keep them engaged. They value their freedom and prefer to make their own decisions, though they are affectionate in their own way.

Pisces (February 19 - March 20): The Dreamer

- **Core Traits:** Compassionate, intuitive, and gentle
- **Influence of the Sun:** Pisces dogs, ruled by Neptune, are the most sensitive and empathetic of the zodiac. These dogs are deeply connected to their owners and can sense their emotions with ease. Pisces dogs are gentle, compassionate, and enjoy providing comfort to those around them. They thrive in peaceful environments and may become stressed if exposed to loud noises or tension. Their dreamy, imaginative nature often leads them to engage in creative play.

How to Use Your Dog's Sun Sign to Enhance Your Relationship

Understanding your dog's Sun sign provides valuable insights into their core personality, allowing you to cater to their specific needs and preferences. By recognizing the strengths and challenges associated with their sign, you can create a nurturing environment that helps them thrive.

1. **Adapt Your Care Routine:** Each Sun sign has different needs when it comes to activity levels, socialization, and emotional support. Tailor your care routine to match your dog's core traits, providing them with the right balance of physical activity, mental stimulation, and affection.

2. **Build a Strong Bond:** By understanding your dog's core personality, you can deepen your bond by responding to their unique emotional needs. Some dogs may need more independence, while others thrive on constant companionship. Recognizing these preferences helps build trust and connection.

3. **Enhance Training:** Knowing your dog's Sun sign can help you adjust your training methods. For example, a stubborn Taurus may need a more patient approach, while an energetic Aries will respond better to fast-paced activities. Customize your training to suit their personality for better results.

4. **Create a Balanced Environment:** Every dog needs a supportive and balanced environment, but how that looks will differ depending on their Sun sign. A Libra dog will thrive in a harmonious, peaceful home, while a Sagittarius dog will need space to explore and roam freely.

Conclusion

The Sun sign plays a significant role in shaping your dog's core personality, influencing everything from their temperament to how they interact with the world. By understanding the traits associated with your dog's Sun sign, you can provide them with the care, attention, and environment they need to thrive. Embrace their unique qualities and enjoy the special bond that comes from recognizing and celebrating their individuality.

Chapter 15: The Moon and Your Dog: The Impact of the Moon on Your Dog's Emotions and Behavior

In astrology, the Moon governs our emotional landscape and subconscious behaviors, influencing how we react to the world on a deeper, more instinctual level. For dogs, the Moon's influence is just as powerful, shaping their emotional responses, habits, and inner life. While the Sun sign governs your dog's core personality, the Moon sign delves into their emotions, instincts, and how they express their feelings. Understanding the Moon's impact on your dog can help you better support their emotional well-being and navigate their moods and behaviors more effectively.

What is the Moon Sign?

The Moon sign in astrology represents the emotional self, guiding how we process feelings, handle security, and relate to our environment on an instinctual level. For dogs, the Moon sign reveals their deepest emotional needs, including how they seek comfort, their emotional triggers, and the behaviors that stem from their emotional core. While your dog's Sun sign might explain their external personality, the Moon sign speaks to their inner emotional world—the part of them that seeks nurturing, safety, and emotional connection.

How the Moon Influences Your Dog's Emotions

The Moon has a profound influence on your dog's emotional state. Much like the tides are affected by the Moon's gravitational pull, your dog's moods and instincts ebb and flow in response to the Moon's phases and their Moon sign. Dogs are highly sensitive creatures, often reacting to subtle changes in their environment. The Moon governs these emotional shifts, influencing everything from your dog's attachment to family members to their response to stress or change.

Emotional Responses Tied to the Moon

The Moon affects your dog's emotional needs, particularly in areas such as:

- **Security and Comfort:** The Moon dictates how your dog finds emotional security. Whether they prefer close cuddles or enjoy their independence, the Moon sign can reveal how they seek comfort and nurturing.

- **Instinctual Behaviors:** The Moon guides your dog's instinctual reactions to new situations, especially in unfamiliar environments. Dogs with a strong Moon influence may rely more on emotional instincts than logic, particularly when they feel threatened or uncertain.

- **Attachment and Bonding:** The Moon influences how your dog forms emotional bonds with you and other pets. Dogs with a strong lunar influence may form deep, emotional connections, whereas others may be more reserved but still deeply attached.

- **Emotional Sensitivity:** The Moon governs emotional sensitivity, which explains why some dogs may be more easily affected by changes in mood, routine, or energy in the household. Understanding your dog's Moon sign can help you predict how they will respond to these shifts.

How the Moon Phases Impact Your Dog's Behavior

In addition to the Moon sign, the phases of the Moon—new, waxing, full, and waning—play a role in your dog's behavior. Dogs are naturally in tune with the cycles of nature, and the lunar phases can subtly influence their moods, energy levels, and overall behavior.

- **New Moon:** The new Moon is a time of introspection and new beginnings. During this phase, your dog may display more reserved or reflective behavior. It's a good time to introduce new routines, commands, or activities, as your dog may be more open to change and growth.

- **Waxing Moon:** As the Moon grows toward fullness, your dog's energy levels and enthusiasm may increase. This is a good time for physical activities, such as longer walks, playtime, or training sessions. Your dog may seem more engaged and eager to learn or explore.

- **Full Moon:** The full Moon is known to heighten emotions and energy levels, both in humans and animals. During this phase, your dog may become more excitable, restless, or even anxious. You may notice an increase in vocalization, such as barking or howling, and heightened sensitivity to changes in their environment. It's important to provide them with extra attention and a calm atmosphere during this phase.

- **Waning Moon:** As the Moon begins to wane, your dog's energy may settle. This is a time for reflection and rest. Your dog may seek more quiet time or engage in calming activities. It's a good time for nurturing and bonding, as your dog may crave emotional closeness.

Understanding Your Dog's Moon Sign

Below is an overview of how each Moon sign affects your dog's emotional responses and behavior. Each Moon sign brings a unique emotional flavor, revealing your dog's deepest instincts, needs, and emotional triggers.

Aries Moon: The Emotional Firestarter

- **Emotional Traits:** Bold, impulsive, and energetic
- **Behavior:** Dogs with an Aries Moon have a fiery emotional nature. They are quick to react to stimuli, whether it's excitement, frustration, or fear. These dogs may display impulsive behaviors, such as barking at sudden noises or acting without thinking. While they are emotionally independent, they still need reassur-

ance during moments of stress. They thrive on action and may need plenty of physical outlets to release pent-up energy.

Taurus Moon: The Comfort Seeker

- **Emotional Traits:** Stable, calm, and affectionate
- **Behavior:** Dogs with a Taurus Moon crave emotional stability and comfort. They are highly affectionate and enjoy routine and familiarity. These dogs are emotionally grounded and rarely overreact, but they can become stubborn when their comfort is disrupted. Taurus Moon dogs thrive on physical closeness, often seeking out cuddles or cozy resting spots. They are sensitive to changes in their environment and may need extra reassurance when routines shift.

Gemini Moon: The Emotionally Curious

- **Emotional Traits:** Restless, curious, and adaptable
- **Behavior:** Dogs with a Gemini Moon have quicksilver emotions, often shifting from one mood to another. They are curious by nature and enjoy mental stimulation. These dogs may have a tendency to get bored easily, leading to restless or mischievous behavior. While they may not be the most emotionally expressive, Gemini Moon dogs are highly observant and enjoy interacting with their surroundings. Mental challenges and engaging activities help keep them emotionally balanced.

Cancer Moon: The Emotional Nurturer

- **Emotional Traits:** Sensitive, nurturing, and protective
- **Behavior:** Cancer Moon dogs are highly sensitive and deeply connected to their families. They are the emotional caregivers of the zodiac and often take on a protective role in the household.

These dogs form strong emotional bonds and may become anxious when separated from their loved ones. Cancer Moon dogs thrive on emotional closeness and may become clingy or moody if they feel neglected. They need a stable, nurturing environment to feel secure.

Leo Moon: The Emotional Performer

- **Emotional Traits:** Confident, dramatic, and affectionate
- **Behavior:** Dogs with a Leo Moon love to be the center of attention. They express their emotions openly and dramatically, often seeking validation and affection from their owners. Leo Moon dogs are affectionate and loyal, but they can be emotionally demanding, craving constant recognition and praise. They thrive in environments where they are given plenty of attention and love to be showered with affection.

Virgo Moon: The Emotionally Grounded

- **Emotional Traits:** Practical, reserved, and attentive
- **Behavior:** Dogs with a Virgo Moon are emotionally grounded and prefer structure and order in their environment. They are sensitive to small changes and may become anxious when things are out of place. Virgo Moon dogs are not overly expressive with their emotions, but they show their love through acts of service, such as staying close to their owners or being attentive to their needs. These dogs thrive on routine and enjoy feeling useful.

Libra Moon: The Emotional Diplomat

- **Emotional Traits:** Balanced, sociable, and peaceful
- **Behavior:** Libra Moon dogs are emotionally balanced and seek harmony in their environment. They dislike conflict and may try

to mediate if they sense tension in the household. These dogs are social creatures and enjoy being around people and other pets. Libra Moon dogs are emotionally expressive but prefer to keep things light and positive. They thrive in peaceful, harmonious environments and may become anxious in chaotic or stressful situations.

Scorpio Moon: The Emotionally Intense

- **Emotional Traits:** Intense, protective, and loyal
- **Behavior:** Dogs with a Scorpio Moon experience emotions with intensity and depth. They are fiercely loyal and protective of their loved ones, often forming deep emotional bonds. Scorpio Moon dogs are emotionally complex and may display behaviors such as guarding or possessiveness. They are highly intuitive and sensitive to the emotions of those around them. These dogs need an environment where they feel emotionally secure and supported.

Sagittarius Moon: The Emotionally Adventurous

- **Emotional Traits:** Optimistic, adventurous, and independent
- **Behavior:** Sagittarius Moon dogs have a free-spirited and emotionally adventurous nature. They are not overly sensitive or clingy and often prefer emotional independence. These dogs thrive on exploration and excitement, and they may become restless or bored if confined to routine. Sagittarius Moon dogs are optimistic and emotionally resilient, but they still need regular stimulation and freedom to express themselves.

Capricorn Moon: The Emotionally Steady

- **Emotional Traits:** Disciplined, patient, and reserved
- **Behavior:** Dogs with a Capricorn Moon are emotionally disciplined and prefer to keep their feelings in check. They are not prone to emotional outbursts and often appear calm and composed. Capricorn Moon dogs value routine and structure, and they thrive in environments where they have a clear role or purpose. While they may not be openly affectionate, they show their love through loyalty and dedication.

Aquarius Moon: The Emotionally Unconventional

- **Emotional Traits:** Independent, quirky, and detached
- **Behavior:** Aquarius Moon dogs march to the beat of their own drum when it comes to emotions. They are emotionally independent and may not seek out affection as much as other signs. These dogs prefer intellectual stimulation and often display quirky, unconventional behaviors. While they may seem emotionally detached, Aquarius Moon dogs are highly observant and care deeply in their own unique way.

Pisces Moon: The Emotional Dreamer

- **Emotional Traits:** Sensitive, intuitive, and compassionate
- **Behavior:** Dogs with a Pisces Moon are the most emotionally sensitive of the zodiac. They are deeply empathetic and often act as emotional sponges, absorbing the feelings of those around them. Pisces Moon dogs are nurturing and compassionate, always seeking to provide comfort and support. These dogs need a calm, peaceful environment where they can feel emotionally secure and loved.

How to Use the Moon's Influence to Support Your Dog

By understanding your dog's Moon sign, you can tailor your care routine to better meet their emotional needs. Here's how to use the Moon's influence to support your dog's emotional well-being:

1. **Provide Emotional Security:** Each Moon sign has different emotional needs, so make sure you provide the right kind of support. For example, Cancer Moon dogs need lots of emotional closeness, while Sagittarius Moon dogs may need more independence.

2. **Understand Their Emotional Triggers:** Knowing your dog's Moon sign can help you identify emotional triggers and predict how they will react to certain situations. This can help you create a calming environment and avoid stressors that may upset them.

3. **Adapt to the Lunar Phases:** Be mindful of how the lunar phases affect your dog's behavior. During the full Moon, your dog may be more excitable or restless, while the new Moon may be a time for calm and introspection. Adjust your activities and routines to match their energy levels during these phases.

4. **Strengthen Your Emotional Bond:** Understanding your dog's emotional nature allows you to build a deeper bond with them. Responding to their emotional needs with love, patience, and understanding will strengthen your connection and improve their emotional well-being.

Conclusion

The Moon plays a significant role in shaping your dog's emotional world, influencing everything from their need for comfort to how they respond to stress and change. By understanding your dog's Moon sign and the lunar phases, you can create an emotionally supportive environment that helps them feel safe, loved, and secure. Embrace the emotional depth of your dog, and use the Moon's wisdom to foster a deeper connection and a more harmonious life together.

Chapter 16: Mercury and Your Dog: Communication and Intelligence in Dogs Ruled by Mercury

Mercury, the planet of communication, intellect, and quick thinking, plays a significant role in shaping how your dog processes information, solves problems, and interacts with the world around them. In astrology, Mercury governs mental agility, learning, and the ways in which beings express their thoughts and feelings. For dogs, the influence of Mercury manifests in their ability to understand commands, solve puzzles, and communicate with their owners. In this chapter, we explore how Mercury affects your dog's communication style and intelligence, helping you better understand and engage with your clever, quick-thinking companion.

The Influence of Mercury on Communication and Intelligence

Mercury is often referred to as the "messenger" in astrology, representing the flow of information, knowledge, and ideas. When this planet governs your dog's astrological chart, it heightens their intellectual abilities and shapes the ways in which they communicate. Dogs ruled by Mercury are typically fast learners, curious about their environment, and highly responsive to verbal and non-verbal cues. Their intelligence often shines through in how quickly they pick up on commands, how they problem-solve, and how they interact with both humans and other animals.

Key Traits of Mercury-Influenced Dogs

Dogs ruled by Mercury—such as those born under Gemini or Virgo—are typically marked by their sharp minds and adaptive communication styles. Here are the primary traits that define Mercury-influenced dogs:

1. **Quick Learners:** Dogs under Mercury's influence have a natural aptitude for learning. They pick up on commands, tricks, and new routines faster than most dogs. They enjoy the challenge of learning new things and are often highly motivated by mental stimulation.

2. **Highly Communicative:** These dogs are excellent communicators, using a combination of body language, vocalizations, and even eye contact to convey their thoughts and feelings. They are especially good at understanding their owner's verbal and non-verbal cues, making them easy to train and interact with.

3. **Curious and Inquisitive:** Curiosity is a hallmark of Mercury-influenced dogs. They love to explore their environment, investigate new smells, and figure out how things work. Their inquisitive nature means they are always looking for mental stimulation and enjoy activities that challenge their minds.

4. **Agile and Adaptive:** Mercury-ruled dogs are mentally agile and can quickly adapt to changes in their environment. Whether it's learning a new routine or solving a puzzle, they are quick to adjust and thrive on mental challenges. This adaptability also makes them great companions in dynamic households.

5. **Problem-Solving Abilities:** These dogs have a keen ability to solve problems. Whether it's figuring out how to open a door or navigating through a puzzle toy, Mercury-influenced dogs excel at tasks that require critical thinking and persistence. They often enjoy games that challenge their intellect and keep them engaged.

6. **Energetic Minds:** Mental energy is a defining trait of Mercury dogs. They have active, energetic minds that are always seeking something to engage with. This intellectual energy means they need regular mental stimulation, as boredom can quickly lead to undesirable behaviors like excessive barking or chewing.

7. **Observant and Perceptive:** Dogs influenced by Mercury are highly observant and can quickly pick up on subtle changes in their environment or their owner's mood. They are often very attuned to their human companions and may even anticipate commands before they are given.

Mercury and Communication Styles

Mercury influences not only a dog's intelligence but also their communication style. Dogs ruled by Mercury tend to be more expressive, using a wide range of vocalizations, body language, and facial expressions to convey their feelings. Here's how Mercury shapes different aspects of communication in dogs:

1. **Vocalization:** Mercury dogs are often more vocal than other dogs, using barks, whines, growls, and other sounds to communicate their needs and emotions. They may bark to get your attention, whine when they're excited, or growl playfully during interactions. Their vocalizations are often varied and expressive, reflecting their complex emotional and intellectual lives.

2. **Body Language:** Dogs with strong Mercury influences are masters of body language. They use their posture, tail movements, ear positions, and even facial expressions to communicate their feelings. For example, a dog may tilt their head when curious or raise their ears when focused. These subtle cues are important for understanding what your dog is thinking or feeling at any given moment.

3. **Eye Contact:** Mercury-ruled dogs are often very good at using eye contact to communicate with their owners. They may gaze at

you to signal they need something or maintain eye contact when they're trying to understand what you're saying. This type of communication can create a deeper bond between you and your dog, as they use their eyes to read and respond to your emotions.

4. **Physical Gestures:** In addition to body language, Mercury dogs may use physical gestures to get your attention. They may paw at you, nudge your hand, or bring you their favorite toy when they want to play. These physical cues are their way of expressing what they need or want in a more direct manner.

Intelligence in Mercury Dogs: Mental Stimulation and Learning

Mercury dogs thrive on mental stimulation and love being challenged intellectually. Their quick minds need regular engagement to stay sharp and content. Without proper mental stimulation, these dogs can become bored, which may lead to restlessness or undesirable behaviors. Here are some ways to keep your Mercury-influenced dog's mind active:

1. **Training and Commands:** Dogs ruled by Mercury are typically eager learners and enjoy the process of mastering new commands and tricks. They respond well to positive reinforcement and often take pride in learning new things. Training sessions that challenge their intellect and offer rewards for success are highly beneficial for these dogs.

2. **Puzzle Toys and Brain Games:** Puzzle toys, brain games, and interactive activities are excellent ways to keep a Mercury dog mentally stimulated. These toys encourage problem-solving and can be used to challenge your dog's intelligence. Whether it's figuring out how to unlock a treat-dispensing puzzle or learning a complex sequence of tasks, these activities engage their mental agility.

3. **Agility Training:** Agility courses are a great way to combine physical exercise with mental stimulation for Mercury dogs. These dogs enjoy the challenge of navigating obstacles, following commands, and using their intelligence to solve problems in real-time. Agility training not only keeps them physically fit but also provides them with the mental challenge they crave.

4. **Interactive Play:** Playtime is an important part of a Mercury dog's life, but they often prefer interactive games that engage their mind. Games like hide-and-seek, fetch with a twist (e.g., hiding the ball), or learning new tricks are perfect for these dogs. Engaging them in creative play helps satisfy their intellectual curiosity.

5. **New Experiences:** Mercury dogs love novelty and are naturally curious about new environments, people, and activities. Regularly introducing them to new experiences—such as exploring different parks, meeting new dogs, or trying out different types of training exercises—keeps their minds sharp and satisfies their curiosity.

Training Mercury Dogs: Tips for Success

Training a Mercury dog can be a rewarding experience, as these dogs are often quick to learn and eager to please. However, their intelligence and curiosity can sometimes make them easily distracted or bored if the training is too repetitive. Here are some tips for successfully training a Mercury-ruled dog:

1. **Keep Training Sessions Short and Engaging:** Mercury dogs have quick minds but can lose interest if training sessions are too long or repetitive. Keep training sessions short (10-15 minutes) and mix up the activities to keep their attention. Variety is key to keeping them engaged and eager to learn.

2. **Use Positive Reinforcement:** Positive reinforcement works best for Mercury dogs. They respond well to praise, treats, and affec-

tion when they successfully complete a task. Reward them immediately after they perform the desired behavior to reinforce the connection between the command and the reward.

3. **Challenge Them with New Tasks:** Mercury dogs love a challenge, so don't be afraid to introduce more complex tasks as they progress in their training. Teach them multi-step commands, advanced tricks, or more difficult problem-solving exercises to keep their minds engaged.

4. **Be Patient and Flexible:** While Mercury dogs are quick learners, they can also be easily distracted by new stimuli. Be patient and flexible during training, allowing them time to refocus if they become distracted. If they seem bored, switch up the routine or introduce a new challenge to regain their interest.

5. **Use Verbal and Non-Verbal Cues:** Mercury dogs are highly attuned to both verbal and non-verbal communication. Use a combination of voice commands and hand signals to communicate with them during training. This helps reinforce the connection between your instructions and their actions, making it easier for them to understand and respond.

Building a Strong Relationship with Your Mercury Dog

Mercury dogs thrive in environments where they can express their intelligence and curiosity. Building a strong relationship with your Mercury dog involves understanding their need for mental stimulation, communication, and exploration. Here's how to strengthen your bond with your Mercury-ruled dog:

- **Communicate Clearly:** Mercury dogs are highly communicative, so engage with them using both verbal and non-verbal cues. Speak to them often, and pay attention to their body language and vocalizations to better understand what they're trying to convey.

- **Challenge Their Minds:** Keep their minds sharp by introducing new activities, toys, and experiences. Mental stimulation is essential for their happiness and well-being, so provide them with puzzles, games, and training exercises that engage their intellect.
- **Be Interactive and Engaged:** Mercury dogs thrive on interaction with their owners. Spend time playing, training, and exploring together to strengthen your bond. They enjoy being mentally and emotionally connected to their human companions.
- **Provide Variety in Their Routine:** Mercury dogs can become bored with routine, so mix things up to keep them engaged. Vary their walks, introduce new toys, and try different training exercises to maintain their interest and enthusiasm.

Conclusion

Dogs ruled by Mercury are intelligent, communicative, and curious creatures who thrive on mental stimulation and engagement. By understanding how Mercury influences your dog's communication style and intellectual needs, you can create a fulfilling environment that keeps their mind sharp and their spirit happy. Embrace their quick-thinking nature, challenge their intellect, and enjoy the deep bond that comes from interacting with a dog who is always eager to learn and explore the world around them.

Chapter 17: Venus and Your Dog: Love, Affection, and Relationships in Dogs Influenced by Venus

Venus, the planet of love, beauty, and harmony, governs how dogs experience affection, form bonds, and seek comfort. In astrology, Venus represents the ways we express love, seek pleasure, and connect with others. For dogs influenced by Venus, this manifests in their strong need for affection, their love of beauty and comfort, and their desire for harmonious relationships with their human companions and other pets. In this chapter, we explore how Venus shapes your dog's affectionate nature, how they form relationships, and what you can do to nurture the loving, gentle side of your Venus-ruled dog.

The Influence of Venus on Love and Affection

Venus is the planet of connection, governing how beings relate to one another in a loving and harmonious way. In dogs, Venus influences their need for companionship, their love of physical affection, and their desire for comfort and luxury. Dogs influenced by Venus are typically affectionate, easy-going, and naturally inclined to form deep emotional bonds with their owners. They seek out pleasure and comfort, often enjoying cozy spaces, soft bedding, and gentle interactions. Venus also enhances their social nature, making them more likely to get along well with other pets and people.

Key Traits of Venus-Influenced Dogs

Dogs ruled by Venus, particularly those born under Taurus or Libra, are known for their affectionate, gentle, and harmonious nature. Here are the primary traits that define Venus-influenced dogs:

1. **Affectionate and Loving:** Venus dogs are extremely affectionate and thrive on physical touch. They love cuddles, belly rubs, and any form of gentle affection from their owners. Their loving na-

ture makes them naturally attuned to their human companions, and they often seek out physical contact to express their love.

2. **Social and Harmonious:** These dogs are highly social and enjoy being in the company of both humans and other animals. They have a natural ability to maintain harmony in social settings and are less likely to engage in aggressive or confrontational behavior. Venus dogs are peace-loving and tend to avoid conflict, preferring a calm and balanced environment.

3. **Comfort-Loving:** Dogs influenced by Venus have a strong appreciation for comfort and luxury. They enjoy soft bedding, cozy blankets, and any environment that offers warmth and relaxation. These dogs are drawn to beautiful, comfortable spaces and often have a sense of aesthetic appreciation, even for their own surroundings.

4. **Easy-Going and Gentle:** Venus-ruled dogs are typically calm, easy-going, and gentle in nature. They are not easily ruffled and prefer to go with the flow rather than engage in stressful or chaotic situations. Their gentleness makes them wonderful companions for families with children, the elderly, or other pets, as they tend to be patient and tolerant.

5. **Sensual and Pleasurable:** Venus dogs are sensual beings who love indulging in physical pleasures. Whether it's enjoying a long nap in a sunbeam, savoring a tasty treat, or receiving a belly rub, these dogs seek out sensory experiences that bring them pleasure and joy. Their love of comfort extends to all their senses, and they are often more aware of textures, smells, and tastes than other dogs.

6. **Loyal and Devoted:** Venus dogs form deep, emotional bonds with their owners and are incredibly loyal and devoted. Once they've bonded with someone, they will remain faithful companions for life, always seeking to offer love and affection. They tend to be emotionally intuitive and often know when their owners need extra comfort or attention.

7. **Balanced and Peaceful:** These dogs have a natural sense of balance and strive to maintain peace and harmony in their environment. They are rarely aggressive and prefer calm, quiet settings where they can relax and enjoy the company of their family. Venus dogs dislike chaos and may become stressed if their environment is too noisy or tense.

Venus and Your Dog's Relationship-Building Style

The way your dog forms relationships is heavily influenced by Venus. Dogs with a strong Venus influence are naturally inclined to create loving, harmonious connections with others. Here's how Venus shapes different aspects of relationship-building in dogs:

1. **Attachment to Owners:** Venus-ruled dogs form deep emotional attachments to their owners. They are highly affectionate and crave close, personal relationships with their human companions. These dogs are often seen following their owners around the house, seeking out cuddles, and wanting to be close at all times. Their attachment is not based on neediness but on a genuine desire to connect emotionally.

2. **Friendly and Sociable:** Dogs influenced by Venus are naturally friendly and enjoy meeting new people and animals. They tend to be warm and welcoming, making them great companions for households with multiple pets or regular visitors. These dogs thrive in social environments where they can interact with others and build meaningful connections.

3. **Peacekeepers in the Pack:** In multi-pet households, Venus dogs often take on the role of the peacekeeper. They dislike conflict and will do what they can to maintain harmony among other pets. Their gentle nature makes them less likely to engage in aggressive behavior, and they often act as calming influences on more excitable or anxious pets.

4. **Emotional Sensitivity:** Venus dogs are emotionally sensitive and can easily pick up on the moods of their owners and those around them. If their human companion is feeling down, a Venus dog will often offer comfort by staying close, offering physical affection, or simply being present. They are attuned to emotional needs and seek to create a sense of emotional balance in the household.

5. **Loyalty and Devotion:** Venus dogs are incredibly loyal and form lifelong bonds with their owners. They are devoted to their family and will go out of their way to ensure their loved ones are happy and comfortable. This loyalty extends to other pets in the household as well, and they often form strong connections with their animal companions.

Venus and Comfort: Creating the Perfect Environment

Dogs influenced by Venus have a deep appreciation for comfort and beauty, and they thrive in environments that reflect these qualities. To keep a Venus-ruled dog happy, it's essential to create a space that meets their need for luxury and relaxation. Here are some tips for creating the perfect environment for your Venus dog:

1. **Soft and Cozy Bedding:** Venus dogs love soft, plush bedding. Provide them with a comfortable bed filled with blankets or cushions where they can relax and feel safe. Their bed should be placed in a quiet, peaceful area of the home where they can retreat when they need to rest.

2. **Beautiful and Calm Surroundings:** Just as Venus governs aesthetics, Venus dogs often appreciate calm, beautiful surroundings. Try to keep their living space tidy and free from excessive noise or chaos. Natural light, soft music, and gentle scents can help create a soothing atmosphere that appeals to their love of beauty and peace.

3. **Physical Comfort and Sensory Pleasures:** Venus dogs enjoy sensory pleasures, so it's important to cater to their senses. Provide them with toys made from soft, pleasing materials, and consider using gentle, calming scents like lavender in their space. Venus dogs also enjoy being pampered, so regular grooming or massages can make them feel loved and cared for.

4. **Gentle Routines and Predictability:** Venus-ruled dogs appreciate a stable, predictable routine that allows them to feel secure. Sudden changes in their environment or routine can cause them stress, so try to keep things as consistent as possible. They thrive when they know what to expect and enjoy gentle, calming activities like leisurely walks and quiet time with their owners.

Nurturing Your Venus Dog's Affectionate Nature

Venus dogs are naturally affectionate and need regular displays of love and attention to feel secure and happy. Here's how you can nurture your Venus dog's loving nature and strengthen your bond:

1. **Physical Affection:** Venus dogs thrive on physical affection. Regular cuddles, petting, and belly rubs are essential for these dogs, as they express their love through touch. Make time each day to give your Venus dog the physical attention they crave, whether it's snuggling on the couch or gently stroking them during quiet moments.

2. **Quality Time Together:** Spending quality time with your Venus dog is just as important as physical affection. They enjoy being close to their owners, whether it's during a walk, a play session, or simply relaxing together. The more time you spend bonding with your Venus dog, the deeper their emotional connection with you will become.

3. **Encouraging Socialization:** Venus dogs are naturally social and enjoy being around other dogs and people. Regular socialization, whether at the dog park or with visitors at home, helps keep them

happy and emotionally balanced. They love making new friends and often thrive in social environments where they can interact with others.

4. **Gentle and Calm Interactions:** Venus dogs respond best to gentle, calm interactions. They are sensitive souls and may become stressed or anxious if handled too roughly or exposed to too much chaos. Always approach your Venus dog with kindness and patience, using soft tones and calm gestures to show your affection.

5. **Praising and Rewarding with Love:** Venus dogs love being appreciated, so use positive reinforcement to show them how much you value their companionship. Praise them when they show good behavior, and reward them with treats or extra affection. This helps reinforce their sense of emotional security and strengthens your bond.

Building a Strong Relationship with Your Venus Dog

Building a deep, loving relationship with a Venus-ruled dog requires understanding their need for affection, comfort, and harmony. Here's how you can strengthen your bond with your Venus dog:

- **Be Present and Affectionate:** Venus dogs thrive on closeness and affection. Be emotionally present for them and show your love through regular physical contact, cuddles, and attention. They need to feel loved and appreciated to form deep bonds with their owners.

- **Create a Peaceful, Beautiful Environment:** Venus dogs are sensitive to their surroundings and prefer calm, peaceful environments. Provide them with a cozy, aesthetically pleasing space where they can feel relaxed and secure. Avoid loud noises or chaotic environments that may cause them stress.

- **Foster Emotional Connections:** Venus dogs are emotionally sensitive and crave deep emotional connections. Spend time bonding with your dog through gentle play, quiet walks, or simply sitting together. They will appreciate the emotional closeness and will return your love tenfold.

- **Maintain Social Harmony:** Venus dogs dislike conflict and strive for harmony in their relationships. Encourage positive social interactions with other pets and people, and avoid exposing them to aggressive or chaotic situations. They thrive in environments where love, peace, and harmony prevail.

Conclusion

Dogs influenced by Venus are affectionate, gentle, and naturally inclined to form deep, loving connections with their owners and companions. By understanding their need for love, comfort, and beauty, you can create a nurturing environment that allows their affectionate nature to flourish. Embrace their love of physical touch, provide them with a calm and cozy space, and enjoy the deep emotional bond that comes from loving a Venus-ruled dog. They will reward you with endless devotion, affection, and harmony, bringing a sense of peace and love to your life that only a Venus dog can provide.

Chapter 18: Mars and Your Dog: Energy, Aggression, and Drive in Mars-Ruled Dogs

Mars, the planet of energy, action, and aggression, plays a pivotal role in shaping your dog's drive, determination, and assertiveness. In astrology, Mars is often associated with physical vitality, courage, and the instinctual forces that propel beings to take action. For dogs, Mars governs their energy levels, how they handle competition or conflict, and their natural instincts for survival, dominance, and territorial behavior. In this chapter, we will explore how Mars influences your dog's behavior, drive, and temperament, helping you better understand their energetic nature and how to channel their intense energy in healthy ways.

The Influence of Mars on Energy and Drive

Mars is the planet that fuels our physical energy and competitive instincts, and its influence on dogs is no different. Dogs ruled by Mars, especially those born under Aries or Scorpio, are characterized by their high energy, assertiveness, and sometimes aggressive tendencies. These dogs are natural go-getters, always ready to take action and pursue their goals with unrelenting determination. Mars also governs their fight-or-flight instincts, which means dogs under its influence can be more territorial, protective, or reactive in the face of perceived threats. Understanding Mars's influence on your dog can help you manage their high energy and strong-willed nature in a positive and constructive way.

Key Traits of Mars-Influenced Dogs

Mars-ruled dogs are known for their energetic, driven, and sometimes assertive personalities. Here are the primary traits that define Mars-influenced dogs:

1. **High Energy and Stamina:** Mars dogs are highly energetic and need plenty of physical activity to keep them satisfied. Whether it's running, playing, or engaging in interactive games, these dogs thrive on movement and often require more exercise than the average dog. Their stamina is impressive, and they may seem tireless in their pursuit of fun or work.

2. **Assertive and Bold:** These dogs are naturally assertive and are not afraid to take the lead or stand their ground. Mars gives them the confidence to be bold, whether in social situations or while protecting their territory. This assertiveness can sometimes come across as bossy or dominant, especially around other animals.

3. **Competitive and Driven:** Mars-ruled dogs are highly competitive and thrive in environments where they can test their skills. They love to compete, whether it's in agility training, fetch, or tug-of-war. Their driven nature makes them focused on achieving goals, whether it's mastering a new command or winning a game.

4. **Protective and Territorial:** Mars dogs have strong territorial instincts and may be quick to defend their home, family, or resources. This protective nature makes them excellent guard dogs, but it can also lead to aggressive or reactive behaviors if not managed properly. Their loyalty to their owners often manifests in a desire to protect their loved ones from perceived threats.

5. **Courageous and Fearless:** Mars instills a sense of fearlessness in these dogs. They are brave and willing to face challenges head-on, whether it's navigating new environments or standing up to larger dogs. This courage makes them resilient and adaptable but can sometimes lead them into risky situations if their instincts aren't tempered by training.

6. **Impulsive and Reactive:** Mars dogs can be impulsive, often acting before they think. This impulsivity can lead to rash behaviors, such as chasing after squirrels, barking at strangers, or jumping into new situations without hesitation. While their spontaneity makes them exciting companions, it can also pose challenges if they're not properly trained to manage their impulses.

7. **Strong-Willed and Determined:** Mars-ruled dogs are known for their strong will and determination. Once they set their mind on something, they will pursue it relentlessly. This determination can be a great asset in training, but it can also make them stub-

born or resistant to commands if they're not interested in cooperating.

Mars and Aggression: Understanding Assertiveness and Reactivity

While Mars is often associated with aggression, it's important to distinguish between healthy assertiveness and problematic aggression in dogs. Mars-ruled dogs are naturally assertive and may display more dominant behaviors, but this doesn't necessarily mean they are aggressive. Instead, Mars gives them the confidence to stand their ground and take action when needed. However, if their energy is not properly managed or if they feel threatened, Mars dogs can become reactive, displaying behaviors such as growling, barking, or even lunging at perceived threats.

1. **Healthy Assertiveness:** Assertiveness is a natural trait for Mars dogs. They are confident, self-assured, and willing to take charge in social situations. This assertiveness is not inherently negative and can be channeled into positive behaviors, such as leadership roles in a multi-pet household or as protectors of the home.

2. **Recognizing Signs of Aggression:** While Mars dogs can be assertive, it's important to recognize when assertiveness crosses the line into aggression. Signs of aggression in Mars-ruled dogs may include excessive growling, snapping, lunging, or aggressive guarding of resources. These behaviors can be triggered by fear, frustration, or a lack of proper socialization, and they should be addressed with training and management techniques.

3. **Managing Reactivity:** Mars dogs can be reactive, especially in situations where they feel threatened or overstimulated. If your dog tends to react aggressively to strangers, other dogs, or sudden noises, it's important to manage their environment and work on desensitizing them to these triggers. Positive reinforcement train-

ing can help reduce reactivity and teach your dog to respond calmly in stressful situations.

Mars and Drive: Channeling Energy and Determination

Mars-ruled dogs are driven by their intense energy and determination, making them natural candidates for activities that require focus, stamina, and a strong work ethic. Whether it's working on a farm, participating in agility competitions, or engaging in obedience training, Mars dogs excel in environments where they can channel their drive into constructive activities.

1. **Exercise and Physical Activity:** Mars dogs need plenty of physical exercise to burn off their excess energy. Long walks, runs, and active play sessions are essential for keeping them physically fit and mentally balanced. These dogs thrive in active households where they can participate in outdoor activities and engage in regular physical challenges.

2. **Agility and Obedience Training:** Mars dogs are excellent candidates for agility and obedience training. Their high energy, drive, and determination make them eager to learn and excel in activities that require focus and discipline. Agility courses, advanced obedience training, and other mentally stimulating activities can help them channel their energy in a positive way.

3. **Interactive Play and Challenges:** In addition to physical exercise, Mars dogs need mental stimulation to stay engaged. Interactive play, such as fetch, tug-of-war, and puzzle toys, can provide them with the challenge they crave. These activities also help reinforce their natural drive and competitiveness, keeping them motivated and focused.

4. **Working Roles:** Mars dogs often excel in working roles that require strength, stamina, and determination. Whether it's herding livestock, guarding property, or performing search-and-rescue tasks, Mars-ruled dogs are well-suited to jobs that allow them to

use their physical and mental abilities in a purposeful way. Providing them with a job or role within the household can help fulfill their need for action and purpose.

Training Mars-Ruled Dogs: Tips for Success

Training a Mars dog can be both rewarding and challenging. Their high energy and determination make them eager learners, but their assertiveness and impulsivity can sometimes lead to stubborn or defiant behaviors. Here are some tips for successfully training a Mars-ruled dog:

1. **Use Positive Reinforcement:** Mars dogs respond best to positive reinforcement techniques that reward good behavior. Use treats, praise, and affection to motivate them and reinforce commands. Avoid harsh training methods or punishment, as this can lead to frustration and exacerbate aggressive tendencies.

2. **Be Consistent and Firm:** While positive reinforcement is key, it's also important to be consistent and firm with your Mars dog. These dogs need clear boundaries and rules to understand what is expected of them. Consistency in training helps them learn faster and prevents confusion or defiance.

3. **Channel Their Energy Productively:** Mars dogs have a lot of energy, so it's essential to provide them with outlets to channel that energy in positive ways. Regular exercise, agility training, and interactive play sessions can help prevent boredom and destructive behaviors.

4. **Work on Impulse Control:** Mars dogs can be impulsive, so teaching them impulse control is crucial. Commands like "stay," "wait," and "leave it" can help them learn to pause before acting on their impulses. Start with short training sessions and gradually increase the difficulty as they improve.

5. **Address Reactivity Early:** If your Mars dog shows signs of reactivity or aggression, it's important to address these behaviors early. Work on socialization with other dogs and people, and use

desensitization techniques to reduce reactivity. Enlisting the help of a professional trainer or behaviorist can be beneficial if aggressive behaviors persist.

Building a Strong Relationship with Your Mars Dog

Building a strong relationship with a Mars-ruled dog involves understanding their need for action, purpose, and assertiveness. Here's how you can create a bond with your Mars dog based on mutual respect and trust:

- **Provide Plenty of Physical Activity:** Mars dogs thrive on action, so make sure they get plenty of exercise and opportunities to burn off energy. Regular walks, playtime, and interactive games help them stay balanced and satisfied.
- **Engage Their Mind and Body:** Mars dogs need both physical and mental stimulation to stay happy. Engage them with challenges that require both strength and intellect, such as agility courses or complex training exercises.
- **Respect Their Assertiveness:** Mars dogs are naturally assertive and confident. Respect their need for independence and leadership while setting clear boundaries to ensure they understand their place in the household.
- **Use Calm, Consistent Training:** Mars dogs respond well to calm, consistent training that rewards good behavior. Be patient and firm, and avoid using harsh methods that could trigger their aggressive tendencies.

Conclusion

Dogs ruled by Mars are energetic, assertive, and driven by a powerful need for action and purpose. By understanding their natural instincts for competition, protection, and movement, you can create a fulfilling environment that allows them to channel their energy in positive ways. Embrace their bold, fearless nature, provide them with plenty of physical and mental stimulation, and enjoy the strong bond that comes from loving a dog who is always ready for action. With proper guidance and training, your Mars dog will become a loyal, protective, and dynamic companion, always eager to face life's challenges head-on.

Chapter 19: Jupiter and Your Dog: Luck, Growth, and Expansion in Dogs Influenced by Jupiter

Jupiter, the planet of expansion, growth, and good fortune, has a profound influence on dogs, shaping their sense of adventure, optimism, and thirst for knowledge. In astrology, Jupiter is known as the planet of abundance and opportunity, representing the quest for meaning, exploration, and personal development. For dogs influenced by Jupiter, this manifests in their optimistic outlook, love for exploration, and a natural ability to find luck and opportunities in their surroundings. In this chapter, we'll explore how Jupiter impacts your dog's personality, behaviors, and the ways in which they grow, learn, and seek new experiences.

The Influence of Jupiter on Growth and Expansion

Jupiter is the largest planet in the solar system, symbolizing growth, expansion, and an endless pursuit of knowledge and adventure. For dogs, Jupiter's influence encourages a sense of curiosity and optimism. These dogs often approach life with an open heart and a desire to explore the world around them. They are natural adventurers, always eager to try new things, meet new people, and discover new places. Dogs under Jupiter's influence tend to have a strong sense of wanderlust and a love for learning, making them adaptable, open-minded, and joyful companions.

Key Traits of Jupiter-Influenced Dogs

Dogs ruled by Jupiter, especially those born under Sagittarius or Pisces, are known for their adventurous, curious, and optimistic personalities. Here are the primary traits that define Jupiter-influenced dogs:

1. **Adventurous and Exploratory:** Jupiter-ruled dogs have an innate desire to explore the world around them. Whether it's sniffing out new scents on a walk, investigating new environments, or embarking on spontaneous adventures, these dogs are always seeking out new experiences. They have a strong sense of curiosity

and love exploring new places, making them excellent companions for active owners who enjoy outdoor activities.

2. **Optimistic and Cheerful:** Jupiter dogs are known for their sunny disposition and positive outlook on life. They are naturally cheerful and often seem to have an unshakable sense of optimism. These dogs rarely dwell on negative experiences and bounce back quickly from challenges, always ready for the next adventure with a wagging tail.

3. **Social and Outgoing:** These dogs love meeting new people and making friends. Jupiter-ruled dogs are naturally sociable and thrive in environments where they can interact with both humans and other animals. They are often the life of the party at the dog park, eager to play and explore with other dogs and people.

4. **Inquisitive and Eager to Learn:** Jupiter dogs have a thirst for knowledge and are always eager to learn new things. They are quick learners and enjoy challenges that stimulate their minds. Whether it's learning new tricks, exploring new environments, or solving puzzles, these dogs are constantly seeking out ways to grow and expand their understanding of the world.

5. **Lucky and Opportunistic:** Jupiter is often associated with luck, and dogs under its influence seem to have a natural ability to find opportunities and good fortune. Whether it's stumbling upon hidden treats, finding the perfect sunbeam to nap in, or winning the affection of everyone they meet, these dogs seem to attract luck wherever they go. Their optimistic attitude often creates opportunities for positive experiences.

6. **Expansive and Energetic:** Jupiter dogs are full of energy and thrive on physical and mental expansion. They need plenty of space to roam and explore, as confinement can stifle their natural curiosity. These dogs enjoy activities that allow them to stretch their legs and minds, such as hiking, agility training, or interactive play.

7. **Generous and Big-Hearted:** Just as Jupiter symbolizes abundance, dogs under this planet's influence are often generous with their love and affection. They have big hearts and are always willing to share their joy with others. Their generous nature makes them excellent companions, always offering unconditional love and loyalty to those around them.

Jupiter and Your Dog's Love for Exploration

One of the most notable traits of Jupiter-ruled dogs is their love for exploration. These dogs have a natural sense of wanderlust and are always eager to venture into new territories. Whether it's exploring a new hiking trail, visiting a new park, or simply investigating a new corner of the yard, Jupiter dogs thrive on the excitement of discovery.

1. **Desire for New Experiences:** Jupiter dogs are constantly seeking out new experiences and environments. They love visiting new places and meeting new people, and they thrive in dynamic environments that offer variety and stimulation. These dogs may become restless or bored if kept in the same environment for too long, so it's important to introduce them to new experiences regularly.

2. **Curiosity and Adventure:** Curiosity drives Jupiter-ruled dogs to explore everything around them. They are natural adventurers, always eager to investigate new smells, sights, and sounds. These dogs are not content to sit still and prefer activities that allow them to roam freely and satisfy their curiosity. Whether it's chasing after butterflies or investigating a new trail, Jupiter dogs are happiest when they're exploring.

3. **Outdoor Enthusiasts:** Jupiter dogs are often happiest when they're outdoors, where they can experience the world in all its expansiveness. They love open spaces where they can run, play, and explore without limitations. Activities such as hiking, running, and long walks are ideal for these dogs, as they allow them to sat-

isfy their need for exploration while burning off their abundant energy.

4. **Social Exploration:** In addition to exploring their physical environment, Jupiter dogs love social exploration. They enjoy meeting new people and other animals, and they are often eager to make new friends wherever they go. These dogs are naturally friendly and outgoing, making them a hit at social gatherings, the dog park, or even during casual walks around the neighborhood.

Jupiter and Growth: Encouraging Your Dog's Development

Jupiter is the planet of growth and expansion, and dogs under its influence have a strong desire to grow, learn, and expand their horizons. Here's how you can encourage your Jupiter dog's personal development:

1. **Mental Stimulation:** Jupiter dogs love mental challenges and need regular stimulation to keep their minds sharp. Engage them in activities that require problem-solving and critical thinking, such as puzzle toys, hide-and-seek games, or interactive training exercises. These dogs enjoy learning new tricks and commands, and they thrive when they are mentally engaged.

2. **Positive Reinforcement Training:** Jupiter dogs respond well to positive reinforcement training. Their optimistic nature means they are eager to please, and they are highly motivated by praise, treats, and affection. Use positive reinforcement techniques to teach them new commands, tricks, and behaviors, and you'll find that they learn quickly and enthusiastically.

3. **Learning Through Exploration:** Encourage your Jupiter dog's natural curiosity by giving them opportunities to learn through exploration. Take them to new environments, introduce them to different types of activities, and allow them to investigate new smells, sights, and sounds. These dogs are natural learners, and

they will appreciate the chance to expand their knowledge of the world.

4. **Adventure-Based Training:** Jupiter dogs excel in training environments that incorporate adventure and exploration. Agility training, scent work, and advanced obedience training are excellent activities for these dogs, as they combine mental and physical challenges with opportunities for exploration. These activities allow Jupiter dogs to grow both mentally and physically, keeping them happy and engaged.

Jupiter and Luck: How Your Dog Attracts Fortune

Jupiter is the planet of luck and good fortune, and dogs influenced by this planet seem to have a natural ability to attract positive experiences and opportunities. Here's how Jupiter enhances your dog's sense of luck and abundance:

1. **Attracting Positive Experiences:** Jupiter dogs have a knack for finding themselves in the right place at the right time. Whether it's discovering hidden treats, finding a favorite toy, or attracting the attention of a kind stranger, these dogs seem to have an innate ability to attract good fortune. Their positive energy and optimistic outlook often lead to lucky encounters and happy experiences.

2. **Optimism and Confidence:** One of the reasons Jupiter dogs seem so lucky is their optimistic and confident nature. These dogs approach life with a sense of enthusiasm and excitement, always expecting the best outcome. Their positive attitude often creates opportunities for success, whether it's winning a game of fetch, making a new friend, or simply enjoying a fun outing.

3. **Taking Advantage of Opportunities:** Jupiter dogs are opportunistic by nature and are always on the lookout for new opportunities. Whether it's finding a sunny spot to nap in or discovering a new game to play, these dogs are quick to seize

opportunities for fun, pleasure, and growth. Their adventurous spirit and willingness to try new things often lead them to lucky discoveries.

4. **Generosity and Abundance:** Just as Jupiter symbolizes abundance, dogs under its influence have a generous, big-hearted nature. They are always willing to share their love, joy, and enthusiasm with those around them, creating an atmosphere of abundance and happiness. This generosity often attracts positive experiences and reinforces their sense of luck and good fortune.

Training Jupiter Dogs: Tips for Success

Training a Jupiter-ruled dog can be a rewarding experience, as these dogs are eager learners with a positive attitude. Here are some tips for successfully training a Jupiter-influenced dog:

1. **Use Adventure-Based Training:** Jupiter dogs respond well to training that incorporates exploration and adventure. Agility training, outdoor obedience classes, and scent work are all excellent ways to engage their minds and bodies while satisfying their need for adventure.

2. **Keep Training Sessions Fun and Positive:** Jupiter dogs thrive on positivity and excitement, so keep training sessions upbeat and engaging. Use treats, praise, and play as rewards to motivate them, and be sure to incorporate plenty of variety to keep them interested.

3. **Encourage Exploration During Training:** These dogs love to explore, so incorporate exploration into your training routine. Take them to new environments, introduce them to different types of challenges, and allow them to investigate their surroundings during training sessions. This will keep them mentally stimulated and eager to learn.

4. **Be Patient with Their Restlessness:** Jupiter dogs can be restless and may become bored if training sessions are too repetitive

or confined. Be patient and flexible, allowing them the freedom to move around and explore during breaks. Short, varied training sessions will keep their attention and prevent boredom.

Building a Strong Relationship with Your Jupiter Dog

Building a strong bond with a Jupiter-ruled dog involves embracing their adventurous, optimistic spirit and providing them with opportunities for growth and exploration. Here's how you can deepen your connection with your Jupiter dog:

- **Embrace Their Love for Adventure:** Jupiter dogs are happiest when they're exploring new environments and experiences. Take them on hikes, visit new parks, and introduce them to different activities to satisfy their sense of wanderlust.
- **Provide Plenty of Mental and Physical Stimulation:** Jupiter dogs need both mental and physical challenges to stay happy. Engage them with interactive play, training exercises, and outdoor adventures to keep their minds and bodies active.
- **Nurture Their Optimistic Spirit:** Jupiter dogs thrive on positivity and love being surrounded by upbeat energy. Offer plenty of praise, affection, and encouragement to reinforce their optimistic outlook and strengthen your bond.
- **Encourage Lifelong Learning:** These dogs love to learn, so continue to challenge them with new experiences, training, and activities throughout their life. They will appreciate the opportunity to grow and expand their horizons, and your relationship will deepen as you embark on new adventures together.

Conclusion

Dogs ruled by Jupiter are adventurous, optimistic, and always eager to explore the world around them. Their love for growth, learning, and new experiences makes them joyful, enthusiastic companions. By understanding their need for adventure, providing them with opportunities for exploration, and nurturing their optimistic spirit, you can create a fulfilling life for your Jupiter dog. Embrace their adventurous nature, celebrate their good fortune, and enjoy the boundless joy and love they bring to your life with their expansive, generous hearts.

Chapter 20: Saturn and Your Dog: Discipline, Responsibility, and Structure in Saturn-Ruled Dogs

Saturn, the planet of discipline, structure, and responsibility, plays a powerful role in shaping a dog's sense of duty, self-control, and work ethic. Known as the planet of boundaries and limitations, Saturn governs the qualities of patience, resilience, and focus. Dogs ruled by Saturn tend to be disciplined, hardworking, and thrive in environments where routine and order are emphasized. While they may not be as outwardly energetic or spontaneous as Jupiter-ruled dogs, Saturn dogs excel in environments that require diligence, reliability, and structure. This chapter explores how Saturn influences your dog's personality, how they approach discipline and responsibility, and how you can create a balanced, structured environment that meets their needs.

The Influence of Saturn on Discipline and Responsibility

Saturn is often associated with lessons of life, discipline, and the mastery of skills through hard work and persistence. Dogs influenced by Saturn embody these qualities, often displaying a strong sense of duty and responsibility toward their family and environment. These dogs thrive when they are given clear boundaries and tasks, enjoying a structured life that allows them to feel useful and focused. Saturn-ruled dogs are not ones for frivolous play or chaotic surroundings—they prefer an environment where rules are clear and where they can fulfill a purpose.

Key Traits of Saturn-Influenced Dogs

Dogs ruled by Saturn, particularly those born under Capricorn or Aquarius, are known for their mature, responsible, and patient nature. Here are the primary traits that define Saturn-influenced dogs:

1. **Disciplined and Hardworking:** Saturn dogs have a strong sense of discipline and are naturally hardworking. They enjoy tasks and responsibilities and take their "jobs" seriously, whether it's guard-

ing the home, learning new commands, or following routines. Their diligent nature makes them excellent working dogs, and they often excel in roles that require focus and reliability.

2. **Structured and Routine-Oriented:** These dogs thrive on routine and structure. They feel most comfortable when their daily schedule is predictable, with regular feeding times, walks, and rest periods. Disruptions to their routine can cause them stress, as they rely on consistency to feel secure and balanced.

3. **Responsible and Reliable:** Saturn-ruled dogs are incredibly responsible and can be trusted to complete tasks or follow commands with precision. They often display a sense of maturity beyond their years, taking their roles within the household seriously. Their reliability makes them dependable companions who can be counted on in various situations.

4. **Reserved and Serious:** Saturn dogs are typically more reserved and serious than their Jupiter or Mars counterparts. They are not as prone to exuberant play or impulsive behavior, preferring calm, focused activities that allow them to demonstrate their skills and intelligence. While they enjoy companionship, they are not overly clingy and tend to have a quiet, contemplative nature.

5. **Patient and Resilient:** One of the key traits of Saturn dogs is their patience. They are willing to wait for rewards and understand that good things come through perseverance and hard work. Their resilience allows them to handle challenging situations without becoming frustrated or overwhelmed, making them excellent problem-solvers.

6. **Self-Controlled and Calm:** Saturn dogs possess a high level of self-control. They are not easily excitable and tend to remain calm even in stressful situations. This ability to maintain composure makes them excellent companions in households with children or other pets, as they are less likely to become reactive or anxious.

7. **Protective and Loyal:** Dogs influenced by Saturn are deeply loyal and protective of their family. While they may not be overly

affectionate or demonstrative, their loyalty is unwavering. They take their role as protectors seriously, often acting as quiet guardians who are always alert to potential threats.

Saturn and Structure: Creating a Routine for Your Dog

Saturn dogs thrive in environments where structure and routine are emphasized. These dogs feel secure when they know what to expect and are happiest when their daily schedule is predictable. Here's how to create a structured routine that meets the needs of your Saturn-ruled dog:

1. **Consistent Feeding Schedule:** Saturn dogs appreciate consistency, so feeding them at the same times each day helps create a sense of security. Ensure that mealtimes are regular and that their feeding area is calm and quiet, free from distractions.

2. **Regular Walks and Exercise:** While Saturn dogs may not require as much physical activity as Mars or Jupiter dogs, they still need regular exercise to maintain their physical and mental well-being. Establish a routine for walks and playtime, ensuring they receive moderate but consistent physical activity each day.

3. **Structured Training Sessions:** Saturn dogs excel in training environments that are well-structured and goal-oriented. They enjoy learning new commands and take pride in mastering tasks. Create a consistent training routine that challenges them mentally and rewards them for their hard work. Focus on commands that require discipline and patience, such as "stay," "wait," and "heel."

4. **Clear Boundaries and Rules:** Saturn dogs feel most comfortable when they understand the rules and boundaries of their environment. Be clear about household rules, such as where they are allowed to go, what behaviors are acceptable, and how they are expected to interact with other pets or people. Consistency in enforcing these boundaries helps them feel secure and in control.

5. **Scheduled Rest and Downtime:** Just as they need structure in their active time, Saturn dogs also benefit from scheduled rest periods. They appreciate having a quiet, designated space where they can retreat to relax and recharge. Ensure they have a comfortable bed in a calm area of the home where they won't be disturbed during rest times.

Saturn and Responsibility: Encouraging Your Dog's Sense of Duty

Saturn-ruled dogs thrive when they are given responsibilities and tasks to complete. Their natural sense of duty makes them eager to contribute to the household, and they often take pride in fulfilling their roles. Here's how to encourage your dog's sense of responsibility:

1. **Assign Them a Job:** Saturn dogs enjoy having a job to do, whether it's helping around the house or participating in structured activities. Consider giving your dog tasks such as carrying a small backpack on walks, assisting with herding animals, or even performing simple commands that require focus and discipline. These tasks give them a sense of purpose and fulfillment.

2. **Engage Them in Working Roles:** Many Saturn dogs excel in working roles, such as guard dogs, service dogs, or therapy dogs. Their reliability, patience, and self-control make them well-suited for roles that require focus and dedication. If your dog enjoys learning and taking on responsibilities, consider enrolling them in training programs for service or therapy work.

3. **Teach Them Advanced Commands:** Saturn dogs love learning advanced commands that challenge their discipline and intelligence. Commands that require precision, such as "fetch," "place," or "leave it," engage their problem-solving skills and reinforce their sense of duty. Teaching them more complex tasks, such as opening doors or retrieving specific objects, also satisfies their need for mental stimulation.

4. **Reward Their Hard Work:** While Saturn dogs are naturally motivated by a sense of duty, it's important to reward their hard work with praise, treats, or affection. Positive reinforcement encourages them to continue performing their tasks with enthusiasm. Saturn dogs may not seek constant attention, but they appreciate recognition for their efforts.

5. **Create Challenges to Build Resilience:** Saturn dogs are naturally resilient and thrive on challenges that test their patience and determination. Introduce puzzle toys, obstacle courses, or advanced training exercises that require them to think critically and stay focused. These activities help them build confidence and reinforce their problem-solving abilities.

Saturn and Patience: How to Work with a Saturn Dog's Calm Nature

One of the defining characteristics of Saturn dogs is their calm, patient nature. These dogs are not easily excitable and are often content to wait for what they want. Here's how to work with their patient temperament and encourage a balanced, well-behaved companion:

1. **Use Patience-Based Training:** Saturn dogs excel in training that emphasizes patience and self-control. Commands such as "stay," "wait," and "down" are ideal for these dogs, as they require focus and discipline. Use positive reinforcement to reward their calm, patient behavior, and avoid rushing through training sessions.

2. **Encourage Calm Behavior in Social Settings:** Saturn dogs are naturally calm and reserved in social settings. They are not likely to become overly excitable around new people or animals, making them excellent companions in busy households or public spaces. Encourage their calm behavior by rewarding them when they remain composed during social interactions.

3. **Provide Quiet, Structured Play:** While Saturn dogs may not engage in high-energy play as frequently as other dogs, they still

enjoy structured, purposeful play sessions. Offer them toys that challenge their intellect, such as puzzle toys or slow-feeder bowls, and engage them in calm activities that require focus and patience.

4. **Be a Calm, Steady Leader:** Saturn dogs respond well to calm, consistent leadership. They thrive in environments where their owners are steady, predictable, and clear about expectations. Avoid using harsh or punitive training methods, as these dogs are sensitive to criticism and prefer a balanced, respectful approach.

Building a Strong Relationship with Your Saturn Dog

Building a strong bond with a Saturn-ruled dog involves understanding their need for structure, discipline, and purpose. These dogs are loyal, protective, and eager to fulfill their role within the household. Here's how you can create a deep, lasting relationship with your Saturn dog:

- **Respect Their Need for Structure:** Saturn dogs feel most secure when they have a clear routine and structure. Provide them with a consistent daily schedule that includes regular exercise, feeding, and training times. This will help them feel safe and grounded.

- **Offer Them a Sense of Purpose:** Saturn dogs thrive when they have responsibilities and tasks to complete. Give them meaningful jobs, whether it's helping around the house, performing tricks, or participating in service work. They will feel fulfilled when they know they are contributing to the household.

- **Be a Calm and Steady Presence:** Saturn dogs respond best to calm, consistent leadership. Be patient and steady in your interactions with them, and avoid raising your voice or becoming frustrated. They will appreciate your calm, measured approach and will respond with loyalty and dedication.

- **Encourage Lifelong Learning:** Saturn dogs enjoy learning new skills, and their disciplined nature means they excel in training throughout their lives. Continue to challenge them with new commands, tasks, and activities to keep their minds sharp and engaged.

Conclusion

Dogs ruled by Saturn are disciplined, responsible, and thrive in structured environments where they can fulfill their roles with dedication and focus. By understanding their need for routine, responsibility, and calm, you can create a fulfilling environment that allows them to thrive. Embrace their patient, hardworking nature, provide them with tasks that challenge their discipline and intelligence, and enjoy the deep sense of loyalty and protection they bring to your life. With the right guidance, your Saturn dog will become a steadfast companion, always ready to fulfill their duties with grace and determination.

Chapter 21: Uranus and Your Dog: Innovation, Change, and Uniqueness in Dogs Influenced by Uranus

Uranus, the planet of innovation, rebellion, and unexpected change, governs the qualities of originality, independence, and adaptability. Known for its disruptive yet liberating energy, Uranus brings an element of surprise and unconventionality to everything it touches. Dogs influenced by Uranus are often quirky, independent thinkers, full of surprises and ready to break the mold of traditional canine behavior. These dogs embrace change, thrive on new experiences, and are unafraid to express their unique personalities. In this chapter, we explore how Uranus shapes your dog's behavior, their love for innovation, and how you can support their need for independence and novelty.

The Influence of Uranus on Innovation and Change

Uranus is often associated with innovation and the breaking down of old structures to make way for new possibilities. For dogs, this planetary influence translates into a love for change, a desire to explore new territories, and an ability to adapt to unpredictable situations with ease. Uranus-ruled dogs are anything but ordinary—they embrace new experiences and often approach life with a sense of curiosity and adventure. Their natural independence makes them less reliant on rigid routines, and they may frequently surprise you with their spontaneous, unconventional behavior.

Key Traits of Uranus-Influenced Dogs

Dogs ruled by Uranus, particularly those born under Aquarius, are known for their unique, rebellious, and innovative natures. Here are the primary traits that define Uranus-influenced dogs:

1. **Innovative and Unconventional:** Uranus dogs are often out-of-the-box thinkers, finding creative ways to solve problems and navigate their world. They may not follow traditional canine be-

havior patterns, instead preferring to create their own rules and routines. Their originality makes them stand out from other dogs, and they often invent new games or approaches to common tasks.

2. **Independent and Self-Sufficient:** These dogs are highly independent and prefer to make decisions on their own. While they enjoy companionship, they are not overly reliant on their owners for constant attention or guidance. Uranus dogs value their freedom and may seek out opportunities to explore or engage in activities without needing direction.

3. **Adaptable and Open to Change:** Uranus dogs thrive in environments that offer change and new experiences. They are highly adaptable and are often excited by the prospect of something new, whether it's a different routine, a new toy, or an unfamiliar place to explore. Unlike Saturn-ruled dogs who prefer structure, Uranus dogs embrace unpredictability and change with enthusiasm.

4. **Rebellious and Free-Spirited:** Uranus-ruled dogs have a natural rebellious streak. They dislike being confined by strict rules or routines and may resist commands that feel too restrictive. These dogs are free spirits, often pushing boundaries and seeking out new ways to assert their individuality. Their rebellious nature is part of their charm, though it can sometimes make training more challenging.

5. **Quirky and Full of Surprises:** One of the most delightful traits of Uranus dogs is their quirky, unpredictable behavior. They are full of surprises and may suddenly invent a new way to play, explore an unconventional hiding spot, or find a unique way to communicate with you. Their spontaneity keeps life interesting, as you never quite know what they'll do next.

6. **Intelligent and Curious:** Uranus dogs are highly intelligent and enjoy mental stimulation. They are naturally curious and love exploring new ideas, environments, and activities. Their sharp

minds and quick learning abilities make them excellent problem solvers, though they may also get bored easily if not provided with enough mental challenges.

7. **Socially Unique:** Uranus dogs tend to approach social interactions in unconventional ways. While they can be friendly and sociable, they may not follow typical social patterns with other dogs or humans. They often march to the beat of their own drum, making friends on their own terms and enjoying a wide range of social experiences.

Uranus and Change: Embracing New Experiences

One of the defining traits of Uranus-ruled dogs is their love for change and new experiences. These dogs thrive in environments that offer variety and opportunities to explore the unknown. Here's how to create a life full of novelty and innovation for your Uranus dog:

1. **Frequent Changes in Routine:** Unlike dogs who prefer strict schedules, Uranus dogs love when routines are mixed up. They are not fazed by changes in their daily schedule and may even become bored with too much predictability. Introduce variety into their routine by altering the time or location of walks, switching up their toys, or trying new activities.

2. **Exploration and Adventure:** Uranus dogs have a natural curiosity about the world around them, and they thrive on exploration and adventure. Take them on hikes, visit new parks, or introduce them to new environments where they can satisfy their urge to explore. These dogs enjoy the thrill of discovering new sights, sounds, and smells, and they are always ready for the next adventure.

3. **Unconventional Play:** Uranus dogs are known for their inventive play styles. Encourage their creativity by offering unconventional toys or setting up play sessions that allow them to think outside the box. Puzzle toys, interactive games, and even obstacle

courses can provide the mental stimulation they crave. They may also enjoy creating their own games, so give them the freedom to experiment during playtime.

4. **Flexibility in Training:** While Uranus dogs can be intelligent and eager learners, they often resist traditional training methods. They prefer learning through exploration and discovery rather than following strict commands. Use positive reinforcement techniques and allow them some autonomy during training sessions. Incorporate variety and creativity into your training routines to keep them engaged.

Uranus and Independence: Supporting Your Dog's Self-Sufficiency

Uranus dogs value their independence and often prefer to make their own decisions. While they still enjoy companionship and love from their owners, they are not as reliant on constant attention as some other dogs. Here's how to support your Uranus dog's independence while still maintaining a strong bond:

1. **Give Them Space:** Uranus dogs appreciate having space to explore and relax on their own terms. Provide them with areas of the house or yard where they can retreat when they want some alone time. Allow them to have the freedom to roam and investigate their environment without feeling confined or restricted.

2. **Encourage Autonomous Play:** These dogs are highly capable of entertaining themselves, so offer them toys and activities that allow for autonomous play. Interactive toys, such as treat-dispensing puzzles or toys that move unpredictably, can keep them engaged and mentally stimulated when they're on their own.

3. **Respect Their Individuality:** Uranus dogs often have unique personalities and preferences that may not align with typical canine behaviors. Respect their individuality and give them the freedom to express themselves in their own way. Whether it's a

quirky habit or an unconventional way of interacting with others, embrace their uniqueness.

4. **Foster Confidence:** Independence doesn't mean isolation—Uranus dogs still need reassurance and support from their owners. Foster their confidence by encouraging their independence while also providing them with affection and positive reinforcement. This helps them feel secure and loved while maintaining their self-sufficient nature.

Uranus and Innovation: Encouraging Creativity and Problem-Solving

Uranus dogs are naturally creative and love problem-solving. Their innovative nature makes them excellent at figuring out new ways to achieve goals, whether it's finding hidden treats or learning a new trick. Here's how to encourage your Uranus dog's creativity and innovation:

1. **Offer Puzzle Toys and Challenges:** Uranus dogs thrive on mental challenges, so puzzle toys are a great way to engage their problem-solving abilities. Look for toys that require them to think critically, such as treat puzzles, interactive feeders, or toys that challenge them to solve problems in order to access rewards.

2. **Encourage Free Play:** Allow your Uranus dog the freedom to engage in free play, where they can explore their surroundings and come up with their own games. Provide them with a variety of toys and objects to interact with, and watch as they invent new ways to entertain themselves. Their creative minds will often surprise you with the solutions they come up with.

3. **Training Through Discovery:** Uranus dogs often resist rigid training methods, preferring to learn through exploration and discovery. Incorporate discovery-based learning into your training routines by allowing them to explore different options when learning new commands or tricks. Use positive reinforcement

to reward their problem-solving efforts and encourage creative thinking.

4. **Introduce New Experiences Regularly:** To keep a Uranus dog mentally stimulated, regularly introduce new experiences and environments. Whether it's a new park, a different walking route, or a novel type of game, these dogs thrive on novelty and will enjoy the opportunity to explore and learn something new.

Uranus and Rebellion: Navigating Their Free-Spirited Nature

One of the challenges of owning a Uranus-ruled dog is their rebellious streak. These dogs often dislike following rules and may resist commands that feel too restrictive or confining. Here's how to work with their free-spirited nature while still maintaining discipline:

1. **Allow for Flexibility in Training:** Uranus dogs often push back against strict training routines. Rather than enforcing rigid commands, try incorporating flexibility into your training sessions. Offer choices and allow them to explore different methods of achieving the desired outcome. This not only keeps them engaged but also satisfies their need for autonomy.

2. **Use Positive Reinforcement:** Punishment or harsh training methods are not effective with Uranus dogs. Instead, use positive reinforcement to encourage good behavior. Reward them with treats, praise, and playtime when they follow commands or exhibit positive behaviors. Their independent nature means they will respond better to rewards than to punishment.

3. **Set Clear Boundaries—With Flexibility:** While Uranus dogs value their independence, they still need clear boundaries. Establish rules that are flexible enough to accommodate their free-spirited nature. For example, if they resist being confined to a crate, provide them with a larger, more open space where they can still feel a sense of freedom.

4. **Channel Their Rebellious Energy Into Positive Outlets:** Uranus dogs have a lot of energy, especially when it comes to challenging rules. Channel their rebellious streak into positive activities, such as agility training, where they can test their limits and push boundaries in a controlled, constructive way. This helps them burn off energy while still reinforcing discipline.

Building a Strong Relationship with Your Uranus Dog

Building a strong bond with a Uranus-ruled dog involves embracing their unique, independent, and innovative nature. Here's how you can strengthen your relationship with your Uranus dog:

- **Celebrate Their Uniqueness:** Uranus dogs are one of a kind, and they thrive when their individuality is recognized and appreciated. Celebrate their quirky habits, spontaneous behaviors, and creative problem-solving abilities. The more you embrace their uniqueness, the stronger your bond will become.
- **Be a Flexible, Supportive Leader:** Uranus dogs need a leader who understands their need for freedom and autonomy. Be supportive and flexible in your approach to training and care, providing them with guidance without being overly restrictive.
- **Provide New Experiences and Challenges:** Keep your Uranus dog mentally stimulated by regularly introducing new experiences and challenges. Whether it's a new game, a different environment, or a unique puzzle toy, these dogs thrive on novelty and exploration.
- **Respect Their Independence:** Uranus dogs value their independence, so give them the space and freedom to make their own choices. Whether it's allowing them to explore on their own or giving them autonomy during playtime, respecting their independence will help build trust and mutual respect.

Conclusion

Dogs ruled by Uranus are unique, independent, and always ready for new experiences. Their love for innovation, change, and spontaneity makes them exciting, unpredictable companions who thrive on freedom and exploration. By understanding their need for autonomy, providing them with mental challenges, and embracing their unconventional nature, you can create a fulfilling life for your Uranus dog. Celebrate their individuality, support their curiosity, and enjoy the endless surprises and creativity they bring to your life.

Chapter 22: Neptune and Your Dog: Dreams, Intuition, and Spirituality in Neptune-Ruled Dogs

Neptune, the planet of dreams, intuition, and mysticism, rules the hidden depths of emotion and spirituality. Known for its influence over the unconscious mind, dreams, and intuition, Neptune brings a sense of mystery, sensitivity, and heightened awareness to those under its influence. Dogs ruled by Neptune are often deeply intuitive, emotionally sensitive, and connected to the unseen. They have a mystical, almost otherworldly quality to them, often seeming to sense things beyond the physical world. In this chapter, we'll explore how Neptune shapes your dog's intuitive abilities, their connection to the spiritual and dream realms, and how you can nurture their sensitive, spiritual nature.

The Influence of Neptune on Intuition and Dreams

Neptune governs the subconscious mind, intuition, and dreams, making dogs influenced by this planet highly sensitive to their surroundings and emotionally in tune with their owners. These dogs often display an uncanny ability to sense emotions, changes in energy, or even impending events. Neptune-ruled dogs are more likely to "feel" their way through life, using their deep connection to their instincts and the unseen to guide their actions. They are also prone to having vivid dreams and may exhibit behaviors that suggest a deep connection to the dream world or other spiritual dimensions.

Key Traits of Neptune-Influenced Dogs

Dogs ruled by Neptune, especially those born under Pisces, are known for their dreamy, sensitive, and intuitive nature. Here are the primary traits that define Neptune-influenced dogs:

1. **Deeply Intuitive and Emotionally Sensitive:** Neptune dogs possess a heightened sense of intuition, often knowing how you feel or what you're thinking before you even say or do anything. They are attuned to subtle shifts in mood or energy and will often react to emotional changes in their environment with empathy

and understanding. These dogs are natural comforters, offering quiet support when they sense their owner is upset or stressed.

2. **Dreamy and Mystical:** Neptune dogs often have a dreamy, almost mystical quality to them. They may seem to be lost in thought or "staring into the distance," as if they are connected to another realm. Their dreaminess can also manifest in their playful or exploratory behavior, where they seem to be engaging with something beyond the physical world.

3. **Spiritual and Calm:** There is a spiritual calmness that defines Neptune dogs. They are not typically hyperactive or overly energetic but instead carry a peaceful, tranquil energy that can soothe those around them. Their spiritual nature may lead them to find quiet places to retreat to, as they often enjoy moments of stillness and reflection.

4. **Vivid Dreamers:** Neptune dogs are likely to be vivid dreamers, and they may display signs of active dreaming, such as twitching, barking softly, or moving their paws as if running while asleep. These dogs are deeply connected to the dream world, and their dreams may even influence their waking behavior.

5. **Empathetic and Compassionate:** Empathy is one of the strongest traits of Neptune dogs. They are incredibly compassionate and often serve as emotional anchors for their owners. When someone in the household is feeling down, a Neptune dog will quietly offer their presence, understanding that sometimes just being close is enough to bring comfort.

6. **Imaginative and Playful:** Neptune dogs often have a rich imagination, which comes through in their playful behavior. They may engage in creative, whimsical games or seem to "play" with invisible companions. Their playtime is often a blend of fantasy and reality, making them endlessly fascinating and charming companions.

7. **Mysterious and Elusive:** Neptune dogs can be a bit elusive at times, seeming to exist in their own world. They may drift in and

out of interactions, appearing distant one moment and deeply connected the next. This mysterious quality only adds to their allure, making them unique and captivating pets.

Neptune and Intuition: Understanding Your Dog's Sixth Sense

One of the most remarkable traits of Neptune-ruled dogs is their powerful intuition. These dogs seem to possess a sixth sense, often predicting events or sensing emotions before they are expressed. Here's how to recognize and nurture your Neptune dog's intuitive abilities:

1. **Recognizing Intuitive Behavior:** Neptune dogs may display intuitive behaviors, such as coming to comfort you before you realize you're upset, reacting to an impending storm or event, or showing awareness of a change in the household long before it occurs. Pay attention to these behaviors, as they reveal your dog's deep connection to their instincts and the unseen.

2. **Respect Their Sensitivity:** Neptune dogs are highly sensitive to their environment and the emotions of those around them. It's important to provide them with a calm, nurturing space where they can feel secure. Avoid loud noises or chaotic environments, as these can overwhelm their sensitive nature. Gentle handling and a peaceful atmosphere will help them feel grounded and emotionally balanced.

3. **Encourage Their Role as Emotional Support:** Neptune dogs are natural emotional support animals, often providing comfort through their quiet, calming presence. Encourage this role by spending time with them during difficult moments and allowing them to offer their unique form of empathy. Their ability to sense when you need comfort can help deepen your bond with them.

4. **Trust Their Instincts:** When your Neptune dog reacts to something seemingly out of the blue, trust that they are sensing something beyond what is immediately visible. Their intuition is often

highly accurate, and they may be aware of things you cannot see or hear. Whether they're warning you of a distant sound or sensing an emotional shift, their instincts are worth paying attention to.

Neptune and Dreams: The Dream World of Your Dog

Neptune is the ruler of the dream realm, and dogs under its influence are often vivid dreamers. Their dreams may be active and engaging, and you may notice them reacting to their dreams in unique ways. Here's how to understand and support your dog's connection to the dream world:

1. **Signs of Active Dreaming:** Neptune dogs often display signs of active dreaming, such as twitching, barking softly, or moving their paws as if they are running while asleep. These behaviors are normal and indicate that your dog is experiencing a vivid dream. It's best not to wake them during these moments, as they are fully immersed in their dream world.

2. **Creating a Dream-Friendly Environment:** To support your Neptune dog's connection to the dream world, provide them with a comfortable, quiet space where they can rest undisturbed. A soft bed in a peaceful corner of the home can help them feel safe and secure while they sleep. Ensuring that they have a calm, serene environment will enhance their ability to connect to the dream realm.

3. **Understanding Dream-Influenced Behavior:** Sometimes, Neptune dogs may carry their dream experiences into their waking life. You might notice them behaving differently after a nap, as if they've brought part of their dream into reality. This can manifest in playful or curious behavior, where they seem to be interacting with something invisible. Respect their dream-influenced playtime, as it's part of their unique connection to the spiritual world.

4. **Dream Interpretation in Dogs:** While we can't fully understand what dogs dream about, Neptune-ruled dogs often display behavior that suggests their dreams are vivid and meaningful. If your dog seems especially active during sleep, it's likely that their dreams are rich with experiences. These dreams may reflect their emotional state, processing of daily events, or even their connection to deeper, spiritual realms.

Neptune and Spirituality: Nurturing Your Dog's Mystical Nature

Neptune dogs have an undeniable connection to the spiritual world. They often display behaviors that suggest they are in tune with energies beyond the physical realm, and they may seem to have a deeper understanding of life's mysteries. Here's how to nurture your Neptune dog's spiritual nature:

1. **Provide a Peaceful, Calm Environment:** Neptune dogs need a tranquil environment where they can connect to their inner world. Create a peaceful home atmosphere with soft lighting, gentle music, and calm energy. This will help your dog feel safe and grounded, allowing them to fully embrace their spiritual side.

2. **Encourage Quiet Time and Reflection:** Neptune dogs benefit from quiet time where they can retreat and relax. Provide them with a comfortable space where they can meditate in their own way, whether it's lounging in a sunbeam or resting in a cozy bed. These moments of stillness allow them to reconnect with their inner self and the spiritual world.

3. **Use Gentle, Calming Communication:** When interacting with a Neptune-ruled dog, it's important to use gentle, calming communication. These dogs are sensitive to tone and energy, so speaking softly and using soothing body language will help them feel at ease. Avoid harsh commands or loud voices, as these can disrupt their sense of peace and balance.

4. **Embrace Their Mystical Side:** Neptune dogs often display a mystical, otherworldly quality. They may seem to sense things beyond the physical, or exhibit behaviors that suggest they are connected to unseen forces. Embrace this side of your dog by allowing them to explore their unique connection to the spiritual world. Whether they're staring off into space or engaging with something invisible, respect their mysterious nature and trust their instincts.

Building a Strong Relationship with Your Neptune Dog

Building a strong bond with a Neptune-ruled dog involves understanding their need for emotional connection, intuition, and spirituality. Here's how you can strengthen your relationship with your Neptune dog:

- **Be Emotionally Present:** Neptune dogs are highly attuned to emotions, so being emotionally present with them is key to building a strong bond. Spend time quietly connecting with your dog, offering them comfort and support when needed. Your emotional presence will help them feel secure and deeply connected to you.

- **Encourage Their Intuitive Abilities:** Neptune dogs often have strong intuitive abilities, so encourage them by trusting their instincts and paying attention to their subtle cues. Whether they're sensing an emotional shift or alerting you to something unseen, acknowledging their intuition will deepen your bond.

- **Create a Calming, Peaceful Environment:** Neptune dogs need a calm, serene space where they can feel safe and relaxed. By providing a peaceful home environment, you allow them to connect more deeply to their spiritual and intuitive nature, which will strengthen your relationship.

- **Respect Their Dreamy, Mystical Side:** Neptune dogs often live in a world of dreams and intuition, so respect their need for quiet reflection and their connection to the unseen. Embrace their mystical side and enjoy the unique, spiritual bond that comes from loving a Neptune-ruled dog.

Conclusion

Dogs ruled by Neptune are deeply intuitive, spiritually connected, and full of dreams and mysteries. Their sensitivity and empathy make them compassionate companions, while their connection to the unseen brings a unique, mystical quality to their personality. By nurturing their intuitive abilities, providing them with a peaceful environment, and embracing their spiritual side, you can create a fulfilling, emotionally rich life for your Neptune dog. Celebrate their gentle, empathetic nature, and enjoy the deep, soulful bond that comes from sharing your life with a dog who is truly in tune with the mysteries of the universe.

Chapter 23: Pluto and Your Dog: Transformation, Power, and Intensity in Pluto-Ruled Dogs

Pluto, the planet of transformation, power, and intensity, governs the deep, hidden forces that shape life's cycles of death and rebirth. Known for its association with profound change, emotional depth, and the subconscious, Pluto's influence brings a level of intensity and depth to those under its rule. Dogs influenced by Pluto are powerful, emotionally complex, and often mysterious. They may possess an intensity that sets them apart from other dogs, as they navigate the world with a deep sense of purpose and emotional power. In this chapter, we explore how Pluto shapes your dog's personality, their approach to transformation and power, and how you can support their need for depth and emotional intensity.

The Influence of Pluto on Transformation and Power

Pluto is the planet of transformation, representing the cycles of destruction and renewal. For dogs ruled by Pluto, this influence manifests as a deep connection to personal growth and change. These dogs often experience periods of transformation, whether it's through their behavior, relationships, or emotional development. Pluto also governs power, and dogs under its influence carry a sense of inner strength and intensity that can be felt by those around them. Pluto dogs are not content with surface-level experiences—they seek depth and meaning in their interactions and relationships, often forming strong emotional bonds with those they trust.

Key Traits of Pluto-Influenced Dogs

Dogs ruled by Pluto, especially those born under Scorpio, are known for their intensity, emotional depth, and transformative nature. Here are the primary traits that define Pluto-influenced dogs:

1. **Intense and Focused:** Pluto dogs possess a level of intensity that sets them apart from other dogs. They are deeply focused on their goals, whether it's mastering a new command, protecting their family, or exploring their environment. Their intensity can some-

times make them seem serious or brooding, but it's a reflection of their deep emotional engagement with the world around them.

2. **Emotionally Deep and Complex:** These dogs are emotionally complex and often display behaviors that suggest they feel things on a deeper level. They may be more sensitive to emotional shifts in their environment and form strong, almost unbreakable bonds with their owners. Pluto dogs often take their relationships seriously, and they value loyalty and trust above all else.

3. **Transformative and Adaptive:** Pluto dogs are not afraid of change—in fact, they embrace it. These dogs often go through periods of transformation, whether it's adjusting to a new environment, overcoming a behavioral challenge, or growing emotionally. They have a unique ability to adapt to difficult situations, emerging stronger and more resilient after each experience.

4. **Powerful and Protective:** Pluto-ruled dogs have a natural sense of power and strength. They are often protective of their family and may take on the role of a guardian, watching over their home with a quiet but intense presence. Their protective instincts are strong, and they will go to great lengths to defend those they love.

5. **Mysterious and Private:** Pluto dogs can be somewhat mysterious, often keeping their thoughts and feelings hidden from the outside world. They may retreat into themselves at times, seeking solitude or quiet reflection. This mysterious nature makes them intriguing companions, as they often reveal their emotional depth slowly and only to those they trust implicitly.

6. **Resilient and Determined:** Resilience is a hallmark of Pluto dogs. They are not easily deterred by challenges or setbacks and will persist in their efforts until they achieve their goals. Whether it's solving a problem, learning a new skill, or protecting their family, Pluto dogs are known for their determination and perseverance.

7. **Possessive and Loyal:** Loyalty is one of the most defining traits of Pluto dogs. Once they've formed a bond with their owner or family, they are fiercely loyal and protective. However, this loyalty can sometimes manifest as possessiveness, as Pluto dogs may become overly attached to their loved ones or resources, such as toys or food.

Pluto and Transformation: Embracing Change in Your Dog's Life

Transformation is a central theme for Pluto-ruled dogs. These dogs often experience significant changes throughout their lives, whether it's in their behavior, environment, or emotional development. Here's how to support your Pluto dog's journey of transformation:

1. **Encourage Growth and Development:** Pluto dogs thrive on personal growth and transformation. Encourage their development by providing them with opportunities to learn new skills, adapt to new environments, and face challenges. Whether it's introducing new commands, enrolling them in agility training, or helping them adjust to a new home, Pluto dogs will embrace these opportunities for growth.

2. **Support Emotional Transformation:** Pluto dogs are emotionally complex and may go through periods of emotional transformation, such as overcoming fear or anxiety. Be patient and supportive during these times, offering them comfort and reassurance as they work through their emotions. These dogs often emerge stronger and more confident after facing emotional challenges.

3. **Respect Their Need for Privacy:** Pluto dogs value their privacy and may retreat into themselves when they need time to process their emotions or experiences. Respect their need for solitude, allowing them space to reflect and recharge. They will return to

you when they're ready, often more focused and emotionally balanced after their time alone.

4. **Recognize Signs of Transformation:** Pluto dogs often exhibit signs of transformation, such as changes in behavior, mood, or energy levels. Pay attention to these shifts, as they may indicate that your dog is going through a period of growth or adaptation. Support them by maintaining a stable, nurturing environment that allows them to feel secure as they navigate change.

Pluto and Power: Understanding Your Dog's Strength and Intensity

Pluto dogs are naturally powerful, both physically and emotionally. They carry a quiet intensity that can be felt by those around them, and they often take on leadership roles within their family or social group. Here's how to harness and support your Pluto dog's sense of power:

1. **Channel Their Power Into Positive Outlets:** Pluto dogs have a lot of energy and emotional intensity, which needs to be channeled into positive outlets. Activities that require focus and discipline, such as advanced obedience training or agility courses, can help them harness their power in a constructive way. These dogs often enjoy tasks that challenge their strength and intelligence.

2. **Encourage Leadership Roles:** Pluto dogs often naturally assume leadership roles, whether it's in a multi-pet household or during playtime at the park. Encourage this sense of leadership by giving them responsibilities, such as guarding the home or leading the way during walks. Their confidence and sense of power will grow when they feel they have an important role to fulfill.

3. **Be a Strong, Calm Leader:** Pluto dogs respect strength and confidence in their owners. To build a strong bond with your Pluto dog, it's important to be a calm, assertive leader who provides clear guidance and boundaries. These dogs need to know that

they can rely on you for stability and support, especially during times of change or stress.

4. **Support Their Protective Instincts:** Pluto dogs are naturally protective and may take their role as a guardian seriously. While it's important to set boundaries to prevent overprotectiveness, you can support their protective instincts by reinforcing their role as a trusted defender of the home. Praise them when they alert you to potential threats, but also teach them when it's appropriate to stand down.

Pluto and Emotional Depth: Nurturing Your Dog's Complex Emotions

Pluto dogs are emotionally deep and often feel things on a more intense level than other dogs. Their emotional complexity can be both a gift and a challenge, as they navigate powerful feelings of loyalty, protectiveness, and love. Here's how to nurture your Pluto dog's emotional depth:

1. **Offer Emotional Support:** Pluto dogs may experience intense emotions, such as fear, anxiety, or possessiveness. Be there for them during these moments, offering comfort and reassurance. Your presence will help them feel safe as they work through their feelings, and they will appreciate your understanding of their emotional needs.

2. **Build a Strong Emotional Bond:** Pluto dogs value loyalty and trust above all else. Building a strong emotional bond with your Pluto dog requires patience, consistency, and understanding. Spend quality time with them, engage in activities that they enjoy, and be emotionally available to them. The deeper your bond, the more secure and confident your Pluto dog will feel.

3. **Respect Their Emotional Boundaries:** While Pluto dogs are deeply loyal, they may also have emotional boundaries that they don't want crossed. They may not always want constant affection

or attention, preferring moments of solitude or quiet reflection. Respect these boundaries, and they will come to trust you even more, knowing that you understand their need for space.

4. **Help Them Navigate Possessiveness:** Pluto dogs can be possessive of their loved ones, toys, or food. While this is a natural expression of their loyalty, it's important to teach them healthy boundaries to prevent over-possessiveness. Work on commands such as "leave it" or "drop it," and reward them for sharing or relinquishing control of their resources.

Building a Strong Relationship with Your Pluto Dog

Building a strong relationship with a Pluto-ruled dog involves embracing their emotional depth, intensity, and transformative nature. These dogs thrive on loyalty, trust, and a sense of purpose. Here's how you can create a deep, meaningful bond with your Pluto dog:

- **Be Patient and Supportive:** Pluto dogs often experience emotional or behavioral transformations that require patience and support. Be there for them during difficult times, offering comfort and guidance as they navigate their emotions.
- **Embrace Their Intensity:** Pluto dogs are intense by nature, and they need an owner who can match their emotional depth and focus. Engage with them in activities that challenge their mind and body, and don't shy away from their powerful, protective nature.
- **Foster a Strong Sense of Trust:** Trust is the foundation of any relationship with a Pluto dog. They need to know that you are loyal and dependable, just as they are. Spend time building trust through consistent, loving care, and they will reward you with unwavering loyalty.
- **Respect Their Need for Solitude:** Pluto dogs often seek moments of quiet reflection or solitude. Respect their need for space and privacy, and they will come to trust and love you even more, knowing that you understand their unique emotional needs.

Conclusion

Dogs ruled by Pluto are powerful, intense, and deeply transformative beings. Their emotional complexity and capacity for growth make them fascinating, loyal companions who thrive on trust, loyalty, and a sense of purpose. By understanding their need for transformation, respecting their emotional depth, and supporting their powerful nature, you can create a fulfilling, meaningful life for your Pluto dog. Embrace their intensity, celebrate their resilience, and enjoy the deep, unwavering bond that comes from sharing your life with a dog who truly understands the transformative power of love and loyalty.

Part 3: Celestial Bodies and Events

Chapter 24: Eclipses and Your Dog: The Impact of Solar and Lunar Eclipses on Your Dog's Behavior

Eclipses—both solar and lunar—have long been associated with powerful shifts in energy and emotions. These celestial events are known for their ability to bring about change, transformation, and heightened awareness in humans, and they can also have a noticeable effect on dogs. Dogs, being highly sensitive to shifts in their environment and the energies around them, often exhibit changes in behavior, mood, and energy during eclipses. In this chapter, we will explore how both solar and lunar eclipses influence your dog's behavior, emotional state, and how you can support them during these potent astrological events.

Understanding Eclipses: A Brief Overview

Eclipses occur when the Sun, Earth, and Moon align in a specific way, causing one celestial body to cast a shadow on another. Solar eclipses happen when the Moon passes between the Earth and the Sun, temporarily blocking the Sun's light. Lunar eclipses occur when the Earth comes between the Sun and the Moon, casting a shadow on the Moon.

In astrology, eclipses are considered highly charged moments that bring sudden changes, revelations, and shifts in energy. They represent moments of realignment and can trigger emotional responses, sudden insights, or changes in behavior. For dogs, these cosmic events can lead to shifts in their energy, emotional state, and general behavior.

The Effects of Solar Eclipses on Your Dog

Solar eclipses are powerful events that can temporarily disrupt the natural flow of light and energy. During a solar eclipse, the sudden blocking of the Sun's light can create an atmosphere of uncertainty or confusion for dogs, as they rely heavily on their senses to navigate the world. Here are some common ways solar eclipses can affect your dog:

1. **Increased Sensitivity and Alertness:** Dogs are highly attuned to their environment, and the sudden changes in light and energy during a solar eclipse may heighten their sensitivity. You may no-

tice your dog becoming more alert, pacing, or looking around as if they are sensing something unusual. This heightened alertness is a natural response to the shift in energy caused by the eclipse.

2. **Anxiety and Restlessness:** Some dogs may experience increased anxiety or restlessness during a solar eclipse. The sudden dimming of light can cause confusion, and your dog may not understand why their environment feels different. Signs of anxiety may include pacing, whining, excessive barking, or seeking comfort from their owner.

3. **Changes in Behavior:** During a solar eclipse, some dogs may display unusual behavior, such as acting more clingy or more distant than usual. They may also become more protective, as the eclipse's energy can trigger a sense of uncertainty. This change in behavior is typically temporary and should subside once the eclipse passes.

4. **Reduced Energy Levels:** While some dogs may become more alert and anxious, others may experience a dip in energy levels during a solar eclipse. They may become lethargic, choose to rest more, or retreat to a quiet spot. This decrease in energy can be a natural response to the sudden shift in the atmosphere.

How to Support Your Dog During a Solar Eclipse

To help your dog feel safe and secure during a solar eclipse, consider the following tips:

1. **Create a Calm Environment:** Ensure that your dog's environment is calm and quiet during the eclipse. Close the blinds or curtains to minimize the sudden change in light, and keep noise levels low to reduce any additional stress.

2. **Provide Comfort and Reassurance:** If your dog seems anxious or unsettled, offer comfort and reassurance. Stay close to them, speak in soothing tones, and provide gentle petting or cuddles if

they seek it out. Your presence will help them feel more secure during the eclipse.

3. **Stick to Their Routine:** Maintaining your dog's regular routine can help alleviate any stress or confusion they may feel during the eclipse. Stick to their usual feeding, walking, and play schedules to provide a sense of normalcy.

4. **Use Calming Aids:** If your dog is particularly sensitive to changes in their environment, consider using calming aids such as a calming collar, diffuser, or natural supplements designed to reduce anxiety. These can help keep your dog relaxed during the eclipse.

The Effects of Lunar Eclipses on Your Dog

Lunar eclipses, which occur when the Earth casts a shadow on the Moon, tend to have a more emotional and introspective impact in astrology. Lunar energy is associated with emotions, instincts, and the subconscious, and a lunar eclipse can heighten these aspects in both humans and animals. For dogs, lunar eclipses can bring about shifts in mood, heightened intuition, and changes in their emotional state.

1. **Heightened Emotional Sensitivity:** During a lunar eclipse, dogs may become more emotionally sensitive and in tune with the feelings of those around them. If you or others in the household are feeling stressed, anxious, or emotional, your dog is likely to pick up on these feelings and respond accordingly. You may notice them becoming more affectionate, seeking comfort, or displaying signs of concern.

2. **Increased Intuition:** Dogs are naturally intuitive, and a lunar eclipse can amplify this trait. Your dog may seem more aware of subtle changes in their environment or more in tune with your emotions. They may display behaviors such as staring intently at you, staying close, or responding to shifts in mood or energy with heightened attentiveness.

3. **Unsettled Sleep Patterns:** The Moon governs the night, and its influence on your dog's sleep patterns can be especially strong during a lunar eclipse. Some dogs may have trouble sleeping or experience restless sleep, while others may be more prone to vivid dreams. You might notice them twitching, whining, or moving more than usual while asleep.

4. **Emotional Fluctuations:** Just as lunar eclipses can bring emotional revelations for humans, they can trigger emotional fluctuations in dogs as well. Your dog may seem more moody, going from calm and content to restless or anxious. These emotional shifts are typically temporary and should return to normal once the lunar eclipse passes.

How to Support Your Dog During a Lunar Eclipse

To help your dog navigate the emotional and energetic shifts of a lunar eclipse, consider the following tips:

1. **Offer Emotional Support:** If your dog seems more emotionally sensitive during a lunar eclipse, be there for them. Offer affection, reassurance, and attention when they seek it out. Your emotional support can help them feel more grounded during this time.

2. **Create a Restful Environment:** Since lunar eclipses can disrupt sleep patterns, create a quiet, restful environment where your dog can relax and rest. Provide them with a comfortable bed in a peaceful area of the home, away from any distractions or noise.

3. **Monitor Their Behavior:** Pay attention to any changes in your dog's behavior during the lunar eclipse. If they seem more emotional or unsettled, provide them with extra care and comfort. These shifts are often temporary and should resolve once the eclipse has passed.

4. **Engage in Calming Activities:** Engage your dog in calming activities, such as gentle play, quiet walks, or relaxation exercises.

Activities that help them release excess energy and calm their mind will be beneficial during a lunar eclipse.

Eclipses and Long-Term Effects on Dogs

While the effects of solar and lunar eclipses on your dog's behavior are typically temporary, they can also trigger deeper emotional or behavioral shifts, especially if your dog is already going through a period of transformation or change. Eclipses can act as catalysts for growth and change, and your dog may experience longer-lasting shifts in their energy or emotional state.

1. **Behavioral Adjustments:** After an eclipse, you may notice subtle changes in your dog's behavior, such as increased awareness, heightened sensitivity, or a stronger bond with you. These changes are often positive and reflect your dog's ability to adapt to new energies and experiences.

2. **Emotional Growth:** Eclipses are known for triggering emotional revelations, and your dog may experience emotional growth or healing during these periods. If your dog has been dealing with anxiety, fear, or emotional trauma, an eclipse may act as a turning point, helping them release old fears and embrace new emotional patterns.

3. **Increased Bonding:** Eclipses can strengthen the bond between you and your dog, as they may become more emotionally attuned to you during these powerful cosmic events. Your dog's heightened sensitivity and intuition can lead to a deeper connection, as they seek comfort and reassurance from you during times of change.

Building a Strong Relationship with Your Dog During Eclipses

Eclipses provide an opportunity to deepen your relationship with your dog by offering them comfort, support, and understanding during these energetically charged times. Here's how to strengthen your bond with your dog during eclipses:

- **Be Present and Attuned:** Your dog will look to you for reassurance during an eclipse, so be emotionally present and attuned to their needs. Offer comfort, gentle words, and affection when they seek it out, helping them feel safe and secure.
- **Respect Their Emotional Shifts:** If your dog experiences emotional or behavioral changes during an eclipse, respect their needs and provide them with the space and care they require. Be patient and understanding as they navigate the shifting energies.
- **Use Eclipses as a Time for Reflection:** Eclipses are a time for transformation and reflection, and you can use these cosmic events as an opportunity to reflect on your relationship with your dog. Consider how you can better support their emotional needs and strengthen your connection moving forward.

Conclusion

Eclipses—both solar and lunar—are powerful astrological events that can have a noticeable impact on your dog's behavior, emotional state, and energy levels. By understanding how these celestial events influence your dog, you can provide the support and care they need during times of change. Whether it's creating a calm environment during a solar eclipse or offering emotional reassurance during a lunar eclipse, your presence and understanding will help your dog navigate these transformative moments with ease. Embrace the opportunity to deepen your bond with your dog, and enjoy the insights and growth that come from sharing life's cosmic shifts with your loyal companion.

Chapter 25: Comets and Your Dog: How Comets Influence Your Dog's Life and Personality

In astrology, comets are often seen as harbingers of sudden change, destiny, and fleeting yet impactful experiences. Comets, with their brilliant appearance and brief journey across the sky, symbolize moments of transformation, dramatic shifts, and powerful energy bursts. Although comets are not as constant or predictable as planets, their presence is significant, and their influence can be felt as sudden bursts of energy or unexpected shifts in life's direction. For dogs, comets can represent times of rapid change, heightened energy, and key moments that leave a lasting impact on their personality and life. In this chapter, we'll explore how comets influence your dog's behavior, their life's trajectory, and how to recognize and navigate these comet-like moments in your dog's journey.

The Astrological Significance of Comets

In astrology, comets are often linked to events that are sudden, intense, and transformative. Unlike planets, which have regular and predictable orbits, comets appear unexpectedly and leave a lasting impression before disappearing once again into the cosmos. The same is true for the influence comets have on your dog's life. Comet energy can manifest as brief but powerful bursts of change, growth, or heightened activity. These are the moments when your dog may undergo sudden shifts in behavior, experience transformative experiences, or display bursts of energy or enthusiasm that seem to come out of nowhere.

Comets are also associated with fate and destiny, often signaling key moments in life where sudden opportunities or challenges arise. For dogs, this can manifest as unexpected life changes, such as moving to a new home, adopting a new family member, or a shift in their emotional or behavioral patterns. While comet energy is fleeting, its impact can be profound, leaving lasting changes that shape your dog's personality and development.

Key Traits of Comet-Influenced Moments in Your Dog's Life

Just as comets streak across the sky in a flash of brilliance, comet-influenced moments in your dog's life are often marked by sudden, intense experiences. These moments may be brief, but they are significant, bringing transformation, excitement, and sometimes challenge. Here are the key traits of comet-influenced moments in your dog's life:

1. **Sudden Shifts in Behavior:** Comet energy often brings sudden, unexpected changes in your dog's behavior. They may display bursts of energy, curiosity, or excitement that seem to come out of nowhere. These shifts can be positive, such as an increased eagerness to play or learn, or more challenging, such as moments of heightened anxiety or restlessness.

2. **Intense, Short-Lived Energy Bursts:** Just as comets blaze brightly for a short time, your dog may experience bursts of energy during comet-influenced moments. They might become more playful, hyperactive, or adventurous, seeking out new experiences with enthusiasm. These energy bursts are usually temporary but can leave a lasting impression on their overall mood and behavior.

3. **Unexpected Changes in Life Circumstances:** Comet energy can bring sudden changes to your dog's life, such as a move to a new home, the arrival of a new pet or family member, or a shift in their daily routine. These changes may come unexpectedly but often lead to personal growth and transformation for your dog. While these shifts may be challenging at first, they often pave the way for positive developments in your dog's life.

4. **Moments of Emotional Intensity:** Comet-influenced moments can also bring heightened emotional intensity. Your dog may become more sensitive or reactive during these times, displaying deeper emotional connections with you or their environment. These moments of emotional intensity can strengthen the

bond between you and your dog, as they seek comfort and support during periods of rapid change.

5. **Transformation and Growth:** Comet energy often marks moments of transformation and growth for your dog. These may be turning points in their behavior, personality, or emotional development. Comet-influenced moments can lead to significant changes, such as overcoming a fear, mastering a new skill, or adjusting to a new environment. These moments, though brief, can have a lasting impact on your dog's growth and maturity.

Recognizing Comet Moments in Your Dog's Life

Comet moments are often brief and may come unexpectedly, but their influence is unmistakable. Recognizing when your dog is experiencing a comet-influenced moment can help you support them through periods of change and growth. Here's how to identify and navigate these key moments in your dog's life:

1. **Pay Attention to Sudden Behavioral Changes:** If your dog suddenly becomes more energetic, curious, or adventurous, they may be experiencing a comet-influenced moment. These bursts of energy are often short-lived but can signal that your dog is going through a period of heightened excitement or transformation. Encourage their playfulness and curiosity, providing them with opportunities to explore and engage with their environment.

2. **Look for Shifts in Routine or Environment:** Comet energy often brings unexpected changes to your dog's life circumstances. If your dog is adjusting to a new home, family member, or daily routine, this could be a comet moment. While these changes may initially be disruptive, they often lead to growth and new experiences. Help your dog adjust by providing consistency and reassurance during times of transition.

3. **Notice Emotional Intensity:** During comet moments, your dog may display heightened emotional sensitivity or intensity.

They may become more attached to you, seeking comfort and reassurance, or they may react more strongly to changes in their environment. Be patient and understanding, offering extra support and affection as your dog navigates these emotional shifts.

4. **Observe Patterns of Rapid Growth:** Comet moments often mark times of rapid transformation in your dog's behavior or personality. If your dog suddenly masters a new command, overcomes a behavioral challenge, or displays newfound confidence, this could be a sign that they are experiencing a comet moment. Celebrate their growth and encourage continued learning and development.

Supporting Your Dog During Comet Moments

Comet moments, while often brief, can be intense and transformative for your dog. To help them navigate these periods of change and growth, it's important to provide the right support and environment. Here are some ways to support your dog during comet-influenced moments:

1. **Offer Opportunities for Exploration:** Comet energy is associated with curiosity and adventure, so provide your dog with opportunities to explore new environments and experiences. Take them on walks in different locations, introduce them to new toys or activities, and encourage their sense of curiosity. These experiences will help them channel their comet energy into positive outlets.

2. **Provide Stability During Change:** While comet moments often bring sudden changes, it's important to provide stability and consistency for your dog. Maintain their regular routines for feeding, exercise, and rest, even as they navigate new circumstances. This will help them feel secure and grounded during periods of rapid transformation.

3. **Be Patient and Understanding:** Your dog may experience emotional or behavioral fluctuations during comet moments, such as increased anxiety, restlessness, or excitement. Be patient and understanding, offering them extra comfort and support. These moments are temporary, and your calm, reassuring presence will help your dog feel more secure.

4. **Encourage Emotional Expression:** Comet moments can bring heightened emotions, and your dog may seek extra affection or attention during these times. Encourage emotional expression by spending quality time with your dog, offering cuddles, and engaging in calming activities. Your support will help them process their emotions and feel more connected to you.

Comet Moments and Long-Term Impact on Your Dog

While comet moments are often brief, their impact on your dog's life can be profound. These periods of intense energy and transformation can lead to long-term changes in your dog's behavior, personality, and emotional development. Here's how comet moments can shape your dog's future:

1. **Lasting Behavioral Changes:** Comet moments often lead to lasting changes in your dog's behavior. They may become more confident, adventurous, or emotionally expressive after experiencing a comet moment. These shifts reflect your dog's ability to adapt to change and grow through new experiences.

2. **Deeper Emotional Connections:** Comet moments can strengthen the bond between you and your dog. The heightened emotional intensity during these periods allows for deeper connections, as your dog may seek extra comfort and reassurance from you. These experiences can create a lasting sense of trust and emotional closeness.

3. **Increased Resilience:** Dogs who experience comet moments often develop greater resilience, as they learn to navigate sudden

changes and challenges. These moments of transformation help your dog build confidence and adaptability, preparing them for future experiences that require flexibility and emotional strength.

Building a Strong Relationship with Your Dog During Comet Moments

Comet moments offer an opportunity to deepen your relationship with your dog by supporting them through periods of change and growth. Here's how to strengthen your bond during comet-influenced moments:

- **Be Present and Engaged:** During comet moments, your dog may seek extra attention or reassurance. Be present and engaged, offering them affection, playtime, and support as they navigate new experiences.
- **Encourage Exploration and Curiosity:** Comet energy is all about adventure and discovery. Encourage your dog's curiosity by providing them with opportunities to explore new environments, toys, and activities. This will help them embrace the comet energy in a positive way.
- **Celebrate Their Growth:** Comet moments often lead to rapid transformation and growth. Celebrate your dog's achievements, whether it's mastering a new skill or overcoming a fear, and encourage their continued development.
- **Provide Emotional Support:** Comet moments can bring heightened emotions, so be there for your dog when they need extra comfort or reassurance. Your emotional support will help them feel secure and loved during periods of change.

Conclusion

Comets, with their sudden, intense energy and brief yet impactful presence, symbolize moments of transformation, excitement, and growth in your dog's life. While comet moments may be short-lived, their influence can lead to lasting changes in your dog's behavior, personality, and emotional development. By recognizing and supporting your dog through these key moments, you can help them navigate the challenges and opportunities that comet energy brings. Embrace the adventure, celebrate their growth, and enjoy the deepened bond that comes from sharing these transformative experiences with your loyal companion.

Chapter 26: Meteor Showers and Your Dog: The Effects of Meteor Showers on Canine Energy and Mood

Meteor showers, with their mesmerizing streaks of light across the night sky, have long been viewed as symbols of transformation, excitement, and cosmic activity. In astrology, meteor showers are often associated with bursts of energy, rapid shifts, and fleeting yet powerful moments that can stir emotions and spark creativity. For dogs, meteor showers may not be something they directly observe, but their energetic influence can still be felt. These celestial events can lead to heightened energy, shifts in mood, and changes in behavior as the atmosphere around them becomes charged with cosmic energy. In this chapter, we will explore how meteor showers impact your dog's energy and mood, and how you can support them during these vibrant cosmic displays.

The Astrological Influence of Meteor Showers

Meteor showers occur when the Earth passes through the debris trail of a comet or asteroid, causing these small particles to burn up as they enter the Earth's atmosphere, creating bright streaks of light in the sky. In astrology, meteor showers represent fleeting yet impactful bursts of energy, moments of rapid change, and the sudden release of potential. These events can act as cosmic catalysts, bringing about swift emotional and energetic shifts.

For dogs, who are highly attuned to changes in the environment and subtle shifts in energy, meteor showers can have a noticeable effect on their behavior and mood. These periods of heightened cosmic activity may cause dogs to become more energetic, restless, or even emotionally sensitive as they react to the increased energy around them.

Key Effects of Meteor Showers on Your Dog

Meteor showers can have a range of effects on your dog, depending on their sensitivity to changes in the environment and their natural temperament. Here are some of the most common effects that meteor showers can have on your dog's energy, behavior, and emotional state:

1. **Increased Energy and Excitement:** During a meteor shower, your dog may experience a sudden surge of energy, becoming more playful, excitable, and enthusiastic. This burst of energy may manifest as zoomies (those joyful bursts of running), increased playfulness, or an eagerness to engage in activities. Meteor showers often act as cosmic energy boosters, stimulating your dog's natural curiosity and sense of adventure.

2. **Restlessness and Hyperactivity:** Some dogs may become restless or hyperactive during meteor showers, displaying behaviors such as pacing, barking, or whining without a clear cause. This restlessness can be a reaction to the heightened energy in the atmosphere, making it difficult for them to relax or settle down.

3. **Heightened Emotional Sensitivity:** Meteor showers can also amplify your dog's emotional sensitivity, making them more attuned to the emotions and energy of those around them. They may become more affectionate, seeking extra attention or comfort from their human companions, or they may display signs of anxiety or nervousness as they react to the intensity of the energy around them.

4. **Temporary Mood Shifts:** Just as meteor showers represent quick, fleeting bursts of cosmic energy, your dog may experience temporary mood shifts during these events. They may swing between excitement and calm, or between playfulness and clinginess. These mood shifts are usually short-lived and return to normal once the meteor shower has passed.

5. **Increased Curiosity and Exploration:** Meteor showers can spark a sense of curiosity and adventure in your dog, leading them to explore their surroundings with renewed interest. You may notice your dog sniffing around more enthusiastically, investigating new areas of the house or yard, or even seeking out new toys or activities to engage with.

How to Support Your Dog During Meteor Showers
Meteor showers, while brief, can create a heightened sense of energy and emotional shifts in your dog. To help them navigate these energetic bursts, it's important to provide the right support and environment. Here are some ways to support your dog during meteor showers:

1. **Channel Their Energy Into Play:** If your dog becomes more energetic or excitable during a meteor shower, channel this energy into playtime. Engage them in their favorite games, such as fetch, tug-of-war, or interactive puzzle toys. Physical activity will help them burn off excess energy and keep them mentally stimulated.

2. **Provide a Calm Space for Rest:** While some dogs may become more active during meteor showers, others may experience restlessness or difficulty settling down. Create a calm, quiet space where your dog can retreat if they feel overwhelmed by the energy. A comfortable bed in a quiet corner of the house can help them relax and feel secure.

3. **Use Calming Techniques for Anxious Dogs:** If your dog displays signs of anxiety or nervousness during a meteor shower, consider using calming techniques such as gentle petting, soothing music, or calming pheromone diffusers. These tools can help reduce anxiety and provide a sense of comfort during periods of heightened cosmic activity.

4. **Engage in Mental Stimulation:** Dogs that become restless or hyperactive during meteor showers may benefit from mental stimulation. Provide them with puzzle toys, treat-dispensing toys, or training exercises that challenge their mind. Mental stimulation can help redirect their energy in a positive way and prevent unwanted behaviors caused by restlessness.

5. **Offer Extra Affection and Comfort:** Meteor showers can amplify your dog's emotional sensitivity, so offering extra affection and comfort can help them feel more secure. Spend quality time

with your dog, offering cuddles, petting, and verbal reassurance to let them know they are safe and loved. This will help them feel grounded during periods of emotional intensity.

Long-Term Effects of Meteor Showers on Your Dog

While meteor showers are brief events, they can have a lasting impact on your dog's energy and mood, especially if your dog is particularly sensitive to changes in the environment. Here's how meteor showers can influence your dog's long-term behavior and emotional state:

1. **Increased Awareness of Cosmic Events:** Dogs that are sensitive to meteor showers may become more attuned to other celestial events, such as eclipses or full moons. You may notice that your dog reacts similarly during other astrological events, displaying heightened energy, restlessness, or emotional sensitivity.

2. **Improved Emotional Resilience:** Experiencing the energetic shifts of meteor showers can help your dog build emotional resilience. As they navigate these periods of heightened energy and emotion, they learn to adapt to change and become more emotionally balanced over time.

3. **Strengthened Bond With You:** Meteor showers can create opportunities for bonding between you and your dog. During these events, your dog may seek comfort, attention, and reassurance, which allows you to deepen your connection through affection and emotional support. This bond can become stronger with each cosmic event you experience together.

4. **Increased Curiosity and Exploration:** The bursts of curiosity and exploration that occur during meteor showers can encourage your dog to become more adventurous in their daily life. You may notice that they are more eager to explore new environments, try new activities, or engage in mentally stimulating games even after the meteor shower has passed.

Building a Strong Relationship With Your Dog During Meteor Showers

Meteor showers offer a unique opportunity to connect with your dog on a deeper level as they navigate the energetic and emotional shifts that come with these celestial events. Here's how to strengthen your bond with your dog during meteor showers:

- **Be Present and Attentive:** Your dog may need extra attention and comfort during meteor showers, so be present and attentive to their needs. Offer them affection, engage in play, and provide reassurance to help them feel secure and grounded.
- **Encourage Exploration and Play:** Meteor showers often bring a surge of energy and curiosity, so encourage your dog to explore their surroundings and engage in playful activities. This will help them channel their comet-like bursts of energy in a positive and enjoyable way.
- **Provide Emotional Support:** If your dog becomes emotionally sensitive or anxious during a meteor shower, offer them the emotional support they need. Cuddles, soothing words, and a calm environment can help them feel more secure and less overwhelmed by the energy shifts.
- **Observe and Learn:** Pay attention to how your dog reacts during meteor showers, as this can give you insight into their sensitivity to cosmic events. By observing their behavior, you can better anticipate their needs during future celestial events and provide the support they require.

Conclusion

Meteor showers are powerful cosmic events that can influence your dog's energy, mood, and behavior in significant ways. While these celestial events may be brief, their impact on your dog can be profound, leading to heightened energy, emotional sensitivity, and temporary shifts in behavior. By recognizing how meteor showers affect your dog and providing the right support, you can help them navigate these cosmic bursts of energy with ease. Embrace the opportunity to bond with your dog during meteor showers, and enjoy the vibrant energy and curiosity that these celestial events bring into both of your lives.

Chapter 27: Retrogrades and Your Dog: Understanding the Impact of Planetary Retrogrades on Your Dog's Life

Planetary retrogrades are significant astrological events that can stir up challenges, delays, and shifts in energy, often leading to a sense of reversal or slowing down of progress. When a planet goes retrograde, it appears to move backward in the sky from our vantage point on Earth, symbolizing a period of review, reflection, and recalibration. While humans experience these shifts in various areas of life—such as communication, relationships, and decision-making—dogs can also feel the energetic effects of retrogrades. For dogs, retrogrades may manifest as changes in behavior, mood, and overall energy. In this chapter, we will explore how different planetary retrogrades affect your dog's life, behavior, and emotions, and offer tips on how to support them during these cosmically challenging periods.

The Nature of Retrogrades: A Brief Overview

Retrogrades occur when a planet appears to move in reverse in its orbit, disrupting the normal flow of energy associated with that planet. Each planet governs a specific area of life, and when it goes retrograde, the energies linked to that planet often experience disruption, delay, or a need for introspection. In astrology, retrogrades are seen as opportunities to reassess, revisit, and revise aspects of life, though they are also known for causing confusion, delays, and emotional upheavals.

For dogs, who are deeply sensitive to changes in energy, retrogrades can create shifts in mood, behavior, and overall well-being. While your dog may not experience the same mental or emotional challenges as humans during retrogrades, they are often attuned to the shifts in energy that these cosmic events bring. The impact of a retrograde will depend on which planet is involved and how its energy influences your dog's natural temperament.

How Retrogrades Affect Your Dog

Retrogrades can affect dogs in various ways, depending on the planet involved and the specific energies it governs. Some retrogrades may cause your dog to become more introspective or anxious, while others may lead to changes in routine or communication challenges. Here are some common effects of planetary retrogrades on your dog's behavior and emotional state:

1. **Increased Sensitivity and Emotional Fluctuations:** During retrogrades, your dog may become more emotionally sensitive, picking up on subtle shifts in the energy around them. This heightened sensitivity can lead to fluctuations in mood, causing your dog to become more clingy, anxious, or restless than usual.

2. **Changes in Routine or Behavior:** Retrogrades often bring disruptions to normal routines, and your dog may react to these changes with confusion or frustration. They may become resistant to their usual walks, meals, or playtimes, or they may display signs of boredom or restlessness as they adjust to the shifting energies.

3. **Communication Challenges:** Some retrogrades, particularly Mercury retrograde, are known for causing communication breakdowns. For dogs, this may manifest as difficulty understanding commands, responding to cues, or maintaining focus during training. You may notice your dog becoming more distracted or uncooperative during these periods.

4. **Physical Discomfort or Lethargy:** Retrogrades can also affect your dog's physical energy, leading to periods of lethargy, discomfort, or sluggishness. Your dog may seem less active or enthusiastic about exercise and play, preferring to rest or retreat to a quiet space.

5. **Heightened Introspection:** Just as retrogrades encourage humans to reflect and introspect, dogs may also display more introspective behavior during these periods. You may notice your dog

spending more time alone, quietly observing their surroundings, or engaging in more thoughtful, slow-paced activities.

Mercury Retrograde: Communication and Routine Disruptions

Mercury retrograde is perhaps the most well-known retrograde, often associated with communication breakdowns, travel delays, and technological malfunctions. Mercury governs communication, information, and daily routines, and when it goes retrograde, these areas can experience disruption. For dogs, Mercury retrograde can bring challenges in communication and routine, making it difficult for them to understand or respond to commands and cues.

1. **Communication Breakdowns:** During Mercury retrograde, your dog may have trouble understanding commands or may seem more distracted during training sessions. They may respond slower to cues, become more easily confused, or seem less focused overall. Be patient with your dog during these periods, and consider simplifying commands or providing extra encouragement.

2. **Routine Disruptions:** Mercury retrograde often disrupts daily routines, which can cause anxiety or restlessness in dogs who thrive on consistency. Your dog may react to changes in their feeding schedule, walk times, or other routines by becoming more clingy or anxious. Stick to their usual routine as much as possible and provide reassurance when disruptions occur.

3. **Sensitivity to Noise and Stimulation:** Some dogs may become more sensitive to noise and stimulation during Mercury retrograde. They may react more strongly to loud sounds, sudden movements, or new environments. If your dog seems more sensitive than usual, create a calm, quiet space where they can retreat and relax.

Venus Retrograde: Emotional Sensitivity and Relationships

Venus retrograde is linked to relationships, love, and emotional connection. During this period, relationships may undergo reassessment, and emotional sensitivities can be heightened. For dogs, Venus retrograde may lead to increased emotional sensitivity and shifts in their relationships with their human companions and other pets.

1. **Increased Affection or Clinginess:** During Venus retrograde, your dog may become more affectionate, seeking extra attention and physical closeness. They may follow you around more frequently, demand more cuddles, or become anxious when left alone. Offer them extra affection and reassurance during this time to help them feel secure.

2. **Changes in Relationships With Other Pets:** Venus retrograde may also affect your dog's relationships with other pets in the household. You may notice changes in how your dog interacts with their furry companions, such as increased playfulness or, conversely, tension and rivalry. Monitor their interactions closely and intervene if necessary to maintain harmony.

3. **Emotional Fluctuations:** Venus retrograde can heighten emotional sensitivity, leading to mood swings or emotional fluctuations in your dog. They may seem more sensitive to your mood and energy, responding with increased empathy or seeking comfort if they sense stress. Be mindful of your own emotional state, as your dog may be picking up on it more acutely during this time.

Mars Retrograde: Energy and Motivation Shifts

Mars retrograde affects energy levels, motivation, and assertiveness. When Mars goes retrograde, there may be a noticeable decrease in drive and enthusiasm, and physical energy may feel sluggish. For dogs, Mars retrograde can lead to shifts in activity levels and changes in how they assert themselves.

1. **Decreased Energy Levels:** Mars retrograde often brings a reduction in energy, and your dog may become less active or less motivated to engage in physical activities. They may prefer resting over playtime, and you may notice a decline in their enthusiasm for walks, games, or exercise. Allow your dog to rest more during this period, and adjust their exercise routine to match their energy levels.

2. **Frustration or Irritability:** Mars governs assertiveness and drive, and during retrograde, your dog may feel more easily frustrated or irritable. This can manifest as impatience during training, resistance to commands, or even minor displays of aggression, such as growling or snapping. Be patient and avoid pushing your dog too hard during this time.

3. **Reevaluation of Boundaries:** Mars retrograde is a good time to reassess boundaries and rules in your dog's life. You may notice that your dog tests limits or challenges authority more frequently during this period. Reinforce boundaries with calm consistency, and avoid overreacting to minor behavioral issues.

Jupiter Retrograde: Growth and Expansion Revisited

Jupiter retrograde encourages introspection and reevaluation of personal growth, expansion, and opportunities. For dogs, Jupiter retrograde may bring a period of internal growth, where they process experiences more deeply and adjust to changes in their environment or behavior.

1. **Quiet Reflection and Introspection:** During Jupiter retrograde, your dog may become more introspective, preferring quiet moments of rest or observation over active play. They may seem more thoughtful, taking their time to process their surroundings

and emotions. Support this introspection by providing a peaceful environment where your dog can reflect and recharge.

2. **Reassessment of Training or Skills:** Jupiter retrograde is a good time to revisit training and skills. If your dog has been working on new commands or behaviors, use this period to reinforce their learning. Take a step back and focus on reviewing previously learned skills rather than pushing for new ones.

3. **Heightened Interest in Exploration:** Jupiter retrograde may also spark a renewed interest in exploration, whether it's exploring new environments or engaging in new activities. Take your dog on walks to different locations, introduce new toys, or try new games to satisfy their curiosity and sense of adventure.

Supporting Your Dog During Retrogrades

While retrogrades can bring challenges, they also offer opportunities for growth, reflection, and deeper connection. Here are some ways to support your dog during planetary retrogrades:

1. **Maintain Consistency in Routines:** Dogs thrive on routine, and maintaining consistency during retrogrades can help them feel more secure. Stick to their regular feeding, exercise, and play schedules to minimize confusion or anxiety caused by energetic shifts.

2. **Offer Extra Patience and Understanding:** Retrogrades can bring mood swings, communication challenges, and emotional sensitivity. Offer your dog extra patience, understanding, and support during these periods. Avoid pushing them too hard in training or expecting perfect behavior during challenging retrogrades.

3. **Create a Calm, Grounded Environment:** During retrogrades, especially Mercury and Venus retrograde, your dog may benefit from a calm, grounded environment. Use calming music, dif-

fusers with relaxing scents, or provide a quiet space where your dog can retreat if they feel overwhelmed.

4. **Focus on Emotional Connection:** Retrogrades are a time for reassessment and reflection, and this applies to your relationship with your dog as well. Spend quality time bonding with your dog through cuddles, gentle play, or quiet walks. Strengthening your emotional connection will help both you and your dog navigate the challenges of retrogrades.

Conclusion

Planetary retrogrades, with their disruptions and cosmic recalibrations, can have a noticeable impact on your dog's behavior, energy, and emotional state. By understanding the influence of retrogrades and offering the right support, you can help your dog navigate these challenging periods with ease. Whether it's Mercury retrograde's communication challenges or Venus retrograde's emotional fluctuations, your presence and patience will provide the comfort and security your dog needs. Embrace retrogrades as opportunities for growth and deeper connection, and enjoy the unique bond that comes from weathering cosmic shifts together with your loyal companion.

Chapter 28: Solar Flares and Your Dog: How Solar Flares Affect Your Dog's Behavior and Health

Solar flares are intense bursts of radiation and energy from the Sun's surface, capable of affecting Earth's magnetic field and disrupting communication systems, electronics, and even human and animal behavior. While these solar outbursts are invisible to the naked eye, they release significant amounts of electromagnetic radiation that can influence the Earth's atmosphere. For dogs, who are highly sensitive to shifts in their environment, solar flares can cause noticeable changes in behavior, mood, and even physical well-being. In this chapter, we'll explore how solar flares impact your dog, what signs to look for during these solar events, and how you can support your dog's health and emotional stability during periods of heightened solar activity.

What Are Solar Flares?

Solar flares occur when there is a sudden release of energy on the surface of the Sun, often associated with sunspots—regions of intense magnetic activity. These flares can last from minutes to hours and can release as much energy as millions of nuclear bombs. The radiation emitted during a solar flare consists of light, heat, and particles, which can travel through space and reach Earth, causing disturbances in the planet's magnetosphere and atmosphere.

While the visible light from a solar flare doesn't pose a direct threat to living organisms, the electromagnetic radiation and charged particles can influence the environment on Earth, affecting electronics, communication systems, and potentially biological rhythms in animals and humans.

The Astrological and Biological Impact of Solar Flares

In astrology, the Sun is a source of life, energy, vitality, and consciousness. Solar flares, as sudden and intense disruptions of solar energy, are seen as catalysts for change, bursts of creativity, and sometimes tension or chaos. While dogs are not conscious of these cosmic events, their heightened sensitivity to environmental changes can make them more susceptible to the energetic effects of solar flares. These effects can manifest as behavioral changes, emotional shifts, and even physical symptoms as their internal rhythms are disrupted.

On a biological level, solar flares can cause geomagnetic storms, which have been linked to increased agitation, sleep disturbances, and anxiety in both humans and animals. Dogs, in particular, may display signs of discomfort or restlessness during periods of high solar activity, as their nervous systems react to changes in the Earth's electromagnetic field.

Common Behavioral and Emotional Effects of Solar Flares on Dogs

Solar flares can influence dogs in a variety of ways, with effects ranging from increased energy and restlessness to anxiety and mood swings. Here are some of the most common behavioral and emotional changes you may notice in your dog during periods of heightened solar activity:

1. **Increased Restlessness and Agitation:** One of the most noticeable effects of solar flares on dogs is an increase in restlessness or agitation. Your dog may pace, whine, or seem unable to settle down during these periods. This heightened energy can be a reaction to the disturbance in the Earth's magnetic field, which affects their natural rhythms.

2. **Heightened Sensitivity to Noise and Stimulation:** During solar flares, dogs may become more sensitive to their surroundings, particularly loud noises or sudden movements. They may startle more easily or react more intensely to environmental stimuli. This increased sensitivity can lead to nervousness or a heightened state of alertness.

3. **Sleep Disturbances:** Just as humans may experience sleep disturbances during geomagnetic storms caused by solar flares, dogs can also have trouble sleeping. You may notice your dog waking up more frequently, moving restlessly during sleep, or struggling to fall asleep during these periods.

4. **Increased Anxiety or Nervousness:** Dogs who are already prone to anxiety may experience heightened nervousness during solar flares. They may seek more reassurance from you, display signs of separation anxiety, or become more reactive to changes in their environment.

5. **Unusual Behavioral Patterns:** Solar flares can also disrupt your dog's usual behavior patterns. For example, they may become more clingy or, conversely, more distant. Some dogs may become more energetic and playful, while others may seem lethargic or withdrawn. These fluctuations are typically temporary but can be noticeable during periods of intense solar activity.

Physical Effects of Solar Flares on Dogs

In addition to behavioral and emotional changes, solar flares can have physical effects on dogs, particularly in terms of their energy levels, health, and well-being. While these effects are generally subtle, they are worth monitoring, especially if your dog seems particularly sensitive to cosmic events.

1. **Lethargy or Fatigue:** Some dogs may experience a decrease in energy during solar flares, becoming more lethargic or fatigued. This can be a result of the body's effort to adapt to the fluctuations in electromagnetic energy. Your dog may sleep more than usual or show less interest in physical activities like walks or playtime.

2. **Digestive Upset:** In rare cases, solar flares may affect your dog's digestive system, leading to mild gastrointestinal discomfort. This could manifest as changes in appetite, slight nausea, or irregular bowel movements. If you notice these symptoms, monitor your dog closely to ensure they are not related to another underlying health issue.

3. **Increased Heart Rate or Respiratory Changes:** Solar flares can sometimes cause subtle changes in heart rate or respiration,

particularly in dogs that are already prone to anxiety or sensitivity. You may notice your dog panting more than usual or breathing more rapidly during periods of solar activity. If these symptoms persist or become severe, it's important to consult a veterinarian.

How to Support Your Dog During Solar Flares

While you can't prevent solar flares from occurring, you can take steps to help your dog feel more comfortable and supported during these periods of heightened cosmic activity. Here are some tips on how to support your dog during solar flares:

1. **Create a Calm Environment:** During solar flares, your dog may benefit from a calm, soothing environment where they can relax and feel safe. Create a quiet space in your home with soft lighting and minimal noise. Providing a comfortable bed or blanket in a peaceful corner can help your dog settle down during periods of restlessness.
2. **Use Calming Tools:** If your dog is prone to anxiety or restlessness during solar flares, consider using calming tools such as pheromone diffusers, calming collars, or natural supplements designed to reduce anxiety. These products can help create a more relaxed atmosphere and ease your dog's nervous system during periods of heightened solar activity.
3. **Engage in Gentle Play or Exercise:** For dogs who display increased energy or restlessness during solar flares, engaging them in gentle play or exercise can help burn off excess energy and reduce anxiety. Try activities like fetch, tug-of-war, or a slow, calming walk to help your dog release pent-up energy and feel more grounded.
4. **Practice Soothing Techniques:** If your dog is feeling anxious or unsettled, practice soothing techniques such as gentle petting, soft verbal reassurances, or a calming massage. Your physical pres-

ence and calming touch can help reassure your dog and reduce their anxiety during solar flares.

5. **Maintain a Consistent Routine:** Dogs thrive on routine, and maintaining a consistent daily schedule can help reduce the stress caused by solar flares. Stick to your dog's usual feeding, walking, and playtime routines as much as possible, providing them with a sense of stability during periods of cosmic disruption.

Monitoring Your Dog's Health During Solar Flares

While most dogs experience only minor disruptions in behavior or mood during solar flares, it's important to monitor their health and well-being during these periods. If you notice any concerning physical symptoms, such as changes in heart rate, persistent gastrointestinal issues, or extreme lethargy, consult with your veterinarian to rule out other potential health problems.

For dogs with preexisting conditions, such as heart disease, anxiety disorders, or sensitivity to environmental changes, solar flares may have a more pronounced effect. In these cases, it's especially important to provide extra care and support, including adjusting their exercise routine, offering calming supplements, or consulting with a veterinarian for additional guidance.

Building a Strong Relationship With Your Dog During Solar Flares

Solar flares, while brief, offer an opportunity to deepen your bond with your dog by providing comfort, support, and understanding during periods of cosmic intensity. Here's how to strengthen your relationship with your dog during solar flares:

- **Be Attuned to Their Needs:** Pay close attention to your dog's behavior and emotional state during solar flares. Being attuned to their needs allows you to offer the right kind of support, whether it's through extra playtime, soothing touch, or creating a peaceful space for them to relax.

- **Offer Comfort and Reassurance:** Dogs often look to their human companions for comfort and reassurance during times of stress or anxiety. Be present and offer gentle words of encouragement, physical affection, and a calm demeanor to help your dog feel secure.
- **Practice Mindful Interaction:** Solar flares can be intense for dogs, but they are also fleeting. Use these moments to practice mindful interaction with your dog, focusing on their needs and emotions. By staying calm and supportive, you can help your dog navigate these periods with greater ease.

Conclusion

Solar flares, with their sudden bursts of energy and cosmic disruption, can have a noticeable impact on your dog's behavior, mood, and physical well-being. By understanding how solar flares affect your dog and offering the right kind of support, you can help them navigate these intense cosmic events with ease. Whether it's creating a calm environment, engaging in gentle play, or offering soothing reassurances, your presence and care will provide the comfort your dog needs during these periods of heightened solar activity. Embrace the opportunity to deepen your bond with your dog as you weather the cosmic energy together, ensuring their well-being and emotional stability during solar flares.

Chapter 29: Equinoxes and Solstices: The Influence of Seasonal Changes on Your Dog

The equinoxes and solstices are pivotal moments in the Earth's annual journey around the Sun, marking significant shifts in light, temperature, and overall energy. The equinoxes occur in spring and autumn, symbolizing balance as day and night become equal in length. The solstices occur in summer and winter, marking the extremes of light and darkness. These celestial events not only influence the environment but also have a profound effect on the behavior, energy levels, and emotional state of living beings, including your dog.

Dogs, being highly sensitive to environmental changes, can react strongly to the shifts in light, temperature, and atmosphere that accompany the equinoxes and solstices. Whether it's the invigorating energy of spring, the long days of summer, the calm of autumn, or the introspective stillness of winter, each season brings new influences on your dog's mood, behavior, and overall well-being. In this chapter, we will explore how seasonal changes affect your dog, what behavioral shifts to expect during the equinoxes and solstices, and how to best support your dog during these transitions.

The Astrological and Natural Significance of Equinoxes and Solstices

In astrology and nature, equinoxes and solstices are seen as powerful times of transformation and change. The equinoxes, which occur in March and September, are moments of balance, where the hours of daylight and darkness are equal. These are periods of transition, signaling the shift from the cold, introspective winter months to the growth and renewal of spring, or from the warm, vibrant summer months into the calm, reflective season of autumn.

The solstices, occurring in June and December, represent the height of the solar cycle. The summer solstice is the longest day of the year, filled with light and activity, while the winter solstice is the shortest day, marking the beginning of a period of introspection and rest. These natural cycles influence not only the Earth's atmosphere but also the rhythms of animals, including dogs, who are highly attuned to the changing seasons.

The Influence of the Spring Equinox on Your Dog

The spring equinox, occurring around March 20th, marks the beginning of spring and a time of renewal, growth, and awakening. As daylight increases and temperatures rise, dogs often respond with increased energy, enthusiasm, and curiosity. This is a period of renewal for both the natural world and your dog's inner world.

1. **Increased Energy and Playfulness:** The longer days and warmer weather of spring often lead to a surge in your dog's energy levels. You may notice your dog becoming more playful, active, and eager to spend time outdoors. This renewed energy is a response to the increased sunlight and the natural sense of awakening that comes with the spring season.

2. **Curiosity and Exploration:** Spring is a time of growth, with new scents, sights, and sounds emerging in the environment. Your dog's natural curiosity may be heightened during this period as they explore the outdoors with renewed interest. Whether it's sniffing the fresh blooms, chasing insects, or enjoying longer walks, spring brings out your dog's adventurous side.

3. **Behavioral Shifts:** As your dog's energy levels increase, you may notice changes in their behavior. They may become more excitable or restless, particularly if they've been less active during the colder winter months. Spring is an ideal time to reintroduce regular outdoor activities and exercise routines to help your dog burn off excess energy.

How to Support Your Dog During the Spring Equinox

To help your dog make the most of the energetic and vibrant spring season, consider the following tips:

1. **Increase Outdoor Activity:** As the weather warms and daylight increases, make the most of the opportunity to spend more time outdoors with your dog. Longer walks, trips to the park, and outdoor play sessions can help your dog burn off excess energy and enjoy the invigorating energy of spring.

2. **Introduce New Experiences:** Spring is a time of growth and exploration, so introduce your dog to new experiences, such as different walking routes, new toys, or interactive games. These new activities will stimulate their curiosity and keep their mind and body engaged.

3. **Maintain a Balanced Diet:** With increased energy comes an increased need for proper nutrition. Ensure that your dog's diet is balanced and appropriate for their energy levels. You may need to adjust their food intake slightly if they're more active in the spring.

The Influence of the Summer Solstice on Your Dog

The summer solstice, occurring around June 21st, marks the longest day of the year and the official start of summer. This is a period of high energy, warmth, and activity, with long days encouraging more outdoor play and exploration. However, the intense heat and extended daylight hours can also bring challenges for your dog.

1. **Heightened Energy Levels:** Just as with the spring equinox, the summer solstice brings a surge in your dog's energy levels, with long days encouraging more activity and play. Dogs may be more eager to go on adventures, take part in outdoor activities, and socialize during the summer months.

2. **Sensitivity to Heat:** While the long days of summer can be enjoyable, the heat can also pose challenges for dogs, particularly those with thick coats or heat sensitivity. It's important to monitor your dog's behavior during hot weather, as they may become more lethargic or seek out cool spots to rest.

3. **Changes in Sleep Patterns:** The extended daylight hours of summer can sometimes disrupt your dog's sleep patterns, particularly if they are sensitive to light. They may take shorter naps during the day or become more restless in the evening as the sun sets later.

How to Support Your Dog During the Summer Solstice

The summer solstice brings plenty of opportunities for fun and adventure, but it's important to keep your dog's health and comfort in mind. Here's how to support your dog during the summer season:

1. **Stay Hydrated and Cool:** Ensure your dog stays hydrated by providing plenty of fresh water throughout the day, especially during hot weather. Consider offering frozen treats or setting up a kiddie pool to help them cool down.

2. **Plan Outdoor Activities Wisely:** Avoid outdoor activities during the hottest parts of the day. Instead, take walks in the early morning or late evening when the temperatures are cooler. Always provide shaded areas for your dog to rest when outside.

3. **Monitor for Signs of Overheating:** Watch for signs of overheating, such as excessive panting, drooling, or lethargy. If your dog shows any signs of heat exhaustion, move them to a cool area, offer water, and seek veterinary care if necessary.

The Influence of the Autumn Equinox on Your Dog

The autumn equinox, occurring around September 22nd, marks the transition from the active energy of summer to the more introspective and calming energy of autumn. As the days grow shorter and temperatures begin to cool, your dog may also experience changes in behavior, mood, and energy levels.

1. **Calming Energy and Reflection:** The cooling temperatures and shorter days of autumn often bring a calming energy, with dogs becoming more relaxed and introspective. This is a time when your dog may slow down, spending more time resting or reflecting on their surroundings.

2. **Increased Appetite:** As the weather cools, your dog's metabolism may shift, leading to an increase in appetite. This is a natural response to prepare for the colder months ahead. Be mindful of their food intake and adjust their diet accordingly to maintain a healthy weight.

3. **Changes in Coat and Shedding:** The transition to cooler weather may trigger changes in your dog's coat, with many dogs shedding their lighter summer fur in preparation for the thicker winter coat. Regular grooming can help manage shedding and keep your dog's coat healthy.

How to Support Your Dog During the Autumn Equinox

To help your dog adjust to the slower pace and cooler temperatures of autumn, consider the following tips:

1. **Maintain Regular Exercise:** While the energy of autumn may be more subdued, it's still important to keep your dog active. Regular walks and playtime will help them stay fit and healthy, even as the weather cools.

2. **Provide Comfort and Warmth:** As temperatures drop, make sure your dog has a warm, comfortable place to rest, especially if they spend time outdoors. Consider providing a cozy bed or blanket to keep them warm during chilly nights.

3. **Adjust Their Diet for Seasonal Changes:** If your dog's appetite increases in autumn, adjust their diet to ensure they are

receiving the right balance of nutrients. Consult with your veterinarian if you're unsure about portion sizes or food choices during the cooler months.

The Influence of the Winter Solstice on Your Dog

The winter solstice, occurring around December 21st, marks the shortest day of the year and the beginning of winter. This is a period of rest, reflection, and introspection, with dogs often responding to the reduced daylight and colder temperatures by becoming more relaxed and contemplative.

1. **Decreased Energy Levels:** The shorter days and colder temperatures of winter often lead to a decrease in your dog's energy levels. They may become less active, preferring to rest indoors and conserve their energy. This is a natural response to the season's slower pace.

2. **Desire for Warmth and Comfort:** During the winter months, dogs may seek out warmth and comfort, curling up in cozy spots around the house or snuggling up with blankets. They may be less interested in outdoor activities, especially during cold or snowy weather.

3. **Emotional Reflection and Bonding:** Winter can be a time of deep emotional reflection for dogs, with many becoming more affectionate and attached to their human companions. The winter solstice offers an opportunity for bonding and quiet moments of connection.

How to Support Your Dog During the Winter Solstice

Winter brings a period of rest and reflection for both you and your dog. Here's how to support your dog during the winter solstice:

1. **Keep Them Warm:** Provide warm bedding and consider using heated blankets or pet-safe heaters to keep your dog comfortable

during cold nights. If your dog has a thin coat, consider using a dog sweater or jacket when going outdoors.

2. **Encourage Gentle Exercise:** While your dog may be less active in winter, it's still important to provide regular exercise. Short walks and indoor play sessions can help keep them physically and mentally stimulated during the colder months.

3. **Focus on Bonding and Affection:** Winter is a time for emotional bonding and connection. Spend quality time with your dog, offering plenty of affection, cuddles, and companionship during this introspective season.

Conclusion

The equinoxes and solstices mark significant shifts in energy and light, influencing not only the natural world but also your dog's behavior, mood, and well-being. By understanding how these seasonal changes affect your dog and offering the right support during each transition, you can help your dog navigate the cycles of the year with ease. Embrace the changing seasons as an opportunity to deepen your bond with your dog, whether through outdoor adventures in spring and summer or quiet moments of reflection in autumn and winter. Through every equinox and solstice, your dog will look to you for guidance, comfort, and companionship as they journey through the rhythms of nature.

Part 4: Moon Phases

Chapter 30: New Moon and Your Dog: The Effects of the New Moon on Your Dog's Behavior and New Beginnings

The new moon marks the beginning of the lunar cycle, a time of renewal, fresh starts, and setting intentions. In astrology, the new moon is a potent time for planting seeds, both literally and figuratively. It symbolizes new beginnings, clean slates, and the opportunity for growth. For dogs, though they may not consciously understand the celestial movements, they are deeply sensitive to the energetic shifts that accompany the lunar phases. The new moon's energy can influence your dog's emotional state, behavior, and even their health, often signaling a time of rest and reflection, followed by the potential for new behaviors, habits, and routines.

In this chapter, we will explore how the new moon affects your dog's behavior, their responses to energetic shifts, and how you can harness the symbolic energy of new beginnings to foster growth and positive changes in your dog's life.

The Astrological and Energetic Influence of the New Moon

Astrologically, the new moon occurs when the Moon is positioned between the Earth and the Sun, and its illuminated side faces away from us, making the Moon appear invisible in the night sky. This period of darkness is associated with introspection, setting intentions, and planting the seeds for future growth. It is a quieter time compared to the full moon's vibrant energy, making it an ideal period for reflection, rest, and preparation for new beginnings.

For dogs, who are highly attuned to the energies around them, the new moon can represent a period of calmness and renewal. Dogs may become more introspective, display changes in their behavior, or even exhibit a need for more rest. Just as humans use the new moon to reflect and set goals, this phase of the lunar cycle can be an excellent time for fostering new habits, training routines, or lifestyle changes for your dog.

How the New Moon Affects Your Dog's Behavior

The new moon's influence on your dog can manifest in various ways, depending on their temperament, environment, and sensitivity to energy shifts. Here are some common ways the new moon may affect your dog's behavior:

1. **Calmness and Introspection:** The new moon is a time of quiet and reflection, and your dog may mirror this energy by becoming calmer and more introspective. They may seek out quiet spaces to rest, observe their surroundings more intently, or simply spend more time in peaceful contemplation. This is an ideal time for your dog to recharge emotionally and physically.

2. **Increased Sensitivity:** Dogs are naturally sensitive to changes in their environment, and during the new moon, this sensitivity can be heightened. Your dog may be more attuned to your emotions or the general energy around them, displaying increased empathy or reactiveness to subtle shifts. This can be a time to nurture their emotional needs and provide them with extra comfort and reassurance.

3. **Rest and Rejuvenation:** Just as the new moon signals a time for rest and renewal for humans, it can also indicate a need for rest in dogs. Your dog may exhibit signs of lethargy or spend more time napping during the new moon. This period of rest is essential for their well-being, allowing them to rejuvenate before the more active phases of the lunar cycle begin.

4. **Focus on New Beginnings:** The energy of the new moon is all about fresh starts and setting intentions. You may notice that your dog is more open to learning new things during this time, whether it's adjusting to a new routine, learning a new command, or adopting a healthier habit. This phase is an ideal time to introduce new training sessions, behaviors, or routines that you want your dog to embrace.

5. **Temporary Changes in Appetite:** Some dogs may experience changes in their appetite during the new moon, either eating more or less than usual. This is typically a temporary shift and may reflect their body's need to adjust to the quieter energy of this phase. Ensure that your dog has access to their usual balanced diet and monitor any significant changes in eating habits.

Harnessing the Energy of New Beginnings for Your Dog

The new moon is a powerful time for setting intentions and creating positive changes. Just as humans use this period to start fresh, you can harness the energy of the new moon to support new beginnings in your dog's life. Whether it's introducing new training methods, adjusting their routine, or helping them overcome behavioral challenges, the new moon offers a symbolic window of opportunity for growth and transformation.

Here's how you can use the new moon's energy to foster positive change in your dog's life:

1. **Start New Training Routines:** If you've been considering introducing a new command, trick, or behavior, the new moon is the perfect time to begin. Dogs are often more receptive to learning during this phase, making it an ideal moment to start training sessions. Whether it's basic obedience or more advanced tricks, use the new moon's energy to set the foundation for success.

2. **Set Intentions for Behavior Improvements:** The new moon is a time for setting intentions, so think about areas of your dog's behavior or routine that you'd like to improve. Perhaps your dog struggles with separation anxiety, leash pulling, or nervousness around new people. Use this phase to create a clear intention for improvement and begin implementing small, manageable changes to address these behaviors.

3. **Establish Healthy Habits:** The new moon is the ideal time to establish healthy habits for your dog, whether it's improving their

diet, increasing exercise, or focusing on mental stimulation. You can introduce healthier foods, longer walks, or more playtime to help your dog embrace a well-balanced lifestyle.

4. **Create a Calming Environment:** Since the new moon brings a sense of quiet reflection, it's important to provide your dog with a calm and peaceful environment. Create a cozy space where they can rest and relax, free from distractions or loud noises. This will help them feel grounded and supported as they recharge during this phase.

5. **Reflect on Your Bond with Your Dog:** The new moon offers a wonderful opportunity to reflect on your relationship with your dog. Consider the emotional connection you share and how you can strengthen your bond. Spend extra time together, offering affection, attention, and reassurance. This is also an excellent time to practice mindful interaction, focusing on being present with your dog.

Emotional Shifts During the New Moon

The new moon's influence on your dog's emotional state can lead to shifts in mood, energy, and emotional expression. These shifts are usually subtle but can be noticeable, especially if your dog is particularly sensitive to lunar cycles.

1. **Increased Affection and Attachment:** During the new moon, your dog may become more affectionate or attached, seeking comfort and closeness from you. This is a natural response to the introspective energy of the new moon, as your dog may feel the need for emotional reassurance and bonding. Offer extra cuddles, attention, and physical contact to help them feel secure.

2. **Moments of Independence:** On the other hand, some dogs may seek out moments of independence during the new moon. They may prefer to spend time alone, quietly observing or resting. If your dog seems more withdrawn, respect their need for solitude

and allow them the space to process their emotions during this reflective time.

3. **Emotional Sensitivity:** The new moon can heighten your dog's emotional sensitivity, making them more reactive to changes in their environment or your own emotional state. Be mindful of your dog's behavior during this time and offer a calm, supportive presence to help them feel balanced and at ease.

Creating Rituals for the New Moon with Your Dog

Just as humans use rituals to mark the new moon and set intentions, you can create simple, meaningful rituals with your dog to honor this phase of the lunar cycle. These rituals can be a way to strengthen your bond, promote calmness, and set the tone for positive changes in your dog's life.

1. **New Moon Walks:** Take your dog for a peaceful walk under the night sky during the new moon. Use this time to reflect on your intentions for your dog's well-being and behavior. The quiet atmosphere of the new moon provides an ideal backdrop for grounding and connection.

2. **Mindful Play Sessions:** Engage your dog in a mindful play session, focusing on their energy, mood, and emotional needs. Whether it's a game of fetch or a puzzle toy, use this time to strengthen your bond and set the tone for new habits or behaviors you want to introduce.

3. **Affectionate Bonding Time:** Spend extra time with your dog during the new moon, offering cuddles, petting, and gentle verbal reassurance. This bonding time helps reinforce emotional security and supports your dog's emotional well-being during this reflective phase.

Supporting Your Dog During the New Moon

To help your dog navigate the energy of the new moon, it's important to create a nurturing and supportive environment that aligns with their emotional and physical needs. Here are some ways to support your dog during the new moon:

1. **Offer a Calm Space for Rest:** The new moon is a time for rest and rejuvenation, so provide your dog with a quiet, comfortable space where they can relax. This could be a cozy corner with their favorite bed, blanket, or toys. The goal is to create a soothing environment that helps them recharge.

2. **Monitor Emotional and Physical Changes:** Pay attention to any changes in your dog's mood, behavior, or physical energy during the new moon. If they seem more introspective or exhibit signs of emotional sensitivity, offer extra support and patience as they adjust to the shifting energy.

3. **Set Positive Intentions for Your Dog's Growth:** Use the new moon as an opportunity to set positive intentions for your dog's growth and well-being. Whether it's improving their training, fostering healthier habits, or deepening your bond, this is the perfect time to focus on new beginnings and set the stage for positive change.

Conclusion

The new moon, with its quiet energy and symbolism of new beginnings, offers a powerful time to reflect on your dog's emotional well-being, behavior, and routines. By understanding how the new moon affects your dog and using this phase to foster new habits, training routines, and emotional growth, you can create a harmonious environment that supports both you and your dog. Embrace the new moon as a time for calm reflection, bonding, and setting intentions, knowing that each new cycle brings the opportunity for positive transformation and deeper connection with your loyal companion.

Chapter 31: Waxing Crescent and Your Dog: Growth and Development During the Waxing Crescent Phase

The waxing crescent moon, which occurs just after the new moon, represents a time of growth, expansion, and development. As the moon gradually becomes more visible in the night sky, it symbolizes the increasing momentum toward new goals, intentions, and possibilities. Astrologically, the waxing crescent phase is a period of motivation, action, and forward movement. For your dog, this phase can signify a time of growth, learning, and developing new behaviors or routines.

Just as the waxing crescent marks the start of the moon's journey toward fullness, your dog may exhibit behaviors and emotions aligned with growth and progress. During this time, they may be more receptive to training, display increased energy, and show curiosity about their surroundings. This chapter will explore the impact of the waxing crescent moon on your dog's behavior and how you can support their emotional and physical development during this phase.

The Astrological and Symbolic Meaning of the Waxing Crescent

In astrology, the waxing crescent moon represents the first stage of manifestation. It is a time to take the seeds of intention planted during the new moon and begin nurturing them into reality. The energy of the waxing crescent is active, creative, and filled with potential. It's a period of preparation, where plans are set into motion, and the first steps are taken toward achieving goals.

For dogs, this phase can be a time of mental and physical development. They are more open to learning, training, and exploring new experiences. This is a powerful time to focus on their growth, whether it's teaching them new behaviors, reinforcing positive habits, or introducing them to new environments.

How the Waxing Crescent Moon Affects Your Dog's Behavior
The waxing crescent moon's influence on your dog can manifest in several ways, from increased curiosity to higher energy levels and openness to new experiences. Understanding these behavioral shifts can help you support your dog's growth and development during this time.

1. **Increased Curiosity and Exploration:** As the waxing crescent phase marks a period of growth, your dog may become more curious about their surroundings. They may show heightened interest in exploring new areas, investigating different scents, or interacting with other animals. This is a time when your dog's natural curiosity is at its peak, making it an ideal moment for new adventures or introducing them to unfamiliar environments.

2. **Heightened Learning Ability:** The waxing crescent moon represents a time of development and learning, and your dog may be more receptive to training during this phase. Whether you're teaching them new commands, reinforcing obedience, or introducing more complex behaviors, they may show a greater ability to focus and absorb new information. This is an ideal time to engage in training sessions and focus on positive reinforcement.

3. **Increased Energy and Playfulness:** Just as the waxing crescent moon's energy is building toward the full moon, your dog's energy levels may increase during this phase. You may notice that your dog is more playful, active, and eager to engage in physical activities. This heightened energy can be channeled into playtime, walks, or other forms of exercise to help them release pent-up energy and stay physically fit.

4. **Development of New Routines and Habits:** The waxing crescent phase is all about establishing momentum, making it a great time to develop new routines or habits for your dog. Whether it's adjusting their feeding schedule, incorporating more exercise into their day, or setting a consistent training routine, this phase offers

an ideal window for creating structure and promoting healthy habits.

5. **Openness to Social Interaction:** During the waxing crescent moon, dogs may be more open to social interactions with other pets or humans. This is a time when they may display increased sociability, enjoying playtime with other dogs, interacting more confidently with strangers, or bonding more deeply with you. It's an excellent period for socialization, especially for young or anxious dogs.

How to Support Your Dog's Growth During the Waxing Crescent Phase

The waxing crescent moon is a powerful time for supporting your dog's development, both mentally and physically. To make the most of this phase, it's important to provide your dog with the right environment and activities that encourage growth, learning, and emotional balance. Here's how you can support your dog during this energetic phase:

1. **Engage in Consistent Training:** Take advantage of your dog's heightened learning ability during the waxing crescent phase by engaging in consistent, focused training sessions. Whether you're teaching them basic commands or more advanced tricks, this is an ideal time to reinforce positive behaviors. Use positive reinforcement techniques such as treats, praise, and playtime to motivate your dog and encourage their progress.

2. **Introduce New Experiences:** Since the waxing crescent is a time of exploration and growth, consider introducing your dog to new experiences, such as visiting a new park, meeting other dogs, or exploring a different walking route. New experiences help stimulate your dog's mind and contribute to their emotional and social development.

3. **Provide Physical and Mental Stimulation:** With increased energy levels during this phase, it's important to provide your dog

with plenty of opportunities for both physical and mental stimulation. Engage them in interactive games, such as fetch or tug-of-war, and offer puzzle toys that challenge their problem-solving skills. This will help them release energy in a productive way while keeping their mind sharp.

4. **Set Clear Goals for Behavior and Routine:** The waxing crescent moon is the perfect time to set clear goals for your dog's behavior and routine. Whether it's improving their leash manners, working on crate training, or establishing a regular feeding schedule, use this phase to build structure and consistency in their daily life. Dogs thrive on routine, and this is the ideal period to reinforce healthy habits.

5. **Encourage Socialization:** If your dog is naturally sociable or needs more socialization, the waxing crescent is a great time to introduce them to new friends—whether human or animal. Arrange playdates with other dogs, take them to dog-friendly events, or spend time bonding with your dog through shared activities. This social interaction will help build their confidence and emotional resilience.

Emotional Shifts During the Waxing Crescent Moon

Just as the waxing crescent moon represents growth and expansion, it can also bring about emotional shifts in your dog. These shifts may manifest as increased excitement, curiosity, or eagerness to bond. Paying attention to your dog's emotional needs during this phase can help you support their development and create a stronger bond.

1. **Increased Excitement and Enthusiasm:** Your dog may exhibit increased enthusiasm during the waxing crescent phase, becoming more excited about their daily activities and interactions. This heightened emotional state can be a positive influence, making them more eager to engage in playtime, training, and bonding. Be

sure to channel this excitement in positive ways by offering them plenty of opportunities to express their energy.

2. **Strengthening Emotional Bonds:** The waxing crescent moon is an ideal time to strengthen your emotional bond with your dog. Spend extra time with them, whether it's through physical affection, shared activities, or simply sitting together in a peaceful environment. This time of growth offers a unique opportunity to deepen your connection and foster trust between you and your dog.

3. **Encouraging Confidence and Independence:** As your dog becomes more confident during the waxing crescent phase, they may show signs of increased independence, exploring their surroundings with more curiosity and self-assurance. Encourage this confidence by giving them the freedom to explore within safe boundaries and rewarding their independent behaviors with praise or treats.

Creating Rituals for the Waxing Crescent Phase with Your Dog

Rituals are a wonderful way to mark the waxing crescent phase and support your dog's growth and development during this time. These rituals can help create a sense of structure and intention, allowing you to focus on nurturing your dog's physical, mental, and emotional well-being.

1. **Growth-Focused Walks:** Take your dog on walks with the intention of growth and exploration. During these walks, allow your dog to take the lead, encouraging them to sniff new scents, investigate their surroundings, and engage with the environment. Use this time to reflect on the progress they've made and the goals you've set for their continued growth.

2. **Intentional Play Sessions:** Engage in play sessions that focus on building skills and strengthening your bond with your dog. Use

toys or games that challenge their mind and body, such as interactive puzzle toys, agility courses, or fetch. As you play, set intentions for what you'd like your dog to learn or achieve during this phase of the lunar cycle.

3. **Affirmations for Growth and Development:** Create a daily ritual of affirming positive intentions for your dog's growth and development. As you spend time with your dog, whether during walks, training, or quiet moments, silently affirm your goals for their well-being. These affirmations could include statements such as, "I support my dog's growth and learning" or "My dog is confident and capable."

Conclusion

The waxing crescent moon is a powerful time for growth, development, and exploration, both for humans and their canine companions. During this phase, your dog may exhibit increased curiosity, energy, and receptiveness to learning, making it an ideal period to focus on training, socialization, and establishing new routines. By understanding the influence of the waxing crescent moon on your dog's behavior and emotional state, you can provide the support and guidance they need to thrive. Embrace this time of expansion, set intentions for your dog's growth, and enjoy the journey of fostering their development as the moon continues its path toward fullness.

Chapter 32: First Quarter and Your Dog: Challenges and Actions During the First Quarter Moon

The first quarter moon represents a critical turning point in the lunar cycle. It is the halfway mark between the new moon and the full moon, where the energy of action, decision-making, and overcoming obstacles comes into play. In astrology, the first quarter moon is a time to confront challenges, take decisive action, and push through any resistance or obstacles that arise on the path to achieving goals. For dogs, this phase of the lunar cycle can manifest as a time of increased activity, determination, and sometimes frustration or challenges in behavior. Understanding how the first quarter moon affects your dog's behavior can help you guide them through this period of heightened energy and ensure their emotional and physical well-being.

In this chapter, we'll explore how the first quarter moon influences your dog's behavior, what challenges they might face during this phase, and how you can support them with appropriate actions to foster growth and harmony.

The Astrological and Energetic Meaning of the First Quarter Moon

Astrologically, the first quarter moon represents a time for action and moving forward. It is a phase of building momentum and taking concrete steps toward the intentions set during the new moon. However, the first quarter moon is also a time when challenges and obstacles can arise, requiring determination, problem-solving, and sometimes a change in approach. This is a phase of growth through action, where effort is needed to overcome resistance and continue progressing toward goals.

For dogs, this phase can signify a time of increased energy, but it can also bring about behavioral challenges or frustration, especially if they encounter obstacles in their daily routines, training, or social interactions. It's important to pay attention to your dog's needs during this time and provide the right support to help them navigate any challenges they may face.

How the First Quarter Moon Affects Your Dog's Behavior

The first quarter moon's energy can influence your dog's behavior in several ways. While the waxing crescent phase focused on growth and exploration, the first quarter moon introduces the need for action, decision-making, and overcoming challenges. Here are some common behavioral traits and challenges your dog may exhibit during this phase:

1. **Increased Determination and Focus:** During the first quarter moon, your dog may display increased determination and focus in their activities. Whether it's mastering a new command, engaging in a favorite game, or pursuing an interesting scent, they may show greater persistence and drive. This determination is beneficial for training, as your dog may be more inclined to push through challenges and learn new skills.

2. **Frustration or Restlessness:** The first quarter moon's energy can also bring about feelings of frustration or restlessness, especially if your dog encounters obstacles in their routine or training. They may become more easily frustrated if they cannot achieve a desired outcome, such as retrieving a toy or mastering a command. This restlessness can manifest as pacing, whining, or an inability to settle down.

3. **Challenging Behaviors:** As your dog works through the energetic challenges of the first quarter moon, they may display more assertive or challenging behaviors. This can include testing boundaries, ignoring commands, or becoming more vocal or demanding. While these behaviors may seem like defiance, they are often a reflection of your dog's need to overcome obstacles or assert their independence during this phase.

4. **Increased Physical Energy:** Just as the first quarter moon brings a surge of action-oriented energy, your dog may experience heightened physical energy during this time. They may be more

eager to engage in play, exercise, or physical challenges such as agility courses or fetch. This increased energy can be positive if channeled into productive activities but may lead to destructive behaviors if not managed properly.

5. **Decision-Making in Training and Behavior:** The first quarter moon is a time for decision-making, and your dog may show signs of needing clear direction and leadership during this phase. They may be more attuned to your commands or cues, seeking guidance on how to proceed when faced with challenges. This is an important time to provide clear, consistent communication and reinforce positive behaviors.

Common Challenges During the First Quarter Moon

While the first quarter moon is a time of action and growth, it can also present challenges for your dog. These challenges are often related to their increased energy and determination, as well as their response to obstacles or frustrations. Here are some common challenges your dog may face during the first quarter moon:

1. **Resistance to Training:** Your dog may exhibit resistance to training during the first quarter moon, especially if they encounter a command or task that feels difficult or unfamiliar. They may become frustrated with repeated attempts or show signs of stubbornness, such as ignoring commands or refusing to engage. It's important to remain patient and provide positive reinforcement to help them overcome this resistance.

2. **Boundary Testing:** The first quarter moon can prompt your dog to test boundaries, whether it's pushing the limits of acceptable behavior, exploring new areas of the house or yard, or ignoring established rules. This boundary testing is a natural part of their desire to assert independence and overcome obstacles, but it requires consistent guidance to maintain structure.

3. **Hyperactivity or Restlessness:** Dogs may experience increased restlessness or hyperactivity during the first quarter moon, making it difficult for them to relax or settle down. They may seek out more physical activity or engage in behaviors such as pacing, barking, or chewing. This restlessness is often a reflection of their need to channel their increased energy into productive outlets.

4. **Emotional Sensitivity:** The challenges of the first quarter moon can also heighten your dog's emotional sensitivity. They may become more reactive to changes in their environment, such as loud noises, new people, or disruptions in their routine. Emotional sensitivity can lead to increased anxiety or nervousness, especially if they feel overwhelmed by the obstacles they are facing.

How to Support Your Dog During the First Quarter Moon

To help your dog navigate the challenges and actions of the first quarter moon, it's essential to provide structure, support, and opportunities for growth. Here are some practical ways to support your dog during this phase of the lunar cycle:

1. **Focus on Problem-Solving Training:** Since the first quarter moon is a time for overcoming obstacles, focus on training exercises that encourage problem-solving. Engage your dog in activities that challenge their mind and body, such as puzzle toys, agility courses, or complex commands. This will help them channel their determination into productive learning experiences.

2. **Provide Clear Boundaries and Guidance:** Your dog may test boundaries during this phase, so it's important to provide clear, consistent guidance. Reinforce established rules and expectations, and avoid giving in to behaviors that push the limits. Positive reinforcement, such as treats, praise, or playtime, can help motivate your dog to stay within the boundaries while still encouraging growth.

3. **Channel Physical Energy Into Exercise:** The increased energy of the first quarter moon can be managed through regular physical exercise. Take your dog on longer walks, engage in active play sessions, or introduce new physical challenges such as running, hiking, or playing fetch. Ensuring your dog has outlets for their energy will reduce restlessness and destructive behaviors.

4. **Practice Patience and Persistence:** During the first quarter moon, your dog may experience frustration or resistance, particularly in training or routine activities. Practice patience and persistence, offering encouragement and rewards when they succeed. Avoid becoming frustrated yourself, as your dog will pick up on your emotions. Instead, remain calm, supportive, and focused on their progress.

5. **Create a Calm, Structured Environment:** To help your dog manage any emotional sensitivity or anxiety during this phase, create a calm and structured environment. Avoid introducing too many new stimuli at once, and maintain a consistent daily routine. Providing a quiet space for rest and relaxation can also help your dog decompress and recharge after periods of activity or stress.

Emotional Shifts During the First Quarter Moon

The first quarter moon's energy can also lead to emotional shifts in your dog, as they process the challenges and actions associated with this phase. These emotional shifts may include increased confidence, frustration, or a desire for reassurance. Paying attention to your dog's emotional state can help you provide the right support during this time.

1. **Increased Confidence:** As your dog overcomes obstacles and engages in problem-solving, they may display increased confidence and self-assurance. Celebrate their successes and reinforce their newfound confidence with praise and rewards, helping them build emotional resilience.

2. **Frustration and Impatience:** Just as the first quarter moon can bring challenges, it can also lead to moments of frustration or impatience for your dog. They may become irritated when they cannot achieve a desired outcome or when faced with repeated failures. Offer reassurance and encouragement, and help them work through their frustrations with patience.

3. **Desire for Emotional Support:** During the first quarter moon, your dog may seek emotional support and reassurance from you, particularly if they are feeling overwhelmed by challenges. Spend extra time bonding with your dog, offering physical affection, soothing words, and companionship to help them feel secure and supported.

Creating Rituals for the First Quarter Moon with Your Dog

Rituals can help you and your dog navigate the action-oriented energy of the first quarter moon, providing structure and intention during this phase of growth. Here are some simple rituals to incorporate into your dog's routine during the first quarter moon:

1. **Action-Focused Walks:** Take your dog on action-focused walks, where you set a clear intention to overcome challenges. Whether it's working on leash training, practicing recall commands, or navigating new environments, use the walk as an opportunity to reinforce positive behaviors and encourage growth.

2. **Goal-Oriented Play Sessions:** Engage in play sessions with specific goals in mind, such as teaching your dog a new trick, improving their agility, or working on problem-solving skills. These goal-oriented sessions can help channel their energy into productive actions and provide a sense of accomplishment.

3. **Affirmations for Strength and Growth:** As you interact with your dog during the first quarter moon, silently affirm their strength and ability to overcome challenges. Statements like, "My dog is resilient and capable" or "We are overcoming obstacles to-

gether" can help set the tone for positive action and growth during this phase.

Conclusion

The first quarter moon is a time for action, decision-making, and overcoming challenges, both for humans and their canine companions. While this phase may bring moments of frustration or resistance for your dog, it also offers opportunities for growth, learning, and increased confidence. By understanding how the first quarter moon affects your dog's behavior and providing the right support, you can help them navigate this phase with resilience and determination. Embrace the challenges of the first quarter moon as opportunities for progress, and enjoy the journey of guiding your dog toward greater growth and well-being.

Chapter 33: Waxing Gibbous and Your Dog: Refinement and Progress in the Waxing Gibbous Phase

The waxing gibbous moon is the final stage before the full moon, marking a period of refinement, adjustment, and progress. In astrology, this phase represents the time when efforts are fine-tuned, loose ends are tied up, and preparations are made for the culmination of the lunar cycle. The energy during this phase is focused on perfecting what has already been started, ensuring that all elements are in place for the upcoming completion represented by the full moon.

For dogs, the waxing gibbous phase is a time of refinement in behavior, routine, and emotional development. It is an ideal period for reinforcing training, solidifying new habits, and addressing any behavioral or emotional challenges that may have surfaced during the earlier phases of the lunar cycle. This chapter will explore how the waxing gibbous moon influences your dog's behavior, how you can support their growth and progress, and what actions you can take to help them prepare for the full moon.

The Astrological and Energetic Meaning of the Waxing Gibbous

The waxing gibbous moon is a time of nearly full illumination, symbolizing the process of refinement and final preparations before the full moon's culmination. It's a phase for reviewing progress, making necessary adjustments, and perfecting the work that began during the new moon. In this phase, attention to detail becomes important, and there is a focus on polishing and improving what has been started.

For dogs, this phase can be a time of mental and emotional refinement. After the challenges and actions of the first quarter moon, the waxing gibbous provides an opportunity to solidify progress and ensure that behaviors, routines, and habits are aligned with growth and well-being. It's also a time when dogs may become more introspective, reflecting on their own emotional state as they prepare for the heightened energy of the full moon.

How the Waxing Gibbous Moon Affects Your Dog's Behavior
The waxing gibbous moon's influence on your dog can manifest as a period of refinement, focus, and preparation. During this phase, dogs are likely to display behaviors that reflect their growing maturity and development, as well as a desire for consistency and stability. Here are some common ways the waxing gibbous moon may affect your dog's behavior:

1. **Increased Focus and Concentration:** The waxing gibbous moon brings a sense of refinement and focus, and your dog may show greater concentration during training sessions or daily routines. They may be more attentive to commands, more patient with tasks, and more determined to complete what they've started. This is an ideal time to reinforce positive behaviors and build on previous training.

2. **Desire for Routine and Consistency:** Dogs thrive on routine, and during the waxing gibbous phase, they may display a stronger desire for consistency in their daily lives. They may become more attuned to their feeding, walking, and play schedules, seeking predictability and stability. This desire for routine helps them feel secure as they prepare for the energetic shift of the full moon.

3. **Emotional Introspection and Calm:** While earlier phases of the lunar cycle may have brought excitement or challenges, the waxing gibbous moon often brings a period of emotional calm and introspection. Your dog may seem more reflective or contemplative during this phase, spending more time quietly observing their surroundings or resting in their favorite spot. This is a time for emotional balance and preparation.

4. **Refinement of Behaviors and Habits:** The energy of the waxing gibbous moon encourages refinement, making this an excellent time to fine-tune your dog's behaviors and habits. If you've been working on training commands or addressing behavioral is-

sues, this phase offers an opportunity to solidify progress and ensure that your dog is on track for long-term success.

5. **Patience and Persistence:** Dogs may display increased patience and persistence during the waxing gibbous phase, particularly in activities that require focus and effort. They may be more willing to stick with a task, such as solving a puzzle toy or practicing a difficult command. This patience is a reflection of their ability to process challenges and work through them with determination.

Common Challenges During the Waxing Gibbous Moon

While the waxing gibbous moon is generally a time of progress and refinement, it can also present some challenges, particularly if there are lingering issues that need to be addressed. These challenges may include behaviors or emotional patterns that require adjustment or fine-tuning before the full moon's culmination.

1. **Difficulty Letting Go of Old Habits:** The waxing gibbous moon is a time for refinement, but some dogs may struggle to let go of old habits or behaviors that are no longer serving them. This can manifest as resistance to change, particularly if they have become attached to certain routines or behaviors. It's important to remain patient and provide gentle guidance as they work through these patterns.

2. **Overthinking or Hesitation:** Just as humans may experience a sense of overthinking during the waxing gibbous phase, dogs may also display hesitation or uncertainty in their actions. They may take longer to make decisions, such as choosing a toy to play with or responding to a command. This hesitation can be a reflection of their desire to perfect their actions, but it may also lead to frustration if not managed properly.

3. **Emotional Sensitivity:** During the waxing gibbous moon, some dogs may experience heightened emotional sensitivity, particularly if they are dealing with unresolved feelings or challenges

from earlier phases of the lunar cycle. This emotional sensitivity can manifest as clinginess, nervousness, or a need for extra reassurance from their human companions.

How to Support Your Dog During the Waxing Gibbous Moon
To help your dog navigate the waxing gibbous phase and make the most of this time of refinement and progress, it's important to provide structure, support, and opportunities for growth. Here are some practical ways to support your dog during this phase:

1. **Reinforce Positive Behaviors:** The waxing gibbous moon is the perfect time to reinforce positive behaviors that you've been working on throughout the lunar cycle. Focus on consistency in training, providing clear commands and rewarding your dog for their progress. This is an excellent time to build on previous successes and ensure that your dog is prepared for the next phase of growth.
2. **Maintain a Consistent Routine:** Dogs thrive on routine, and during the waxing gibbous phase, it's especially important to maintain consistency in their daily activities. Stick to their regular feeding, exercise, and play schedules to provide a sense of stability and predictability. This will help your dog feel grounded and secure as they work through this phase of refinement.
3. **Encourage Problem-Solving and Focus:** The increased focus and concentration during the waxing gibbous moon can be channeled into activities that encourage problem-solving and mental stimulation. Offer puzzle toys, interactive games, or training exercises that challenge your dog's mind and allow them to refine their skills. These activities will help them stay engaged and mentally sharp.
4. **Offer Emotional Reassurance:** If your dog is displaying emotional sensitivity during the waxing gibbous moon, provide them with extra reassurance and support. Spend quality time with

them, offering affection, soothing words, and physical touch to help them feel secure. This emotional connection will help them process any lingering feelings and prepare for the full moon's energetic culmination.

5. **Monitor and Adjust as Needed:** During the waxing gibbous phase, it's important to monitor your dog's behavior and make adjustments as needed. If you notice any challenges or setbacks, take the time to address them before they become more pronounced. This phase is all about refinement, so use it as an opportunity to fine-tune your dog's behavior and routine.

Emotional Shifts During the Waxing Gibbous Moon

The waxing gibbous moon's energy can bring about emotional shifts in your dog, particularly as they process the progress they've made and prepare for the upcoming full moon. These emotional shifts may include feelings of calm, reflection, or sensitivity. Paying attention to your dog's emotional state during this phase can help you provide the right support and guidance.

1. **Increased Calm and Reflection:** Many dogs become more emotionally balanced during the waxing gibbous phase, displaying a sense of calm and reflection. They may spend more time quietly resting or observing their surroundings, processing the growth they've experienced during the lunar cycle. This is a time for emotional grounding and preparation.

2. **Desire for Reassurance:** Some dogs may seek extra reassurance during the waxing gibbous moon, particularly if they are feeling emotionally sensitive. They may become more affectionate or clingy, seeking out physical touch and comfort from their human companions. Offering extra affection and attention can help them feel supported during this introspective phase.

3. **Emotional Growth and Maturity:** As the waxing gibbous moon represents a time of refinement, it also offers an opportu-

nity for emotional growth and maturity. Your dog may display signs of increased emotional resilience, handling challenges with greater patience and composure. Celebrate their emotional growth and provide positive reinforcement for their progress.

Creating Rituals for the Waxing Gibbous Phase with Your Dog

Rituals can help you and your dog navigate the energy of the waxing gibbous moon, providing structure and intention during this phase of refinement and progress. Here are some simple rituals to incorporate into your dog's routine during the waxing gibbous phase:

1. **Refinement-Focused Training Sessions:** Use this time to engage in training sessions that focus on refining skills and behaviors. Choose a specific command or behavior to work on, and dedicate time each day to perfecting it. These sessions should be focused on consistency and patience, helping your dog feel confident in their abilities.
2. **Affirmations for Progress and Growth:** As you interact with your dog during the waxing gibbous moon, silently affirm their progress and growth. Statements like, "My dog is progressing beautifully" or "We are refining our skills together" can help set the tone for positive action and continued development.
3. **Quiet Reflection and Bonding Time:** Spend quiet moments of reflection with your dog, offering affection and bonding through shared activities. Whether it's sitting together in a peaceful environment or taking a leisurely walk, use these moments to connect emotionally and reinforce your bond.

Conclusion

The waxing gibbous moon is a time of refinement, progress, and preparation for the culmination of the lunar cycle. For your dog, this phase offers an opportunity to fine-tune behaviors, solidify habits, and prepare for the full moon's energetic climax. By understanding how the waxing gibbous moon influences your dog's behavior and providing the right support, you can help them navigate this phase with confidence and ease. Embrace this time of refinement as an opportunity to strengthen your bond with your dog and guide them toward continued growth and well-being.

Chapter 34: Full Moon and Your Dog: The Peak of Energy and Emotions During the Full Moon

The full moon is the most energetically charged phase of the lunar cycle, symbolizing completion, culmination, and heightened emotions. In astrology, the full moon is a time of intensity, where the energies that have been building during the earlier phases reach their peak. For many, this period is associated with emotional release, illumination of hidden truths, and dramatic shifts in behavior. For dogs, the full moon can lead to an increase in energy, heightened emotional sensitivity, and sometimes behavioral changes that reflect the intensity of this cosmic event.

In this chapter, we will explore how the full moon affects your dog's behavior, energy levels, and emotional state. We'll also provide guidance on how to support your dog during this intense lunar phase and how to navigate the challenges and opportunities that arise as your dog experiences the peak of the lunar cycle.

The Astrological and Energetic Significance of the Full Moon

The full moon is a time of maximum lunar illumination, symbolizing the culmination of the lunar cycle. Astrologically, it is associated with bringing hidden emotions or unresolved issues to the surface, allowing for clarity, release, and completion. The energy of the full moon is often intense, with people and animals alike experiencing heightened emotions and a surge in physical energy.

For dogs, this energetic shift can lead to noticeable changes in their behavior. Some dogs may become more excitable, while others may exhibit signs of restlessness or anxiety. This phase is often one of heightened activity, where the emotions and energy that have been building throughout the lunar cycle come to a head. Understanding these shifts and knowing how to manage them can help you provide the right support for your dog during this time.

How the Full Moon Affects Your Dog's Behavior

The full moon's energy can influence your dog in several ways, from increased physical activity to emotional sensitivity and even temporary changes in behavior. While each dog may respond to the full moon differently, there are some common behavioral traits and shifts that are often observed during this phase.

1. **Increased Energy and Hyperactivity:** Many dogs experience a surge of energy during the full moon, becoming more active, playful, or even hyperactive. This heightened energy may manifest as increased enthusiasm during walks, more frequent play sessions, or a desire to engage in physical activities for longer periods of time. It's important to provide outlets for this energy to prevent it from turning into restlessness or destructive behaviors.

2. **Restlessness and Difficulty Settling Down:** The full moon's intense energy can also make it difficult for some dogs to relax or settle down, leading to restlessness. Your dog may pace, whine, or show signs of being unable to find a comfortable spot to rest. This restlessness is often a reflection of the emotional and physical energy they are feeling during this phase.

3. **Heightened Emotional Sensitivity:** Just as humans may feel more emotionally sensitive during the full moon, dogs can also experience heightened emotions. They may become more reactive to stimuli, such as loud noises, changes in routine, or the emotions of the people around them. This emotional sensitivity can manifest as clinginess, anxiety, or increased need for reassurance from their human companions.

4. **Increased Social Interaction:** Some dogs may become more sociable and seek out interaction with other animals or people during the full moon. This can be a time of increased playfulness, where your dog is more eager to engage with you, other pets, or

even strangers. It's a great time to take advantage of their social energy by scheduling playdates or trips to the dog park.

5. **Behavioral Challenges:** While the full moon's energy can lead to increased excitement and playfulness, it can also bring about behavioral challenges. Some dogs may display more stubbornness or difficulty following commands during this phase, as their heightened energy makes it harder for them to focus. Patience and understanding are key during this time, as your dog may need extra guidance and reinforcement.

Common Challenges During the Full Moon

While the full moon brings an abundance of energy, it can also present certain challenges, particularly if your dog is sensitive to the shifts in their environment. These challenges may include increased anxiety, hyperactivity, or difficulty managing their emotional state. Recognizing these challenges and taking proactive steps can help ensure your dog remains balanced and calm during this energetic phase.

1. **Anxiety and Nervousness:** The full moon's intensity can exacerbate feelings of anxiety or nervousness in some dogs. They may become more easily startled by noises, more reactive to changes in their environment, or display signs of separation anxiety if left alone. Providing comfort and reassurance is crucial to helping your dog manage these heightened emotions.

2. **Sleep Disruptions:** Just as humans may experience trouble sleeping during the full moon, dogs can also have difficulty settling down for restful sleep. They may wake up more frequently during the night or struggle to find a comfortable sleeping position. Offering a calming environment and maintaining a consistent bedtime routine can help alleviate sleep disturbances.

3. **Aggression or Irritability:** In rare cases, the heightened energy of the full moon can lead to irritability or aggressive behavior in dogs, especially if they are already prone to such behaviors. This

may manifest as snapping, growling, or becoming more territorial around other pets or people. It's important to monitor your dog's interactions closely and intervene if needed to prevent conflict.

4. **Overstimulation:** The abundance of energy during the full moon can lead to overstimulation in some dogs, particularly those who are naturally high-energy or sensitive to their surroundings. They may become overwhelmed by too much activity, noise, or social interaction, leading to behaviors such as excessive barking, zoomies, or difficulty calming down.

How to Support Your Dog During the Full Moon

To help your dog navigate the intense energy of the full moon, it's important to provide structure, reassurance, and appropriate outlets for their physical and emotional needs. Here are some practical ways to support your dog during this phase:

1. **Provide Extra Physical Activity:** Since many dogs experience a surge of energy during the full moon, increasing their physical activity can help channel that energy in a productive way. Take them on longer walks, engage in extra play sessions, or introduce new physical challenges such as agility courses. This will help them burn off excess energy and reduce restlessness.

2. **Create a Calming Environment:** To counterbalance the full moon's intensity, create a calming environment for your dog at home. Dim the lights, play soothing music, and provide a quiet space where they can retreat if they feel overwhelmed. Calming pheromone diffusers or sprays can also be helpful in reducing anxiety and promoting relaxation.

3. **Stick to a Consistent Routine:** Maintaining a consistent daily routine during the full moon can help your dog feel more grounded and secure. Stick to regular feeding times, walks, and play sessions to provide a sense of stability amidst the heightened

energy. Consistency in routine will also help prevent feelings of anxiety or unease.

4. **Offer Emotional Reassurance:** During the full moon, your dog may seek extra emotional reassurance from you, especially if they are feeling emotionally sensitive or anxious. Spend quality time with them, offering physical affection, soothing words, and gentle touch. This bonding time can help them feel secure and supported during this intense phase.

5. **Use Calming Tools:** If your dog is particularly sensitive to the full moon's energy, consider using calming tools such as anxiety wraps, calming collars, or natural supplements designed to reduce stress. These tools can help provide extra support and comfort, especially if your dog is prone to anxiety or restlessness during this phase.

Emotional Shifts During the Full Moon

The full moon's emotional intensity can bring about noticeable shifts in your dog's mood and behavior. These emotional shifts may include increased excitement, sensitivity, or a desire for emotional closeness. Paying attention to your dog's emotional state during the full moon will help you provide the right support and ensure their well-being.

1. **Heightened Excitement and Enthusiasm:** Many dogs experience heightened excitement and enthusiasm during the full moon, displaying more playful and energetic behaviors. They may seek out more interaction with you or other pets, showing a strong desire to engage in physical activities. Embrace this enthusiasm by providing them with outlets for play and exercise.

2. **Increased Emotional Sensitivity:** Emotional sensitivity is often heightened during the full moon, and your dog may be more attuned to your emotions or the energy in their environment. They may seek extra comfort or become more reactive to changes in

mood or routine. Offering a calm, reassuring presence can help them feel emotionally balanced.

3. **Desire for Emotional Closeness:** Some dogs may become more affectionate or clingy during the full moon, seeking out physical contact and emotional closeness with you. This is a reflection of their need for reassurance and connection during this intense phase. Offering extra cuddles, petting, and verbal affirmations can help strengthen your bond during this time.

Creating Rituals for the Full Moon with Your Dog

Rituals can help you and your dog navigate the energy of the full moon, providing structure and intention during this emotionally charged phase. Here are some simple rituals to incorporate into your dog's routine during the full moon:

1. **Full Moon Walks:** Take your dog on a full moon walk, using this time to reflect on the progress and growth you've both experienced throughout the lunar cycle. The heightened energy of the full moon can make outdoor walks more invigorating, offering a chance to burn off excess energy while connecting with the natural world.

2. **Affectionate Bonding Time:** Spend extra time bonding with your dog during the full moon, offering physical affection and verbal reassurance. Whether it's cuddling on the couch, petting, or simply sitting together in a quiet space, these moments of connection can help your dog feel secure and grounded during this intense phase.

3. **Calming Rituals Before Bed:** If your dog is prone to restlessness or sleep disturbances during the full moon, create a calming bedtime ritual to help them wind down. This could include a gentle massage, calming music, or a warm, cozy bed in a quiet part of the house. Establishing a relaxing routine will help them settle in for a restful night's sleep.

Conclusion

The full moon is a time of heightened energy and emotional intensity, both for humans and their canine companions. While this phase can bring about challenges such as restlessness, anxiety, or behavioral shifts, it also offers opportunities for growth, emotional connection, and energetic release. By understanding how the full moon influences your dog's behavior and providing the right support, you can help them navigate this phase with confidence and ease. Embrace the energy of the full moon as a time for bonding, play, and emotional closeness, and enjoy the journey of guiding your dog through the peak of the lunar cycle.

Chapter 35: Waning Gibbous and Your Dog: Reflection and Gratitude in the Waning Gibbous Phase

The waning gibbous moon occurs just after the peak of the full moon and symbolizes a time of reflection, gratitude, and emotional processing. In astrology, the waning gibbous phase represents the process of harvesting the fruits of your efforts, reviewing what has been accomplished, and letting go of anything that no longer serves a purpose. It is a time to express gratitude for progress made and to begin preparing for the next lunar cycle. For dogs, this phase can be a time of emotional balance, introspection, and a shift from high-energy activity to calm reflection.

During the waning gibbous moon, your dog may display behaviors that reflect this shift in energy, such as becoming more relaxed, emotionally sensitive, and introspective. This chapter will explore how the waning gibbous phase affects your dog's behavior and emotional state, and how you can support them in this time of reflection and gratitude.

The Astrological and Energetic Meaning of the Waning Gibbous

In astrology, the waning gibbous moon follows the intense, peak energy of the full moon and is a time for reflection and release. This phase is often associated with reviewing progress, expressing gratitude for achievements, and letting go of anything that has been outgrown or no longer aligns with current goals. It is a calming period where the heightened emotions of the full moon begin to settle, and there is space to process experiences and prepare for the next phase of growth.

For dogs, this phase can bring a sense of emotional balance and calm, as the energy of the full moon dissipates and they transition into a quieter, more reflective state. This is an ideal time for your dog to emotionally process the experiences of the lunar cycle, settle into their routine, and find comfort in familiar patterns. It's also a time for bonding, as your dog may seek more emotional connection with you during this reflective phase.

How the Waning Gibbous Moon Affects Your Dog's Behavior

The waning gibbous moon's influence on your dog can manifest as a period of emotional balance, calmness, and a desire for routine and connection. During this phase, dogs often become more introspective and may display behaviors that reflect their need for emotional processing and relaxation. Here are some common ways the waning gibbous moon may affect your dog's behavior:

1. **Increased Calmness and Relaxation:** After the energetic peak of the full moon, the waning gibbous phase often brings a sense of calmness and relaxation. Your dog may seem more content to rest, nap, or quietly observe their surroundings. This is a time when they may need less physical activity and more opportunities for emotional recovery.

2. **Desire for Routine and Familiarity:** Dogs thrive on routine, and during the waning gibbous phase, they may display a stronger desire for familiar patterns and consistency in their daily life. They may prefer sticking to established routines, such as their usual walk times, feeding schedule, or favorite resting spots. This desire for routine helps them feel grounded and secure as they process the energy of the previous lunar phases.

3. **Emotional Reflection and Sensitivity:** The waning gibbous moon is a time of emotional reflection, and your dog may become more emotionally sensitive during this phase. They may be more attuned to your emotions and the energy around them, responding with increased empathy or a need for reassurance. This emotional sensitivity can be an opportunity for deeper bonding and emotional connection.

4. **Desire for Emotional Connection:** During the waning gibbous moon, many dogs seek emotional connection and may become more affectionate or clingy. They may want to spend more time close to you, seeking out physical contact or quiet moments of companionship. This phase is an ideal time for bonding, offer-

ing your dog the emotional support they need as they reflect and process their experiences.

5. **Refinement of Behaviors and Habits:** The reflective nature of the waning gibbous phase makes it a good time to refine behaviors and habits that have been established during the earlier phases of the lunar cycle. If you've been working on training or improving certain behaviors, this phase offers an opportunity to review progress and make any necessary adjustments.

Common Challenges During the Waning Gibbous Moon

While the waning gibbous phase is generally a time of calm reflection, there can be some challenges associated with emotional sensitivity or difficulty letting go of unresolved issues. These challenges may manifest in your dog's behavior or emotional state, particularly if they are struggling to process the heightened energy of the full moon.

1. **Emotional Sensitivity and Vulnerability:** Some dogs may experience heightened emotional sensitivity during the waning gibbous phase, becoming more reactive to changes in their environment or the emotions of those around them. This emotional sensitivity can lead to feelings of vulnerability, causing them to seek extra reassurance or become more anxious in unfamiliar situations.

2. **Difficulty Letting Go of Stress or Anxiety:** If your dog experienced stress or anxiety during the full moon, they may have difficulty letting go of those emotions during the waning gibbous phase. They may continue to display signs of restlessness or nervousness, especially if they have not yet fully processed the intensity of the previous phase.

3. **Over-Attachment or Clinginess:** While the waning gibbous moon is a time for emotional connection, some dogs may become overly attached or clingy during this phase. They may seek constant attention or become distressed when left alone, reflecting

their need for emotional reassurance. It's important to provide comfort while also maintaining healthy boundaries.

How to Support Your Dog During the Waning Gibbous Moon
To help your dog navigate the reflective and calming energy of the waning gibbous moon, it's important to provide emotional support, maintain consistent routines, and create a nurturing environment. Here are some practical ways to support your dog during this phase:

1. **Maintain a Consistent Routine:** Dogs thrive on routine, and maintaining a consistent daily schedule during the waning gibbous phase can help your dog feel grounded and secure. Stick to regular feeding times, walks, and play sessions, providing a sense of familiarity and stability as your dog processes the energy of the lunar cycle.

2. **Offer Emotional Reassurance:** During this emotionally reflective phase, your dog may seek extra reassurance and comfort. Spend quality time bonding with them, offering physical affection, soothing words, and gentle touch. Whether it's cuddling on the couch or sitting quietly together, this emotional connection will help your dog feel supported and secure.

3. **Encourage Quiet Reflection and Rest:** The waning gibbous moon is a time for rest and recovery, so provide your dog with plenty of opportunities for quiet reflection and relaxation. Create a calm, comfortable space where they can retreat to rest, nap, or observe their surroundings in peace. This time of rest is essential for their emotional and physical well-being.

4. **Refine Training and Behaviors:** The reflective energy of the waning gibbous moon makes it an ideal time to review and refine your dog's training and behaviors. Focus on reinforcing positive habits and making any necessary adjustments to address areas where improvement is needed. This is a time for refinement, rather than introducing new behaviors or commands.

5. **Practice Gratitude and Positive Reinforcement:** Express gratitude for your dog's progress and achievements during the lunar cycle. Use positive reinforcement to acknowledge their growth and development, offering praise, treats, or affection for their efforts. This practice of gratitude will help your dog feel appreciated and supported as they continue to grow.

Emotional Shifts During the Waning Gibbous Moon

The waning gibbous moon's energy can bring about emotional shifts in your dog, particularly as they process the experiences of the full moon and reflect on their growth. These emotional shifts may include increased calmness, sensitivity, or a desire for emotional connection. Paying attention to your dog's emotional state during this phase will help you provide the right support and ensure their well-being.

1. **Increased Calmness and Emotional Balance:** Many dogs become more emotionally balanced during the waning gibbous phase, displaying a sense of calm and relaxation. They may be content to rest and reflect, finding comfort in familiar routines and environments. This is a time for emotional recovery and balance.

2. **Heightened Sensitivity to Your Emotions:** During the waning gibbous moon, dogs may become more attuned to the emotions of their human companions. They may be more sensitive to changes in your mood or energy, responding with increased empathy or a desire to offer comfort. Be mindful of your own emotional state, as your dog may mirror your feelings during this phase.

3. **Desire for Emotional Bonding:** The reflective nature of the waning gibbous moon often leads dogs to seek out deeper emotional connections with their human companions. They may become more affectionate, spending extra time close to you or

seeking physical touch. This is an ideal time to strengthen your bond and provide emotional support.

Creating Rituals for the Waning Gibbous Phase with Your Dog

Rituals can help you and your dog navigate the energy of the waning gibbous moon, providing structure and intention during this phase of reflection and gratitude. Here are some simple rituals to incorporate into your dog's routine during the waning gibbous phase:

1. **Gratitude Walks:** Take your dog on gratitude walks, using this time to reflect on the progress you've both made during the lunar cycle. As you walk, silently express gratitude for your dog's growth, achievements, and companionship. This practice of gratitude will help you both connect with the reflective energy of the waning gibbous moon.

2. **Affectionate Bonding Time:** Spend extra time bonding with your dog during the waning gibbous moon, offering physical affection and verbal reassurances. Whether it's cuddling on the couch, petting, or simply sitting together in a quiet space, these moments of connection will help your dog feel supported and appreciated during this reflective phase.

3. **Reflective Play and Rest:** Engage in gentle play sessions that allow your dog to release any lingering energy, followed by quiet moments of rest. This balance of activity and relaxation will help your dog process their emotions and prepare for the next phase of the lunar cycle.

Conclusion

The waning gibbous moon is a time for reflection, gratitude, and emotional balance, both for humans and their canine companions. During this phase, your dog may display a sense of calmness, emotional sensitivity, and a desire for routine and connection. By understanding how the waning gibbous moon influences your dog's behavior and providing the right support, you can help them navigate this phase with ease. Embrace this time of reflection as an opportunity to strengthen your bond with your dog, express gratitude for their growth, and prepare for the next chapter in the lunar cycle.

Chapter 36: Last Quarter and Your Dog: Letting Go and Releasing During the Last Quarter Moon

The last quarter moon is the final stage of the lunar cycle before the new moon, marking a time of release, letting go, and making space for new beginnings. In astrology, this phase is associated with closure, introspection, and the shedding of old habits or patterns that no longer serve a purpose. It is a time to reflect on what has been accomplished during the lunar cycle and to let go of anything that may be holding back progress. For dogs, the last quarter moon can bring about a period of emotional release, where they process their experiences and transition into a calmer, more introspective state.

During the last quarter moon, your dog may exhibit behaviors that reflect this need for emotional release and letting go. This chapter will explore how the last quarter moon affects your dog's behavior, emotional state, and energy levels, and how you can support them as they navigate this phase of the lunar cycle.

The Astrological and Energetic Significance of the Last Quarter Moon

In astrology, the last quarter moon represents a time for letting go, making final adjustments, and preparing for the new moon's fresh start. The energy during this phase is often quieter and more introspective, as it encourages us to reflect on the lessons of the lunar cycle and release any unresolved emotions, thoughts, or behaviors that may have accumulated. It is a period of emotional cleansing, where we can gain clarity on what needs to be released in order to move forward.

For dogs, this phase can also be a time of emotional processing and letting go. After the intensity of the full moon and the reflection of the waning gibbous, the last quarter moon offers an opportunity for your dog to release any lingering emotional tension or stress. This is a phase of quiet reflection, where they may become more introspective and seek out rest or solitude.

How the Last Quarter Moon Affects Your Dog's Behavior

The last quarter moon's influence on your dog can manifest as a time of emotional release, calmness, and the shedding of old patterns or habits. During this phase, your dog may show behaviors that reflect their need to process emotions and release any built-up tension from the previous phases of the lunar cycle. Here are some common ways the last quarter moon may affect your dog's behavior:

1. **Emotional Release and Processing:** The last quarter moon is a time for emotional release, and your dog may need to process any unresolved emotions or experiences from the lunar cycle. They may become more introspective, spending time quietly resting or reflecting. This phase is essential for their emotional well-being, allowing them to release stress or tension that has accumulated.

2. **Increased Calmness and Desire for Solitude:** As your dog moves through the last quarter moon, they may become more calm and less inclined to engage in high-energy activities. They may seek out quiet spaces or moments of solitude, where they can rest and recharge. This desire for calmness and solitude is a natural response to the release of emotional energy during this phase.

3. **Letting Go of Old Habits:** Just as the last quarter moon encourages the shedding of old patterns for humans, your dog may also show signs of letting go of behaviors or habits that are no longer serving them. This could be a time when certain behavioral challenges or repetitive actions begin to diminish, as your dog moves toward a more balanced and refined state.

4. **Emotional Sensitivity and Vulnerability:** During the last quarter moon, your dog may become more emotionally sensitive, particularly if they are processing deeper emotions or experiences. They may need extra reassurance, comfort, and attention from

you during this phase, especially if they seem more vulnerable or uncertain.

5. **Desire for Routine and Structure:** The last quarter moon can also bring a desire for routine and structure, as your dog seeks consistency to help them process their emotions. Maintaining a steady routine during this phase can provide them with the stability they need to feel secure and supported as they navigate this period of release.

Common Challenges During the Last Quarter Moon

While the last quarter moon is generally a time for emotional release and letting go, it can also present certain challenges, particularly if your dog is struggling with unresolved emotions or behaviors. These challenges may manifest in their behavior or emotional state, requiring extra support and guidance during this phase.

1. **Resistance to Change:** Some dogs may struggle with letting go of old habits or behaviors during the last quarter moon, especially if those patterns have become deeply ingrained. They may resist changes to their routine or training, displaying signs of frustration or reluctance to adapt. Patience and consistency are key to helping your dog navigate this resistance.

2. **Emotional Sensitivity or Anxiety:** As your dog processes their emotions during the last quarter moon, they may become more emotionally sensitive or anxious. They may seek out extra comfort or display signs of clinginess, such as following you around more closely or becoming distressed when left alone. Providing emotional reassurance and maintaining a calm environment can help ease their anxiety.

3. **Restlessness or Difficulty Relaxing:** While many dogs may become more calm and introspective during the last quarter moon, others may struggle with restlessness or difficulty relaxing. This restlessness can be a result of emotional tension that has not yet

been fully released. Offering opportunities for gentle play, exercise, or calming activities can help them release this energy.

How to Support Your Dog During the Last Quarter Moon

To help your dog navigate the emotional release and letting go that occurs during the last quarter moon, it's important to provide emotional support, maintain a consistent routine, and create a calm environment. Here are some practical ways to support your dog during this phase:

1. **Provide Emotional Reassurance:** During the last quarter moon, your dog may need extra emotional reassurance as they process their experiences and release any lingering tension. Spend quality time bonding with them, offering physical affection, soothing words, and gentle touch. This emotional connection will help them feel supported and secure during this phase of release.

2. **Maintain a Consistent Routine:** Maintaining a consistent daily routine during the last quarter moon can help your dog feel grounded and secure as they navigate this period of emotional release. Stick to regular feeding times, walks, and play sessions, providing a sense of familiarity and stability.

3. **Encourage Rest and Relaxation:** The last quarter moon is a time for rest and recovery, so provide your dog with plenty of opportunities to relax and recharge. Create a calm, comfortable space where they can retreat to rest or nap, and avoid overstimulating activities that may disrupt their emotional balance.

4. **Let Go of Old Patterns:** Use the energy of the last quarter moon to help your dog let go of any old behaviors or patterns that are no longer serving them. Whether it's addressing a behavioral challenge or refining their training, this is an ideal time to gently guide your dog toward healthier habits and emotional balance.

5. **Offer Calming Activities:** If your dog is experiencing restlessness or emotional sensitivity during the last quarter moon, offer calming activities to help them release any remaining tension. Gentle walks, quiet playtime, or puzzle toys can provide a soothing outlet for their energy and help them feel more grounded.

Emotional Shifts During the Last Quarter Moon

The last quarter moon's energy can bring about emotional shifts in your dog, particularly as they process their experiences and release any lingering emotions from the lunar cycle. These emotional shifts may include feelings of calmness, vulnerability, or emotional release. Paying attention to your dog's emotional state during this phase will help you provide the right support and ensure their well-being.

1. **Increased Calmness and Emotional Release:** Many dogs become more emotionally balanced during the last quarter moon, displaying a sense of calmness and emotional release. They may be content to rest and reflect, processing their experiences from the lunar cycle and releasing any built-up tension.

2. **Heightened Sensitivity and Vulnerability:** During the last quarter moon, your dog may become more emotionally sensitive or vulnerable, especially if they are processing unresolved emotions. They may seek extra comfort or reassurance, displaying clingy behaviors or a need for physical affection.

3. **Desire for Emotional Closeness:** Some dogs may seek out more emotional closeness during the last quarter moon, wanting to spend extra time near you or engaging in quiet bonding activities. This desire for emotional connection reflects their need for support as they navigate this phase of emotional release.

Creating Rituals for the Last Quarter Moon with Your Dog

Rituals can help you and your dog navigate the energy of the last quarter moon, providing structure and intention during this phase of release and letting go. Here are some simple rituals to incorporate into your dog's routine during the last quarter moon:

1. **Letting Go Walks:** Take your dog on letting go walks, using this time to reflect on what you both need to release from the lunar cycle. As you walk, silently express intentions of release and emotional cleansing, allowing your dog to process their experiences and shed any lingering tension.

2. **Affectionate Bonding Time:** Spend extra time bonding with your dog during the last quarter moon, offering physical affection and verbal reassurances. Whether it's cuddling on the couch, petting, or simply sitting together in a quiet space, these moments of connection will help your dog feel supported and secure as they release and let go.

3. **Calming Rituals Before Bed:** If your dog is experiencing restlessness or emotional sensitivity during the last quarter moon, create a calming bedtime ritual to help them wind down. This could include a gentle massage, calming music, or a warm, cozy bed in a quiet part of the house.

Conclusion

The last quarter moon is a time for emotional release, letting go, and preparing for the fresh start of the new moon. For your dog, this phase offers an opportunity to process their experiences, release any lingering tension, and find emotional balance. By understanding how the last quarter moon influences your dog's behavior and providing the right support, you can help them navigate this phase with ease. Embrace this time of release as an opportunity to strengthen your bond with your dog and guide them toward emotional clarity and well-being.

Chapter 37: Waning Crescent and Your Dog: Rest and Rejuvenation in the Waning Crescent Phase

The waning crescent moon is the final stage of the lunar cycle before the new moon, symbolizing rest, reflection, and rejuvenation. In astrology, the waning crescent moon is a time for turning inward, conserving energy, and preparing for the fresh start of the new lunar cycle. It is a period of quiet introspection, where the focus shifts from external activities to internal healing and emotional renewal. For dogs, this phase represents a time of rest and recovery, allowing them to release any lingering emotional or physical energy from the previous phases and prepare for the new beginnings that the next lunar cycle will bring.

During the waning crescent moon, your dog may exhibit behaviors that reflect their need for rest, relaxation, and emotional recovery. This chapter will explore how the waning crescent moon affects your dog's behavior and emotional state, and how you can support their need for rejuvenation during this quiet and introspective phase of the lunar cycle.

The Astrological and Energetic Significance of the Waning Crescent

In astrology, the waning crescent moon is a time of closure and rest before the new moon begins a fresh cycle of growth and activity. The energy of this phase is low, encouraging rest, contemplation, and emotional healing. It is a time to reflect on the lessons of the lunar cycle, release any residual stress or emotional tension, and conserve energy for the new beginnings that lie ahead.

For dogs, the waning crescent phase can be a time of emotional processing and physical recovery. After the intensity of the full moon and the emotional release of the last quarter moon, the waning crescent offers an opportunity for your dog to recharge, both physically and emotionally. This is a time when your dog may become more introspective, seeking rest and quiet moments of solitude. Supporting your dog during this phase is essential to their overall well-being, allowing them to transition smoothly into the new lunar cycle.

How the Waning Crescent Moon Affects Your Dog's Behavior

The waning crescent moon's influence on your dog can manifest as a period of rest, emotional introspection, and low energy. During this phase, dogs often become more focused on conserving their energy, finding comfort in routine, and seeking emotional balance. Here are some common ways the waning crescent moon may affect your dog's behavior:

1. **Increased Need for Rest and Relaxation:** The waning crescent moon encourages rest and rejuvenation, and your dog may show a greater need for sleep, naps, and relaxation during this phase. They may be less interested in physical activities and more content to rest in their favorite spot, allowing their body and mind to recover from the earlier phases of the lunar cycle.

2. **Emotional Reflection and Processing:** Just as the waning crescent moon is a time for emotional healing, your dog may become more introspective and reflective during this phase. They may exhibit signs of processing their emotions or experiences from the previous phases, spending more time quietly observing or resting. This introspection is essential for their emotional well-being and allows them to release any lingering stress or tension.

3. **Lower Energy Levels:** During the waning crescent moon, your dog's energy levels may naturally decline as they focus on conserving their strength for the new lunar cycle. They may be less inclined to engage in high-energy activities, preferring slower, more calming activities that allow them to recharge both physically and mentally.

4. **Increased Sensitivity and Vulnerability:** Some dogs may display heightened emotional sensitivity during the waning crescent phase, particularly if they are processing unresolved emotions. They may seek extra comfort, reassurance, or physical affection from you, displaying signs of vulnerability or a need for emo-

tional support. Offering them a calming presence can help them feel secure during this introspective time.

5. **Desire for Routine and Stability:** The waning crescent moon is a time for grounding and stability, and your dog may show a stronger desire for routine and consistency in their daily life. They may prefer sticking to familiar patterns, such as their usual feeding, walking, and resting schedules, finding comfort in the stability of their routine.

Common Challenges During the Waning Crescent Moon

While the waning crescent moon is generally a time of rest and rejuvenation, it can also present challenges if your dog is struggling with emotional or physical exhaustion. These challenges may manifest in their behavior or emotional state, requiring extra attention and care during this quiet phase.

1. **Restlessness Despite Fatigue:** While the waning crescent moon encourages rest, some dogs may experience restlessness even though they are physically or emotionally tired. This restlessness can be a result of unresolved emotional tension or difficulty relaxing. Offering a calm, soothing environment can help them release any lingering stress and settle into a more restful state.

2. **Clinginess or Emotional Sensitivity:** During the waning crescent moon, your dog may become more emotionally sensitive or clingy, seeking constant attention or reassurance from you. This emotional sensitivity can be a reflection of their need for comfort and emotional security during this introspective phase. Providing extra affection and support can help them feel more grounded.

3. **Difficulty Engaging in Activities:** While some dogs may be content to rest during the waning crescent moon, others may struggle to engage in activities or focus on training. This lack of motivation can be a sign that your dog is emotionally or physically exhausted and needs more time to recharge. Allowing them

the space to rest without pushing them into activities will help them recover.

How to Support Your Dog During the Waning Crescent Moon

To help your dog navigate the rest and rejuvenation that occurs during the waning crescent moon, it's important to provide a calm, nurturing environment and offer opportunities for emotional healing and physical recovery. Here are some practical ways to support your dog during this phase:

1. **Encourage Rest and Relaxation:** The waning crescent moon is a time for rest, so encourage your dog to relax and take it easy. Provide them with a comfortable space where they can retreat to rest and nap without being disturbed. This could be their favorite bed or a quiet corner of the house where they can feel safe and secure.

2. **Maintain a Calm, Stable Environment:** During this phase, it's important to maintain a calm and stable environment for your dog. Avoid overstimulating activities or changes to their routine that could disrupt their emotional balance. Instead, focus on creating a peaceful atmosphere with soft lighting, calming music, and a predictable schedule.

3. **Offer Emotional Reassurance:** If your dog is displaying signs of emotional sensitivity or vulnerability during the waning crescent moon, offer them extra emotional reassurance. Spend quality time bonding with them, offering physical affection, soothing words, and gentle touch. This emotional connection will help them feel supported as they process their emotions.

4. **Limit High-Energy Activities:** Since the waning crescent moon is a time for conserving energy, limit high-energy activities that could exhaust your dog further. Instead, focus on gentle walks, quiet playtime, or activities that promote relaxation and

emotional well-being. This will help your dog conserve their energy and prepare for the next lunar cycle.

5. **Provide Emotional Healing Tools:** If your dog is struggling with emotional tension or stress during the waning crescent moon, consider using emotional healing tools such as calming pheromone diffusers, anxiety wraps, or natural supplements designed to reduce stress. These tools can help create a calming environment and support your dog's emotional recovery.

Emotional Shifts During the Waning Crescent Moon

The waning crescent moon's energy can bring about emotional shifts in your dog, particularly as they process their experiences and prepare for the new lunar cycle. These emotional shifts may include increased calmness, sensitivity, or a desire for emotional connection. Paying attention to your dog's emotional state during this phase will help you provide the right support and ensure their well-being.

1. **Increased Calmness and Emotional Balance:** Many dogs become more emotionally balanced during the waning crescent moon, displaying a sense of calmness and relaxation. They may be content to rest and reflect, finding comfort in familiar routines and environments. This is a time for emotional recovery and balance.

2. **Heightened Sensitivity and Vulnerability:** During the waning crescent moon, your dog may become more emotionally sensitive or vulnerable, especially if they are processing unresolved emotions. They may seek extra comfort or reassurance, displaying clingy behaviors or a need for physical affection.

3. **Desire for Emotional Connection:** Some dogs may seek out more emotional connection during the waning crescent moon, wanting to spend extra time near you or engaging in quiet bonding activities. This desire for emotional connection reflects their

need for support as they navigate this phase of rest and rejuvenation.

Creating Rituals for the Waning Crescent Phase with Your Dog

Rituals can help you and your dog navigate the energy of the waning crescent moon, providing structure and intention during this phase of rest and rejuvenation. Here are some simple rituals to incorporate into your dog's routine during the waning crescent phase:

1. **Restful Walks:** Take your dog on slow, calming walks during the waning crescent moon, allowing them to move at their own pace and enjoy the peaceful environment. These walks can be a time for quiet reflection, both for you and your dog, offering an opportunity to release any lingering tension.

2. **Affectionate Bonding Time:** Spend extra time bonding with your dog during the waning crescent moon, offering physical affection and verbal reassurances. Whether it's cuddling on the couch, petting, or simply sitting together in a quiet space, these moments of connection will help your dog feel supported and secure as they rest and rejuvenate.

3. **Calming Rituals Before Bed:** Create a calming bedtime ritual to help your dog wind down during the waning crescent moon. This could include a gentle massage, calming music, or a warm, cozy bed in a quiet part of the house. Establishing a relaxing routine will help your dog settle in for a restful night's sleep.

Conclusion

The waning crescent moon is a time for rest, rejuvenation, and emotional recovery, both for humans and their canine companions. During this phase, your dog may display a need for calmness, introspection, and emotional support as they prepare for the new lunar cycle. By understanding how the waning crescent moon influences your dog's behavior and providing the right support, you can help them navigate this phase with ease. Embrace this time of rest as an opportunity to strengthen your bond with your dog, guide them toward emotional balance, and prepare for the fresh start that the new moon will bring.

Part 5: Astrological Compatibility

Chapter 38: Dog-to-Dog Compatibility: Understanding How Different Zodiac Signs Interact in the Canine World

Astrology not only helps us understand our individual dogs' traits, behaviors, and needs, but it also provides valuable insights into how different dogs interact with one another. Just as astrological signs influence human compatibility, they play a role in the dynamics between dogs as well. Understanding how different zodiac signs interact in the canine world can provide key insights into your dog's friendships, play styles, and social behaviors.

In this chapter, we will explore how the zodiac signs influence dog-to-dog interactions, focusing on compatibility between signs, how different signs approach play and companionship, and how to foster healthy relationships between dogs with different astrological traits. By recognizing the unique qualities of each sign, you can better understand how your dog relates to others and promote harmonious relationships.

The Importance of Dog Compatibility

In the canine world, social compatibility plays a significant role in establishing friendships, hierarchies, and cooperation among dogs. While much of dog-to-dog interaction is influenced by environmental factors, such as socialization, upbringing, and training, astrological traits can provide deeper insights into why certain dogs naturally bond or face challenges with each other. By considering astrological compatibility, you can tailor playdates, group activities, or even multi-dog households in ways that promote peace and minimize conflict.

Dog Compatibility by Zodiac Sign

Each zodiac sign carries unique traits that influence how dogs interact with others. Some dogs may be naturally more assertive and dominant, while others may prefer calm, cooperative play. Let's take a look at how each zodiac sign influences dog-to-dog interactions and which signs they are most and least compatible with.

Aries (March 21 - April 19): The Leader of the Pack
Personality: Aries dogs are energetic, bold, and always ready to take charge. They enjoy action-packed play and tend to assert themselves in social settings. As natural leaders, they may initiate games and compete for dominance with other dogs, often becoming the "alpha" in group settings.

Compatible Signs:

- **Leo:** Both Aries and Leo dogs are full of energy and enthusiasm, making them excellent playmates. They thrive on competition but can respect each other's boldness.
- **Sagittarius:** Sagittarius dogs match Aries' adventurous spirit, making for lively and exciting play sessions. They enjoy exploring together and embarking on outdoor adventures.
- **Gemini:** Playful and curious, Gemini dogs get along well with Aries, matching their high energy and love for mental stimulation.

Challenging Signs:

- **Taurus:** Taurus dogs prefer a more relaxed and predictable routine, which can clash with Aries' impulsive and energetic nature.
- **Cancer:** Cancer dogs are sensitive and nurturing, preferring calm and gentle companionship, which may not align with Aries' intense play style.

Taurus (April 20 - May 20): The Peaceful Companion
Personality: Taurus dogs are known for their steady, calm demeanor. They enjoy routines, and comfort, and tend to be more laid-back in social settings. While they may not be the most adventurous dogs, they are loyal and form deep bonds with dogs that respect their space and routine.

Compatible Signs:

- **Cancer:** Both Taurus and Cancer dogs appreciate calm environments and form strong emotional bonds. They can enjoy each other's company in peaceful, quiet ways.
- **Virgo:** Virgo's attention to detail and Taurus' love for routine create a harmonious relationship. Both signs value stability and predictable behavior, making them excellent companions.
- **Pisces:** Pisces dogs are gentle and intuitive, aligning well with Taurus' calm and affectionate nature.

Challenging Signs:

- **Aries:** Aries' intense energy and assertiveness may overwhelm the laid-back Taurus, leading to conflicts over pace and control.
- **Aquarius:** Aquarius dogs are independent and unpredictable, which can frustrate Taurus' need for consistency and routine.

Gemini (May 21 - June 20): The Social Butterfly

Personality: Gemini dogs are playful, curious, and highly sociable. They enjoy mental stimulation, new experiences, and constant interaction with others. These dogs thrive in dynamic environments where they can explore different play styles and form connections with multiple dogs.

Compatible Signs:

- **Libra:** Gemini and Libra dogs share a love for socializing and playing, making them perfect companions for group activities. Their playful and diplomatic natures create a balanced friendship.
- **Aries:** Both Aries and Gemini dogs are full of energy and curiosity. They engage in mentally stimulating games and enjoy active play together.
- **Leo:** Leo's confidence and Gemini's sociability create a playful and vibrant dynamic. They love to entertain each other with games and social interactions.

Challenging Signs:

- **Virgo:** Virgo's practical and focused nature may conflict with Gemini's playful unpredictability, leading to misunderstandings.
- **Scorpio:** Scorpio dogs prefer deep, focused interactions, which can clash with Gemini's need for variety and constant social engagement.

Cancer (June 21 - July 22): The Nurturer
Personality: Cancer dogs are deeply emotional, nurturing, and sensitive. They form strong bonds with other dogs and prefer quiet, emotionally secure environments. Cancer dogs may shy away from loud or chaotic social settings, seeking out calm and understanding companions.

Compatible Signs:

- **Taurus:** Both Cancer and Taurus dogs enjoy peaceful environments and emotional connection, creating a bond based on mutual trust and affection.
- **Pisces:** Pisces' intuitive and gentle nature aligns with Cancer's sensitivity, making them ideal companions for emotional support.
- **Virgo:** Virgo's practical care complements Cancer's nurturing tendencies, creating a harmonious balance in their relationship.

Challenging Signs:

- **Aries:** Aries' high-energy and assertiveness can overwhelm the sensitive Cancer, leading to conflicts over play style and boundaries.
- **Sagittarius:** Sagittarius' need for adventure and independence may clash with Cancer's preference for security and emotional connection.

Leo (July 23 - August 22): The Confident Playmate

Personality: Leo dogs are bold, confident, and love to be the center of attention. They enjoy active, playful interactions and often take on leadership roles in social groups. Leo dogs thrive on praise and enjoy showing off their skills to other dogs and humans alike.

Compatible Signs:

- **Aries:** Both Aries and Leo share a love for energetic, competitive play. They enjoy engaging in playful dominance games and respect each other's confidence.
- **Gemini:** Leo's vibrant personality and Gemini's sociability make for a fun-loving and interactive dynamic. They both enjoy engaging with others in playful, high-energy ways.
- **Libra:** Libra's diplomatic nature and Leo's leadership complement each other, allowing for harmonious social interactions and balanced play.

Challenging Signs:

- **Scorpio:** Scorpio's intense emotional nature may conflict with Leo's need for lighthearted play and attention, leading to misunderstandings.
- **Capricorn:** Capricorn's serious and reserved nature can clash with Leo's desire for attention and praise, leading to a disconnect in social interactions

Virgo (August 23 - September 22): The Careful Planner
Personality: Virgo dogs are practical, methodical, and focused. They enjoy structured environments and prefer calm, organized play. Virgo dogs may not be as adventurous as other signs, but they appreciate routines, learning new tasks, and forming close, steady relationships with other dogs.
Compatible Signs:

- **Taurus:** Virgo and Taurus dogs share a love for structure and routine, creating a peaceful and stable companionship. They both enjoy a calm environment and appreciate predictability.
- **Capricorn:** Both Virgo and Capricorn are grounded, focused, and serious, which helps them form a disciplined and harmonious relationship.
- **Cancer:** Cancer's nurturing nature aligns well with Virgo's practical care, creating a balanced relationship based on mutual support and respect.

Challenging Signs:

- **Gemini:** Gemini's unpredictability and love for variety may frustrate Virgo's need for routine and structure, leading to conflict in play styles.
- **Sagittarius:** Sagittarius' free-spirited and adventurous nature may clash with Virgo's careful and cautious approach to social interactions.

Libra (September 23 - October 22): The Diplomat

Personality: Libra dogs are charming, sociable, and diplomatic. They enjoy balance and harmony in social settings and prefer to avoid conflict. Libra dogs thrive in group environments where they can play and interact with multiple dogs, always striving to maintain peace and fairness in their interactions.

Compatible Signs:

- **Gemini:** Libra and Gemini dogs share a love for socializing and playing, creating a dynamic and fun-loving relationship. They both enjoy interacting with others in a balanced way.
- **Leo:** Leo's confidence and Libra's diplomatic nature create a playful yet harmonious dynamic, where both dogs can enjoy each other's company without competing for attention.
- **Sagittarius:** Sagittarius' adventurous spirit and Libra's sociable nature make them great companions for playful and interactive games.

Challenging Signs:

- **Capricorn:** Capricorn's reserved and serious nature may conflict with Libra's need for social interaction and playful engagement.
- **Scorpio:** Scorpio's intense and emotionally focused nature may not align with Libra's lighthearted approach to social interactions, leading to misunderstandings.

Scorpio (October 23 - November 21): The Intense Companion
Personality: Scorpio dogs are intense, focused, and emotionally driven. They form deep bonds with those they trust and can be highly protective of their companions. Scorpio dogs may not be the most playful or sociable, but they value loyalty and seek meaningful, one-on-one connections with other dogs.

Compatible Signs:

- **Cancer:** Scorpio and Cancer dogs share a deep emotional bond, both valuing loyalty and connection. They provide each other with emotional security and understanding.
- **Pisces:** Both Scorpio and Pisces are intuitive and emotionally sensitive, making for a deep and meaningful companionship where they support each other's emotional needs.
- **Virgo:** Virgo's practical care complements Scorpio's emotional intensity, creating a balanced relationship that is grounded in trust and mutual support.

Challenging Signs:

- **Gemini:** Gemini's playful and lighthearted nature may clash with Scorpio's need for deep emotional connection, leading to misunderstandings in social interactions.
- **Leo:** Leo's need for attention and playful dominance may not align with Scorpio's more serious and focused approach to relationships.

Sagittarius (November 22 - December 21): The Adventurer
Personality: Sagittarius dogs are adventurous, independent, and always ready for new experiences. They thrive on outdoor exploration, physical challenges, and spontaneous play. Sagittarius dogs may not always seek out deep emotional connections, but they enjoy playful and active interactions with other dogs.

Compatible Signs:

- **Aries:** Sagittarius and Aries share a love for adventure and high-energy play, making them ideal companions for outdoor activities and exploration.
- **Leo:** Both Sagittarius and Leo enjoy lively and playful interactions, where they can engage in fun, competitive games without feeling constrained.
- **Libra:** Libra's sociable and easygoing nature complements Sagittarius' adventurous spirit, allowing for playful and harmonious companionship.

Challenging Signs:

- **Cancer:** Cancer's need for emotional connection and security may conflict with Sagittarius' independent and free-spirited nature, leading to a disconnect in social interactions.
- **Taurus:** Taurus' preference for routine and stability may not align with Sagittarius' desire for adventure and spontaneity, leading to challenges in compatibility.

Capricorn (December 22 - January 19): The Responsible Friend

Personality: Capricorn dogs are disciplined, serious, and focused. They prefer structured environments and tend to take a more reserved approach to social interactions. While they may not be the most playful, Capricorn dogs value loyalty, trust, and long-lasting relationships with other dogs.

Compatible Signs:

- **Virgo:** Capricorn and Virgo dogs share a love for structure and discipline, creating a harmonious relationship based on mutual respect and routine. They enjoy calm and predictable interactions.
- **Taurus:** Both Capricorn and Taurus appreciate stability and consistency, making them compatible companions who enjoy peaceful and grounded relationships.
- **Scorpio:** Scorpio's emotional depth complements Capricorn's seriousness, creating a balanced relationship where both signs provide loyalty and trust.

Challenging Signs:

- **Leo:** Leo's playful and attention-seeking behavior may not align with Capricorn's more serious and focused nature, leading to misunderstandings in social interactions.
- **Sagittarius:** Sagittarius' free-spirited and adventurous nature may conflict with Capricorn's need for structure and discipline, creating tension in play styles.

Aquarius (January 20 - February 18): The Independent Thinker

Personality: Aquarius dogs are independent, quirky, and full of surprises. They enjoy socializing on their own terms and often approach play in unconventional ways. Aquarius dogs value freedom and may not always follow the rules of group play, preferring to engage in activities that stimulate their curiosity and intellect.

Compatible Signs:

- **Gemini:** Aquarius and Gemini dogs share a love for mental stimulation and social interaction, creating a dynamic and playful relationship where they can explore new ideas and activities together.
- **Libra:** Libra's sociable and easygoing nature complements Aquarius' independent and quirky behavior, allowing for harmonious interactions that respect each dog's unique approach to play.
- **Sagittarius:** Sagittarius' adventurous spirit aligns with Aquarius' love for exploration and new experiences, making them ideal companions for outdoor activities and spontaneous play.

Challenging Signs:

- **Taurus:** Taurus' need for routine and predictability may not align with Aquarius' independent and unpredictable nature, leading to challenges in compatibility.
- **Cancer:** Cancer's emotional sensitivity and need for connection may clash with Aquarius' detached and independent approach to relationships, leading to misunderstandings.

Pisces (February 19 - March 20): The Gentle Companion

Personality: Pisces dogs are gentle, intuitive, and emotionally sensitive. They form deep emotional bonds with their companions and prefer calm, peaceful environments. Pisces dogs are nurturing and enjoy quiet, affectionate interactions with other dogs, often providing emotional support to those around them.

Compatible Signs:

- **Cancer:** Pisces and Cancer dogs share a deep emotional bond, both valuing emotional connection and nurturing relationships. They provide each other with emotional security and support.
- **Taurus:** Taurus' calm and grounded nature complements Pisces' gentle and intuitive approach to relationships, creating a peaceful and harmonious companionship.
- **Scorpio:** Both Pisces and Scorpio are emotionally sensitive and intuitive, making for a deep and meaningful relationship where they can support each other's emotional needs.

Challenging Signs:

- **Gemini:** Gemini's playful and lighthearted nature may clash with Pisces' need for emotional depth and connection, leading to challenges in social interactions.
- **Aries:** Aries' assertive and high-energy behavior may overwhelm Pisces' gentle and sensitive nature, creating tension in play styles.

How to Foster Healthy Dog-to-Dog Relationships

Understanding the unique traits and compatibility of each zodiac sign can help you foster healthy relationships between dogs, whether they are part of the same household or regular playmates at the park. Here are some tips to ensure harmonious interactions between dogs of different astrological signs:

1. **Respect Individual Play Styles:** Each zodiac sign has its own preferred play style and energy level. By recognizing and respecting these differences, you can create play sessions that cater to each dog's needs and preferences. For example, high-energy Aries and Leo dogs may enjoy active games, while calmer Taurus and Cancer dogs may prefer gentle interactions.

2. **Monitor for Signs of Overstimulation:** Some dogs may become overwhelmed or overstimulated by certain play styles or personalities. Pay attention to body language and behavior to ensure that all dogs are comfortable and enjoying the interaction. If necessary, intervene to provide a break or redirect attention to a different activity.

3. **Encourage Positive Socialization:** Positive reinforcement and structured socialization can help dogs of different signs learn to interact in healthy ways. Reward good behavior and encourage cooperative play, especially in group settings where different personalities are interacting.

4. **Provide Emotional Support:** Dogs, like humans, have emotional needs. Ensure that each dog receives the emotional support they require, whether it's through affection, routine, or calm environments. Sensitive signs like Cancer and Pisces may need extra reassurance, while independent signs like Aquarius and Sagittarius may appreciate more freedom and autonomy.

Conclusion

Understanding dog-to-dog compatibility through the lens of astrology can provide valuable insights into your dog's social behavior, preferences, and interactions with other dogs. By recognizing the unique traits and compatibility of each zodiac sign, you can foster harmonious relationships between dogs, create positive play experiences, and ensure that your canine companions thrive in their social lives. Embrace the diverse personalities of each sign and celebrate the special bonds that form between dogs in the astrological canine world.

Chapter 39: Dog-to-Human Compatibility: How Your Dog's Sign Affects Their Relationship with Human Family Members

Astrology is a powerful tool for understanding the dynamic between dogs and their human family members. Each dog's astrological sign reveals unique traits that influence how they bond, communicate, and form relationships with the people around them. Understanding your dog's sign can provide deeper insights into their behavior, preferences, and needs, allowing you to foster a stronger, more harmonious relationship with them.

In this chapter, we will explore how each zodiac sign shapes the relationship between dogs and their human companions. By understanding the natural compatibility between different signs, you can better meet your dog's emotional and physical needs, strengthen your bond, and create a nurturing environment where both you and your dog thrive.

Aries Dogs (March 21 - April 19): The Energetic Leader

Personality: Aries dogs are energetic, bold, and eager to take charge. They are natural leaders who thrive on action and adventure. These dogs need human family members who can match their energy level and offer plenty of physical activities to keep them engaged. Aries dogs are also competitive and may enjoy challenges, making them ideal for families who love outdoor activities and sports.

Best Human Matches:

- **Leo:** Leo humans appreciate the confidence and enthusiasm of an Aries dog, making for a vibrant and dynamic relationship. Both enjoy play and adventure.
- **Sagittarius:** Sagittarius humans are adventurous and independent, traits that align well with Aries' love of action and new experiences.
- **Gemini:** Gemini's playful, curious nature keeps Aries dogs mentally stimulated, creating an exciting, high-energy dynamic between dog and human.

Challenges:

- **Taurus:** Taurus' preference for calm and routine may clash with Aries' need for constant activity and exploration.
- **Capricorn:** Capricorn's disciplined and structured approach may frustrate Aries, who thrives on spontaneity and independence.

Taurus Dogs (April 20 - May 20): The Loyal Companion
Personality: Taurus dogs are calm, affectionate, and reliable. They enjoy stability and routine, making them excellent companions for human family members who value loyalty and consistency. These dogs thrive in environments where they can enjoy comfort, regular meals, and predictable schedules. Taurus dogs are patient and form deep emotional bonds with their humans, often becoming protective of their family.

Best Human Matches:

- **Cancer:** Cancer humans share Taurus' need for emotional connection and security, creating a nurturing and affectionate bond between them.
- **Virgo:** Virgo's love for routine and attention to detail aligns well with Taurus' preference for structure and predictability in daily life.
- **Pisces:** Pisces' gentle, intuitive nature complements Taurus' calm demeanor, creating a peaceful and emotionally fulfilling relationship.

Challenges:

- **Gemini:** Gemini's need for variety and change may clash with Taurus' love for routine and stability, leading to tension over lifestyle preferences.
- **Sagittarius:** Sagittarius' free-spirited and adventurous nature may feel overwhelming to the grounded Taurus, who prefers a slower pace of life.

Gemini Dogs (May 21 - June 20): The Playful Communicator
Personality: Gemini dogs are sociable, curious, and highly communicative. They thrive on mental stimulation and enjoy interacting with their human family members through play, training, and exploration. These dogs need human companions who can keep up with their constant need for new experiences and learning. Gemini dogs are adaptable and can fit into a variety of family dynamics, making them versatile companions.

Best Human Matches:

- **Libra:** Libra humans appreciate Gemini's sociable and playful nature, creating a dynamic where both enjoy constant interaction and mental stimulation.
- **Aquarius:** Aquarius' love for intellectual engagement complements Gemini's curiosity, leading to a relationship full of exploration and discovery.
- **Aries:** Aries' energetic approach to life aligns with Gemini's playfulness, resulting in a lively and active partnership between dog and human.

Challenges:

- **Virgo:** Virgo's practical and focused nature may clash with Gemini's need for variety and unpredictability, leading to frustration over routine.
- **Capricorn:** Capricorn's disciplined, structured approach may feel limiting to Gemini, who thrives on freedom and constant change.

Cancer Dogs (June 21 - July 22): The Nurturing Soul
Personality: Cancer dogs are deeply emotional, sensitive, and nurturing. They form strong emotional bonds with their human family members and often act as protectors and emotional supporters. Cancer dogs are intuitive and can pick up on the moods of the people around them, making them ideal companions for families that value empathy and emotional connection. They need stability and reassurance from their human companions.

Best Human Matches:

- **Taurus:** Taurus' calm, grounded nature provides Cancer with the stability and security they need to feel emotionally secure.
- **Pisces:** Both Cancer and Pisces value emotional connection, creating a deep, intuitive bond where each supports the other's emotional needs.
- **Scorpio:** Scorpio's loyalty and emotional depth align with Cancer's need for emotional support, forming a strong, protective relationship.

Challenges:

- **Aries:** Aries' high-energy and assertiveness may overwhelm the sensitive Cancer, leading to a mismatch in emotional needs.
- **Sagittarius:** Sagittarius' independence and love for adventure may clash with Cancer's desire for emotional closeness and security.

Leo Dogs (July 23 - August 22): The Confident Performer

Personality: Leo dogs are confident, bold, and love being the center of attention. They thrive on praise and affection from their human family members and enjoy showing off their skills. Leo dogs need human companions who appreciate their larger-than-life personality and are willing to shower them with attention. These dogs are natural leaders and enjoy being in the spotlight, making them excellent companions for outgoing, confident families.

Best Human Matches:

- **Aries:** Both Aries and Leo enjoy action, play, and competition, making for a dynamic and fun-loving relationship.
- **Sagittarius:** Sagittarius' adventurous spirit complements Leo's boldness, creating an exciting and energetic dynamic between dog and human.
- **Libra:** Libra's sociable and diplomatic nature aligns with Leo's need for attention, creating a balanced and harmonious relationship.

Challenges:

- **Scorpio:** Scorpio's intense emotional nature may conflict with Leo's need for lighthearted play and constant praise, leading to misunderstandings.
- **Capricorn:** Capricorn's reserved and disciplined approach may not align with Leo's desire for attention and admiration.

Virgo Dogs (August 23 - September 22): The Practical Perfectionist

Personality: Virgo dogs are practical, disciplined, and focused. They thrive in structured environments where they can engage in purposeful activities, such as training or working alongside their human family members. These dogs enjoy routines and appreciate attention to detail. Virgo dogs are loyal and prefer calm, predictable environments where they can form close, steady relationships with their human companions.

Best Human Matches:

- **Taurus:** Virgo and Taurus share a love for routine and stability, creating a peaceful and harmonious bond between them.
- **Capricorn:** Both Virgo and Capricorn value discipline and structure, making them compatible companions who enjoy organized and purposeful activities together.
- **Cancer:** Cancer's nurturing nature complements Virgo's practical care, creating a balanced relationship where emotional and physical needs are met.

Challenges:

- **Gemini:** Gemini's unpredictable and playful nature may clash with Virgo's need for routine and order, leading to frustration in daily interactions.
- **Sagittarius:** Sagittarius' adventurous and spontaneous approach may conflict with Virgo's preference for structure and careful planning.

Libra Dogs (September 23 - October 22): The Social Diplomat
Personality: Libra dogs are charming, sociable, and diplomatic. They thrive on interaction and enjoy being around people and other animals. These dogs are natural peacemakers, preferring to avoid conflict and maintain harmony in their environment. Libra dogs are ideal for families who value socialization and balance, and they need human companions who appreciate their easygoing, cooperative nature.

Best Human Matches:

- **Gemini:** Both Libra and Gemini enjoy socializing and mental stimulation, creating a lively and engaging relationship full of interaction.
- **Leo:** Leo's confidence and Libra's diplomacy create a harmonious and balanced dynamic where both dog and human enjoy each other's company.
- **Aquarius:** Aquarius' independent but sociable nature aligns well with Libra's need for companionship and balanced interactions.

Challenges:

- **Capricorn:** Capricorn's disciplined, serious nature may feel too rigid for Libra's need for balance and social interaction, leading to tension in the relationship.
- **Scorpio:** Scorpio's emotional intensity may clash with Libra's preference for lighthearted, conflict-free interactions, leading to misunderstandings.

Scorpio Dogs (October 23 - November 21): The Intense Protector

Personality: Scorpio dogs are intense, loyal, and deeply emotional. They form strong bonds with their human family members and are highly protective of those they love. These dogs need human companions who can match their emotional depth and provide them with a sense of security. Scorpio dogs thrive in environments where they feel a deep connection to their humans, and they may be wary of strangers or new situations.

Best Human Matches:

- **Cancer:** Both Scorpio and Cancer value emotional connection and loyalty, creating a deep, intuitive bond between them.
- **Pisces:** Pisces' gentle, intuitive nature complements Scorpio's emotional intensity, resulting in a relationship full of understanding and emotional support.
- **Virgo:** Virgo's practical care provides a stabilizing influence for Scorpio's emotional depth, creating a balanced relationship.

Challenges:

- **Gemini:** Gemini's playful, lighthearted nature may clash with Scorpio's need for emotional connection and intensity, leading to misunderstandings.
- **Leo:** Leo's need for attention and constant praise may conflict with Scorpio's focus on emotional depth and loyalty.

Sagittarius Dogs (November 22 - December 21): The Adventurous Spirit

Personality: Sagittarius dogs are adventurous, independent, and always ready for new experiences. They thrive on outdoor activities, exploration, and spontaneous play. Sagittarius dogs need human companions who enjoy adventure and can provide them with the freedom to explore their environment. These dogs are ideal for families who value independence and outdoor activities, and they form strong bonds through shared experiences.

Best Human Matches:

- **Aries:** Both Sagittarius and Aries share a love for adventure and action, making them ideal companions for outdoor exploration and high-energy play.
- **Leo:** Leo's confidence and Sagittarius' adventurous spirit create a dynamic relationship full of excitement and mutual admiration.
- **Aquarius:** Aquarius' independent nature complements Sagittarius' need for freedom, resulting in a relationship where both dog and human enjoy exploring new experiences together.

Challenges:

- **Cancer:** Cancer's emotional need for security and stability may clash with Sagittarius' desire for independence and adventure, leading to tension in the relationship.
- **Taurus:** Taurus' preference for routine and predictability may feel limiting to Sagittarius, who thrives on spontaneity and change.

Capricorn Dogs (December 22 - January 19): The Responsible Partner

Personality: Capricorn dogs are disciplined, focused, and responsible. They thrive in structured environments where they can take on meaningful roles, such as guarding the home or assisting with daily routines. Capricorn dogs need human companions who appreciate their loyalty, work ethic, and need for routine. These dogs are ideal for families who value discipline and enjoy engaging their dog in purposeful activities.

Best Human Matches:

- **Virgo:** Capricorn and Virgo share a love for structure and discipline, creating a harmonious relationship where both dog and human appreciate routine and order.
- **Taurus:** Both Capricorn and Taurus enjoy stability and consistency, making them ideal companions for families who value peaceful, grounded relationships.
- **Scorpio:** Scorpio's loyalty and emotional depth complement Capricorn's disciplined approach, creating a relationship built on trust and mutual respect.

Challenges:

- **Leo:** Leo's playful, attention-seeking behavior may clash with Capricorn's more serious and focused nature, leading to misunderstandings in the relationship.
- **Sagittarius:** Sagittarius' free-spirited and adventurous approach may feel chaotic to Capricorn, who prefers structure and routine.

Aquarius Dogs (January 20 - February 18): The Independent Thinker

Personality: Aquarius dogs are independent, quirky, and full of surprises. They enjoy intellectual stimulation and social interaction but value their autonomy. Aquarius dogs need human companions who respect their independence while providing opportunities for exploration and mental engagement. These dogs thrive in environments where they can explore new ideas and activities, making them ideal for families who value creativity and freedom.

Best Human Matches:

- **Gemini:** Aquarius and Gemini share a love for intellectual stimulation and social interaction, creating a dynamic relationship full of exploration and discovery.
- **Libra:** Libra's sociable and easygoing nature aligns well with Aquarius' independent, yet social behavior, resulting in a balanced and harmonious relationship.
- **Sagittarius:** Sagittarius' adventurous spirit complements Aquarius' love for exploration, making them excellent companions for outdoor activities and new experiences.

Challenges:

- **Taurus:** Taurus' need for routine and predictability may feel limiting to Aquarius, who thrives on freedom and spontaneity.
- **Cancer:** Cancer's emotional sensitivity and need for connection may clash with Aquarius' detached and independent nature, leading to misunderstandings.

Pisces Dogs (February 19 - March 20): The Gentle Dreamer
Personality: Pisces dogs are gentle, intuitive, and emotionally sensitive. They form deep bonds with their human family members and thrive in peaceful, nurturing environments. Pisces dogs need human companions who can provide them with emotional security and a calm atmosphere. These dogs are ideal for families who value empathy, emotional connection, and quiet companionship.

Best Human Matches:

- **Cancer:** Pisces and Cancer share a deep emotional bond, both valuing emotional connection and nurturing relationships. They provide each other with emotional security and support.
- **Taurus:** Taurus' calm and grounded nature complements Pisces' gentle and intuitive approach to relationships, creating a peaceful and harmonious companionship.
- **Scorpio:** Scorpio's emotional intensity aligns with Pisces' deep emotional sensitivity, creating a relationship where both dog and human provide loyalty and understanding.

Challenges:

- **Gemini:** Gemini's playful and lighthearted nature may clash with Pisces' need for emotional depth and connection, leading to challenges in forming a close bond.
- **Aries:** Aries' assertive and high-energy behavior may overwhelm Pisces' gentle and sensitive nature, leading to tension in their relationship.

How to Foster Strong Dog-to-Human Relationships

Understanding the astrological traits of both your dog and yourself can enhance the bond between you and your canine companion. Here are some tips to ensure a harmonious relationship between you and your dog, based on their zodiac sign:

1. **Meet Their Emotional Needs:**

   Each zodiac sign has unique emotional needs. Sensitive signs like Cancer and Pisces may need extra reassurance, while independent signs like Aquarius and Sagittarius require more freedom. By recognizing and addressing these needs, you can create a stronger emotional bond.

2. **Tailor Activities to Their Preferences:**

   Active and adventurous signs like Aries, Leo, and Sagittarius will appreciate outdoor activities and high-energy play, while calmer signs like Taurus, Virgo, and Capricorn thrive on routine and structured activities. Tailoring activities to your dog's preferences will keep them happy and engaged.

3. **Communicate Based on Their Traits:**

   Communication is key to building a strong relationship with your dog. Signs like Gemini and Libra enjoy social interaction and mental stimulation, so engaging in training and play that challenges their mind is important. For more introspective signs like Scorpio and Capricorn, quiet bonding moments may be more meaningful.

4. **Provide Consistent Routines:**

   Many signs, especially Taurus, Virgo, and Capricorn, thrive on routine and structure. Ensuring that feeding, walks, and playtime occur regularly will help them feel secure and balanced. For more free-spirited signs like Sagittarius and Aquarius, adding variety and adventure into their routine is key.

Conclusion

Understanding your dog's astrological sign can provide deep insights into their relationship with human family members. By recognizing the unique traits of each sign and catering to their emotional and physical needs, you can foster a harmonious and fulfilling bond with your canine companion. Embrace your dog's personality, celebrate their strengths, and create a nurturing environment where your dog can thrive alongside their human family.

Chapter 40: Dog-to-Environment Compatibility: Creating the Perfect Living Environment Based on Your Dog's Astrological Sign

Just as humans have preferences for the type of environment that best suits their personality and lifestyle, dogs also have environmental needs that align with their astrological signs. By understanding your dog's zodiac sign, you can create a living environment that supports their well-being, comfort, and overall happiness. The right environment can enhance their emotional stability, reduce stress, and encourage positive behaviors. Whether your dog thrives in a quiet, cozy home or prefers outdoor adventures and constant stimulation, tailoring their surroundings to match their astrological traits can make a significant difference in their daily life.

In this chapter, we will explore how each zodiac sign influences a dog's environmental preferences, providing insights into what types of living spaces, activities, and routines will best support their astrological needs. By designing an environment that aligns with your dog's natural tendencies, you can help them feel secure, engaged, and content.

Aries Dogs (March 21 - April 19): The Adventurous Explorer

Personality: Aries dogs are bold, energetic, and always ready for adventure. They thrive in environments that allow for physical activity and exploration. These dogs need space to run, play, and engage in high-energy activities. A home environment with access to the outdoors, such as a large yard or nearby park, is ideal for Aries dogs. They enjoy challenges and stimulation, so interactive toys and obstacle courses can keep them engaged.

Ideal Environment:

- **Outdoor Space:** A large yard or regular trips to a park where they can run and explore freely.
- **Adventure Opportunities:** Access to hiking trails, beaches, or new places to explore will keep Aries dogs mentally and physically stimulated.
- **Active Household:** A home with active family members who enjoy physical activities and can keep up with their energy level.

Key Features to Include:

- High-energy toys like Frisbees, balls, and agility equipment.
- A dog-friendly garden or outdoor space where they can roam and burn off energy.
- Rotating interactive toys to keep them mentally stimulated and challenged.

Taurus Dogs (April 20 - May 20): The Comfort Seeker
Personality: Taurus dogs are calm, steady, and enjoy the finer things in life. They thrive in comfortable, cozy environments where they can relax and enjoy a stable routine. Taurus dogs appreciate consistency and will feel happiest in a home that offers them plenty of soft, comfortable places to rest. These dogs also enjoy routines and will appreciate a predictable schedule for walks, meals, and naps.

Ideal Environment:

- **Comfortable and Cozy:** A home with soft bedding, cozy corners, and a calm, peaceful atmosphere.
- **Routine and Predictability:** A stable environment with consistent feeding and walk times, allowing them to feel secure.
- **Quiet Spaces:** Areas where they can rest undisturbed, away from loud noises or frequent disruptions.

Key Features to Include:

- High-quality, comfortable beds placed in quiet corners of the home.
- A cozy nook where they can retreat when they need alone time.
- Consistent daily routines for walks, meals, and relaxation.

Gemini Dogs (May 21 - June 20): The Social Butterfly

Personality: Gemini dogs are curious, playful, and love mental stimulation. They thrive in dynamic environments that offer variety and constant engagement. These dogs enjoy social interactions and need opportunities to explore new sights, sounds, and experiences. A busy household with multiple people or other pets can keep a Gemini dog entertained, as they love to engage with their environment and those around them.

Ideal Environment:

- **Interactive and Stimulating:** A home filled with toys, puzzles, and opportunities for mental engagement.
- **Social Interaction:** A household with plenty of people or other pets to interact with, ensuring they always have company.
- **Variety and Change:** Regular changes to their environment, such as new toys, rearranged furniture, or new experiences, keep them mentally stimulated.

Key Features to Include:

- Interactive toys and puzzles that challenge their intelligence.
- Social activities like trips to dog parks, playdates with other dogs, or interaction with visitors.
- Access to windows or lookout spots where they can observe the outside world.

Cancer Dogs (June 21 - July 22): The Homebody

Personality: Cancer dogs are deeply emotional, nurturing, and enjoy quiet, comfortable environments where they feel secure. These dogs are very sensitive to their surroundings and thrive in homes that provide emotional warmth and stability. A home that offers cozy resting spots, calm energy, and emotional connection with their human family is ideal for Cancer dogs. They may prefer homes with quiet corners where they can retreat and feel safe.

Ideal Environment:

- **Safe and Secure:** A calm, peaceful home where they feel emotionally secure and close to their family.
- **Emotional Bonding:** Spaces where they can spend quiet time with their family members, whether curled up on the couch or resting nearby.
- **Comfortable Retreats:** Soft, comfortable bedding in quiet areas where they can retreat when feeling emotionally overwhelmed.

Key Features to Include:

- A cozy bed placed in a quiet, low-traffic area of the home.
- A home where they can stay close to their family, as they thrive on emotional connection.
- A calm, predictable environment free from sudden loud noises or frequent changes.

Leo Dogs (July 23 - August 22): The Royalty

Personality: Leo dogs are bold, confident, and love being the center of attention. They thrive in environments that allow them to show off their skills and receive praise. Leo dogs enjoy spaces where they can be seen, whether it's a favorite spot by the window or a place near the heart of the home where family members frequently gather. They love attention and will appreciate an environment that recognizes their need for affection and admiration.

Ideal Environment:

- **Central Location:** A place where they can be at the center of family activity, receiving attention and praise.
- **Space to Show Off:** Areas where they can display their skills, such as a yard for running or performing tricks.
- **Comfortable Seating:** As royalty, Leo dogs appreciate comfortable resting places, especially those that are visible to the rest of the household.

Key Features to Include:

- A window seat or perch where they can observe their kingdom.
- Regular opportunities for praise and positive attention, through training, play, or grooming sessions.
- Soft bedding placed in a prominent area of the house where they can comfortably rest and be admired.

Virgo Dogs (August 23 - September 22): The Neat Freak

Personality: Virgo dogs are practical, organized, and thrive in clean, structured environments. They appreciate order and predictability, making them excellent companions for households that value cleanliness and routine. Virgo dogs are sensitive to their surroundings and prefer environments that are tidy and well-maintained. They may become stressed in chaotic or cluttered environments, so a clean and well-organized home is ideal for them.

Ideal Environment:

- **Tidy and Organized:** A clean, clutter-free home where everything has its place.
- **Routine and Structure:** A home with a consistent routine, ensuring they know when to expect walks, meals, and rest times.
- **Calm and Predictable:** A peaceful environment where they can avoid chaos or sudden changes.

Key Features to Include:

- A designated space for their belongings, such as toys, bedding, and bowls.
- A regular schedule for feeding, exercise, and grooming.
- Calm and quiet areas where they can retreat if they need a break from noise or activity.

Libra Dogs (September 23 - October 22): The Harmonizer
Personality: Libra dogs are social, charming, and seek harmony in their environment. They thrive in aesthetically pleasing, balanced spaces where they can interact with their human companions and feel at peace. Libra dogs enjoy being surrounded by beauty and comfort, and they prefer homes that are well-decorated and calming. They appreciate environments where there is a balance between activity and relaxation, allowing them to engage socially but also rest when needed.

Ideal Environment:

- **Beautiful and Balanced:** A home with a harmonious, aesthetically pleasing design that makes them feel calm and comfortable.
- **Social Spaces:** Areas where they can interact with their family members and other pets, as they thrive on companionship.
- **Comfortable Resting Spots:** Soft bedding in quiet corners where they can rest after socializing.

Key Features to Include:

- A balanced living space with comfortable furniture and calming decor.
- Access to both active areas where they can socialize and quiet areas where they can retreat.
- Toys and accessories that are not only functional but also aesthetically pleasing, creating a harmonious environment.

Scorpio Dogs (October 23 - November 21): The Intense Protector

Personality: Scorpio dogs are intense, loyal, and protective. They thrive in environments that offer emotional security and privacy. These dogs need a home where they feel safe and can retreat to quiet, private spaces when they need alone time. Scorpio dogs form deep emotional bonds with their family members, so they prefer environments where they can be close to their humans while also having access to secure, enclosed spaces where they can rest undisturbed.

Ideal Environment:

- **Private and Secure:** A home with quiet, private spaces where they can retreat when feeling overwhelmed or needing rest.
- **Emotional Bonding:** Spaces where they can stay close to their family members and form strong emotional connections.
- **Protection Zones:** Enclosed areas or corners where they feel safe and protected.

Key Features to Include:

- A private, enclosed bed or crate where they can rest without disturbances.
- A home with low foot traffic, ensuring they have quiet areas to retreat to when needed.
- Regular interaction with their family members, as they need emotional bonding to feel secure.

Sagittarius Dogs (November 22 - December 21): The Free Spirit

Personality: Sagittarius dogs are adventurous, independent, and always ready for exploration. They thrive in environments that offer plenty of space and opportunities for outdoor activities. These dogs love freedom and need a home with access to nature, whether it's a large backyard, regular trips to hiking trails, or outdoor adventures. Sagittarius dogs enjoy environments that allow for physical activity and mental stimulation, as they get bored easily in confined spaces.

Ideal Environment:

- **Outdoor Access:** A home with a large yard or access to outdoor spaces where they can run, explore, and play.
- **Adventure Opportunities:** A household that enjoys outdoor activities, such as hiking, camping, or long walks in nature.
- **Spontaneous Atmosphere:** An environment that embraces spontaneity, allowing them to explore new places and experiences.

Key Features to Include:

- A secure backyard where they can roam freely and explore.
- Regular outings to parks, beaches, or hiking trails to satisfy their need for adventure.
- Interactive toys and puzzles to keep them mentally engaged when indoors.

Capricorn Dogs (December 22 - January 19): The Responsible Worker

Personality: Capricorn dogs are disciplined, focused, and responsible. They thrive in structured environments where they can take on meaningful roles or tasks, such as guarding the home or assisting with daily routines. Capricorn dogs appreciate order and routine and prefer homes that are organized and peaceful. They feel most comfortable in environments where they have a clear sense of purpose and stability.

Ideal Environment:

- **Structured and Organized:** A home with a clear routine and designated spaces for their belongings.
- **Purposeful Roles:** Opportunities to take on roles, such as guarding the home or participating in training or tasks.
- **Calm and Disciplined:** A peaceful, well-ordered environment where they can avoid chaos and distractions.

Key Features to Include:

- A designated spot for their bed, food bowls, and toys, ensuring everything has its place.
- Regular training sessions or activities that give them a sense of purpose and responsibility.
- A quiet, structured environment where they can feel secure and focused.

Aquarius Dogs (January 20 - February 18): The Independent Innovator

Personality: Aquarius dogs are independent, quirky, and full of surprises. They thrive in environments that offer freedom, mental stimulation, and the ability to explore their surroundings. Aquarius dogs enjoy homes where they can express their individuality, engage with interactive toys, and have the freedom to come and go as they please. They prefer environments that challenge their intellect and provide opportunities for independent play.

Ideal Environment:

- **Freedom and Flexibility:** A home that allows for exploration and independence, such as a yard or open spaces.
- **Mental Stimulation:** A variety of interactive toys and puzzles to keep them intellectually engaged.
- **Creative Atmosphere:** An environment that encourages innovation, such as introducing new toys, changing routines, or offering new experiences.

Key Features to Include:

- Access to outdoor spaces where they can explore independently.
- Interactive toys and puzzles that challenge their intelligence and curiosity.
- Freedom to choose their activities, whether it's playing, resting, or exploring.

Pisces Dogs (February 19 - March 20): The Dreamer
Personality: Pisces dogs are gentle, intuitive, and emotionally sensitive. They thrive in peaceful, nurturing environments where they feel safe and emotionally secure. Pisces dogs enjoy quiet, calm spaces where they can relax and dream, and they often form strong emotional bonds with their human companions. These dogs prefer homes that provide emotional comfort and security, with soft bedding and quiet corners where they can retreat when they need alone time.

Ideal Environment:

- **Calm and Peaceful:** A quiet, serene home where they can feel emotionally secure and protected.
- **Soft and Cozy:** Comfortable, soft bedding in quiet areas where they can relax and rest.
- **Emotional Connection:** Spaces where they can stay close to their family members, forming strong emotional bonds.

Key Features to Include:

- A cozy bed or blanket in a peaceful corner of the home.
- Calming music or soft lighting to create a relaxing atmosphere.
- Access to quiet spaces where they can retreat when they need emotional rest.

Conclusion

Understanding your dog's astrological sign can provide valuable insights into their environmental preferences, helping you create the perfect living space that supports their well-being, comfort, and happiness. By tailoring your dog's environment to their astrological traits, you can ensure that they feel secure, engaged, and content in their home. Whether your dog thrives in a bustling, social environment or prefers a quiet, cozy retreat, creating a space that aligns with their needs will enhance their emotional and physical health, fostering a stronger bond between you and your canine companion.

Conclusion

Chapter 41: Bringing It All Together: Synthesizing All the Information to Better Understand and Care for Your Dog

Understanding your dog's astrological sign is a powerful tool for enhancing your relationship with them. Throughout this book, we have explored the influence of the zodiac on your dog's personality, behavior, preferences, and needs. From how your dog interacts with other dogs and humans, to their ideal living environment, and the role of planetary influences like the Sun, Moon, and planets—every detail we've covered provides a deeper understanding of how astrology can shape your dog's world.

In this final chapter, we will bring together all the key insights to help you synthesize this information into practical steps for caring for your dog. By combining astrological knowledge with everyday pet care, you can create a nurturing environment that aligns with your dog's natural tendencies, making them feel understood, loved, and supported.

The Importance of Knowing Your Dog's Zodiac Sign

Your dog's zodiac sign reveals core aspects of their personality, guiding you in how to best care for, train, and bond with them. By paying attention to their astrological traits, you can:

- **Enhance Communication:** Dogs express themselves in various ways, and knowing their astrological sign can help you understand how they communicate, their emotional needs, and how they respond to your cues. For example, a Gemini dog may communicate more with playful behavior, while a Cancer dog might express emotions through close physical proximity.

- **Support Emotional Well-Being:** Each sign has its emotional needs. Sensitive signs like Pisces and Cancer thrive on emotional connection and reassurance, while more independent signs like Sagittarius and Aquarius appreciate space and freedom.

- **Tailor Activities to Personality:** Knowing your dog's sign can help you tailor activities that match their natural preferences. Active and adventurous signs, like Aries or Leo, need plenty of physical play, while calmer signs, such as Taurus or Virgo, prefer structured routines and peaceful environments.

- **Improve Social Interactions:** Understanding your dog's compatibility with other dogs and humans based on their zodiac sign can guide you in fostering harmonious relationships. You'll know what to expect in dog-to-dog interactions and which family members may naturally bond more closely with your dog.

Key Themes Across the Zodiac: A Quick Recap

Each sign provides a unique blueprint for understanding your dog. Let's briefly recap the core traits of each sign and how they affect your dog's behavior, environment, and relationships:

- **Aries (March 21 - April 19):** Bold, energetic, and adventurous. Aries dogs thrive on physical activity, mental challenges, and leadership roles.
- **Taurus (April 20 - May 20):** Loyal, calm, and comfort-seeking. Taurus dogs prefer routine, comfort, and stability in a peaceful home environment.
- **Gemini (May 21 - June 20):** Social, curious, and playful. Gemini dogs need mental stimulation, social interaction, and variety in their daily lives.
- **Cancer (June 21 - July 22):** Nurturing, emotional, and protective. Cancer dogs crave emotional connection, a secure home, and calm surroundings.
- **Leo (July 23 - August 22):** Confident, bold, and attention-seeking. Leo dogs love to be in the spotlight, receiving praise and admiration in an active, social environment.
- **Virgo (August 23 - September 22):** Practical, disciplined, and focused. Virgo dogs thrive on routine, organization, and purposeful tasks.

- **Libra (September 23 - October 22):** Sociable, charming, and balanced. Libra dogs enjoy harmony, aesthetics, and companionship in a peaceful, well-organized home.
- **Scorpio (October 23 - November 21):** Intense, loyal, and protective. Scorpio dogs need emotional security, private spaces, and deep connections with their family.
- **Sagittarius (November 22 - December 21):** Adventurous, independent, and free-spirited. Sagittarius dogs love outdoor exploration, new experiences, and mental stimulation.
- **Capricorn (December 22 - January 19):** Disciplined, responsible, and loyal. Capricorn dogs thrive on structure, routine, and purposeful roles in a quiet, organized home.
- **Aquarius (January 20 - February 18):** Independent, quirky, and intellectual. Aquarius dogs need freedom, mental stimulation, and room to explore and be creative.
- **Pisces (February 19 - March 20):** Gentle, intuitive, and emotionally sensitive. Pisces dogs prefer calm, peaceful environments with strong emotional connections.

Practical Tips for Integrating Astrology Into Dog Care

Understanding your dog's zodiac sign can transform how you approach their care and daily routine. Here are practical ways to integrate astrology into various aspects of your dog's life:

1. Routine and Daily Life

Each dog's sign dictates their ideal routine. Some dogs need a fast-paced, ever-changing environment, while others thrive in a predictable and steady setting.

- **Active Dogs (Aries, Leo, Sagittarius):** Incorporate plenty of physical exercise, outdoor adventures, and spontaneous activities.
- **Calm Dogs (Taurus, Virgo, Pisces):** Stick to regular, calming routines with consistent feeding, walking, and resting schedules.

- **Sociable Dogs (Gemini, Libra, Aquarius):** Provide opportunities for social interactions through playdates, visits to the park, or family gatherings.

2. Training and Discipline

Each zodiac sign responds differently to training. Tailor your approach based on your dog's temperament:

- **Focused Signs (Virgo, Capricorn):** These dogs appreciate structure and discipline. Use consistent, clear commands and reward systems to encourage positive behavior.
- **Playful Signs (Gemini, Aries, Leo):** Make training sessions fun and dynamic. Use games and praise to keep them engaged and excited to learn.
- **Sensitive Signs (Cancer, Scorpio, Pisces):** Use gentle, patient methods, and focus on building trust. Avoid harsh reprimands, as these dogs can become emotionally affected by negative training experiences.

3. Emotional Bonding and Connection

Understanding your dog's emotional needs based on their sign will help you strengthen your bond.

- **Emotionally Sensitive Dogs (Cancer, Pisces, Scorpio):** Spend quality time offering physical affection, calm energy, and reassurance. These dogs need emotional closeness to feel secure.
- **Independent Dogs (Sagittarius, Aquarius, Aries):** Give them the space to explore and engage on their terms. They value freedom but will come to you for bonding when they are ready.
- **Sociable Dogs (Gemini, Libra, Leo):** Engage in interactive play and spend time with them in group settings, as these dogs enjoy being surrounded by family members or other pets.

4. Living Environment

Create a home environment that aligns with your dog's astrological needs:

- **Adventure Seekers (Aries, Sagittarius):** Ensure they have access to outdoor spaces where they can burn off energy. Regular trips to parks or hiking trails are ideal.
- **Homebodies (Taurus, Cancer, Virgo):** Provide cozy, comfortable areas where they can relax and feel secure. A quiet home with soft bedding and peaceful corners is best.
- **Mentally Stimulated Dogs (Gemini, Aquarius):** Rotate interactive toys and puzzles to keep them engaged and curious. Give them access to stimulating environments that encourage exploration and learning.

Building a Strong, Lasting Relationship With Your Dog

By synthesizing all the information about your dog's astrological sign, you can cultivate a deep, harmonious relationship that nurtures their unique qualities. Here are a few final tips to bring it all together:

- **Stay Attuned to Their Needs:** Astrology gives you insight into your dog's emotional, physical, and mental needs. By being attuned to these aspects, you can anticipate their preferences and moods, helping them feel understood and cared for.
- **Adapt as They Grow:** Just as humans evolve, so do dogs. As they grow and mature, their astrological influences may shift subtly. Pay attention to how their behavior changes over time and adjust your care accordingly.
- **Celebrate Their Uniqueness:** Each dog is special and deserves to be celebrated for who they are. Astrology helps you recognize their individuality and provides guidance on how to support their natural strengths and address their challenges.

Conclusion: A Deeper Connection Through Astrology

Astrology offers a unique lens through which we can understand and care for our dogs. By integrating the wisdom of the zodiac into everyday life, you can foster a deeper connection, provide tailored care, and ensure your dog thrives in all aspects of their life. Whether it's understanding their emotional needs, adjusting their environment, or guiding their behavior, the stars provide valuable insights that enhance the human-dog relationship.

With all this knowledge in hand, you're now equipped to offer your dog the love, support, and care that best suits their astrological sign. Embrace this newfound understanding, and watch as your bond with your dog strengthens and flourishes.

Chapter 42: AstroPaws Community: Resources, Support Groups, and Online Communities for Dog Astrology Enthusiasts

As dog lovers and astrology enthusiasts, combining these passions creates a unique and vibrant community of like-minded individuals who share a deep connection to both the stars and their furry companions. The **AstroPaws Community** is growing, with people around the world engaging in discussions, sharing insights, and offering support as they learn how astrological influences shape the lives and behaviors of their dogs. Whether you're new to dog astrology or a seasoned enthusiast, connecting with others in this space can deepen your understanding, provide valuable resources, and offer a sense of camaraderie with fellow astrology fans.

In this chapter, we will explore the resources, support groups, and online communities available for dog astrology enthusiasts. You'll find information on where to connect with others, how to stay updated on astrological trends that impact dogs, and ways to actively participate in a thriving community that celebrates both astrology and canine care.

Why Join the AstroPaws Community?

Being part of the AstroPaws community offers numerous benefits, whether you're looking for advice, seeking to share experiences, or hoping to learn more about how astrology influences your dog's behavior. Here are just a few reasons why joining this community can enhance your journey:

- **Shared Knowledge:** By joining an online group or community, you can learn from others who have studied dog astrology and gain valuable insights from their experiences.
- **Support and Guidance:** Community members often provide emotional and practical support when dealing with challenging dog behaviors or when looking for ways to understand your dog's astrological traits better.

- **Latest Astrological Trends:** Keep up with the latest astrological movements (like retrogrades, eclipses, or full moons) and how they might affect your dog's mood, energy, or behavior.
- **Friendship and Camaraderie:** Connect with other dog lovers who are just as passionate about astrology as you are, forging friendships and bonds through shared interests.

Online Resources for Dog Astrology Enthusiasts

The internet is full of valuable resources that provide information and insights into dog astrology. From websites to blogs, there are plenty of places where you can expand your knowledge, stay informed, and explore different facets of dog astrology.

1. Dog Astrology Websites

A number of websites are dedicated to the intersection of astrology and pet care, offering horoscopes, behavior tips, and in-depth analyses of how different planetary movements impact pets. Some of the most popular websites include:

- **AstroPets.com:** This site provides daily and weekly astrological updates on how celestial events affect your dog, as well as detailed zodiac breakdowns for all types of pets.
- **StarryPaws.net:** Offering detailed horoscopes for dogs based on their birth sign, StarryPaws provides comprehensive articles and tools for tracking planetary influences on your dog's mood and behavior.
- **Pet Astrology Blog:** This blog focuses on understanding how the Moon's phases, eclipses, and planetary retrogrades influence dogs' emotional and physical well-being.

2. Online Dog Astrology Horoscopes

Many astrology-focused websites offer dog horoscopes alongside human ones. Some of the top astrology sites also cater to pet astrology, providing monthly or weekly updates on what to expect for dogs of different zodiac signs. Popular choices include:

- **Astro.com Pet Horoscopes:** Check regular dog horoscopes for insights into your dog's moods, preferences, and the best time for training or bonding.
- **AstrologyZone Pets:** Susan Miller's AstrologyZone often includes updates on how celestial movements affect pets, including dogs. This can be helpful for timing major decisions like training sessions, adoption, or changes in routine.

3. Books on Dog Astrology

For those looking to deepen their knowledge of astrology and pets, several books combine these two interests. Some recommended titles include:

- **"Star Signs for Pets: How Astrology Shapes Your Pet's Personality"** by Jackie Ford – A book that dives deep into each zodiac sign and its influence on pets, with a special section on dogs.
- **"Astrology for Dogs: Unlocking the Mysteries of the Canine Zodiac"** by Helena Kingsley – A comprehensive guide to understanding how astrological traits shape your dog's behavior, needs, and compatibility with humans and other pets.

Support Groups and Forums

If you're looking for a more interactive experience, support groups and online forums are excellent places to connect with other dog astrology enthusiasts. Here, you can ask questions, share stories, and engage in lively discussions about astrological trends and their impact on dogs. Some popular platforms include:

1. Facebook Groups

Facebook is home to a wide array of groups focused on astrology and pets, where you can find daily updates, participate in discussions, and get advice from experienced members.

- **Dog Astrology Enthusiasts:** A growing community where members post daily dog horoscopes, share stories about how astrology has helped them understand their pets, and offer advice on managing behavior based on zodiac signs.
- **Astrology for Pets and Owners:** This group caters to both dog and cat owners, providing insights on how astrological movements affect pets and how owners can align with their animals' celestial energy.

2. Reddit Communities

Reddit offers a number of astrology-related subreddits where users discuss how the stars impact not only humans but also pets, especially dogs. Some notable communities include:

- **r/AstrologyPets:** A subreddit dedicated to discussing pet astrology, with a focus on how different zodiac signs affect dogs' personalities, health, and behavior. Members often share stories and ask questions about specific astrological events and their influence on dogs.
- **r/DogAstrology:** A smaller but dedicated community where dog owners discuss astrology as it relates to their furry friends, with regular threads on dog horoscopes, moon phases, and compatibility with other pets and humans.

3. Astrology Forums

Astrology forums often have sections dedicated to pet astrology, where users can post about their experiences, ask questions, and share insights.

- **AstroSeek Forum – Pet Astrology:** This forum includes a special section on astrology and pets, where dog lovers exchange ideas, offer advice, and explore astrological events' impact on their dogs' moods and behaviors.
- **AstroCafe Forum – Pets and the Stars:** An active community where users discuss celestial influences on their pets, with regular updates on planetary movements and what they mean for your dog.

In-Person Meetups and Workshops

For those looking to connect offline, local meetups and workshops are great ways to engage with other dog astrology enthusiasts. Some communities offer in-person events that combine pet care with astrology, such as:

- **Dog Astrology Workshops:** These workshops provide hands-on guidance on understanding your dog's zodiac sign and how to incorporate astrological insights into your dog's daily care. Some workshops may also offer personalized astrological readings for dogs.
- **Astrology and Pet Wellness Events:** Many holistic pet care events include discussions on astrology and how to use it to enhance your dog's emotional and physical health. Check local pet wellness centers or metaphysical shops for upcoming events.

Building Your Own AstroPaws Community

If you can't find a local group or forum that resonates with you, why not start your own AstroPaws community? By creating a group, blog, or social media account dedicated to dog astrology, you can bring together fellow enthusiasts who share your passion. Here are a few tips to get started:

1. **Create a Facebook Group or Instagram Account:** Start by sharing insights, daily horoscopes, or stories about your own dog and how astrology influences their behavior. Invite friends and fellow dog lovers to join, and encourage discussions around astrological trends.

2. **Host Virtual Meetups:** Use platforms like Zoom or Google Meet to host virtual discussions, where community members can share tips, insights, and stories about their dogs and astrology.

3. **Start a Blog or YouTube Channel:** Share your knowledge and passion for dog astrology by creating a blog or YouTube channel dedicated to the topic. Offer tips, horoscopes, and advice on how to understand dogs based on their astrological sign.

Conclusion: Joining the AstroPaws Movement

The AstroPaws community is an exciting and ever-growing space where dog lovers and astrology enthusiasts come together to share knowledge, provide support, and celebrate their love for both the stars and their furry companions. Whether you're engaging in online discussions, attending workshops, or creating your own community, being part of this movement allows you to deepen your understanding of your dog and connect with others who share your passion.

As you continue your journey in dog astrology, remember that you're not alone. There's a whole world of fellow enthusiasts eager to learn, share, and grow with you. By joining the AstroPaws community, you'll gain valuable insights, form meaningful connections, and discover even more ways to enrich your dog's life through the lens of astrology.

Chapter 43: Future of Dog Astrology: Emerging Trends and Research in the Field of Canine Astrology

Dog astrology has experienced a surge in popularity as more people seek to understand their canine companions through the lens of the zodiac. The growing interest in pet astrology reflects a broader trend of blending ancient wisdom with modern science, as pet owners increasingly look to astrology for insights into their dogs' behavior, emotional needs, and overall well-being. As the field of canine astrology evolves, new trends, technologies, and research are emerging that could revolutionize our understanding of how celestial movements affect our dogs.

In this chapter, we will explore the future of dog astrology, including upcoming trends, innovative tools, and areas of potential research. From personalized dog horoscopes and AI-powered astrology apps to deeper studies on astrological influence, the future of canine astrology holds exciting possibilities for dog lovers and astrology enthusiasts alike.

The Rising Popularity of Dog Astrology

In recent years, astrology has seen a resurgence in mainstream culture, and this growing interest has extended to pets, especially dogs. As more pet owners turn to astrology for insights into their dogs' personalities, the demand for personalized astrological services and products has grown. Many are finding that astrology offers a deeper understanding of their dog's needs, helping them navigate everything from training and socialization to emotional bonding and health care.

Several factors have contributed to the rising popularity of dog astrology:

- **Holistic Pet Care:** More pet owners are adopting holistic approaches to their dogs' health and well-being, which includes using astrology as a tool for emotional and behavioral insights.
- **Personalized Pet Services:** With the rise of personalized pet care, owners are seeking tailored services, such as astrological readings and pet horoscopes, to better meet their dogs' unique needs.

- **Social Media Influence:** Astrology-themed content is trending on social media platforms, with influencers and pet lovers sharing dog horoscopes, zodiac-themed pet products, and astrological insights.

This surge in popularity is fueling a demand for more sophisticated tools and services, setting the stage for the next wave of dog astrology advancements.

Emerging Trends in Dog Astrology

As dog astrology continues to evolve, several key trends are emerging that reflect the growing interest and innovation in this field. These trends indicate a future where dog astrology is not only more accessible but also more personalized and scientifically informed.

1. Personalized Dog Horoscopes

While general dog horoscopes based on zodiac signs are already popular, the future of dog astrology is moving toward highly personalized readings. These horoscopes take into account not only your dog's sun sign but also their entire birth chart, including the positions of the moon, planets, and astrological houses at the time of their birth. This comprehensive approach can offer deeper insights into your dog's personality, behavior, and emotional needs.

- **Detailed Birth Charts for Dogs:** Just as human birth charts provide a detailed astrological profile, birth charts for dogs are becoming more common. These charts offer personalized predictions about behavior patterns, compatibility with other pets, and even insights into health and well-being based on planetary influences.

- **Custom Horoscopes by Breed:** Some emerging services are blending astrology with breed-specific characteristics to provide even more accurate and tailored horoscopes. For example, how a Virgo personality manifests in a high-energy breed like a Border

Collie might differ from how it manifests in a laid-back breed like a Basset Hound.

2. AI-Powered Astrology Apps for Dogs

As technology becomes more integrated into pet care, AI-powered apps are playing a significant role in advancing dog astrology. These apps offer pet owners easy access to personalized astrological readings, daily horoscopes, and behavior tips based on their dog's astrological profile.

- **Real-Time Astrological Insights:** Some apps allow users to input their dog's birth information to receive real-time astrological updates that predict how planetary movements, such as retrogrades or lunar phases, will impact their dog's mood and behavior.

- **Customized Behavior Suggestions:** AI-based astrology apps can provide recommendations for training, socialization, and emotional care based on both astrological transits and real-time data about the dog's daily behavior patterns.

- **Integration with Wearable Technology:** Future astrology apps may integrate with wearable pet technology, such as smart collars, to track physical activity, mood, and health indicators. By combining this data with astrological forecasts, these apps can offer holistic care advice that addresses both physical and emotional needs.

3. Zodiac-Themed Pet Products

As pet owners embrace astrology, the market for zodiac-themed pet products is expanding. From zodiac-inspired toys and clothing to astrological pet care kits, these products allow owners to celebrate their dog's sign in fun and practical ways.

- **Astrology-Themed Toys and Accessories:** Look for zodiac-inspired designs in everything from dog toys to collars, leashes, and bedding. These products often highlight the traits of each sign, allowing owners to express their dog's astrological personality.

- **Pet Care Kits Based on Zodiac Signs:** Some companies are creating pet care kits tailored to each zodiac sign. These kits may include grooming products, calming aids, and treats selected based on the unique needs of each sign. For example, a Cancer-themed kit might include calming aromatherapy oils and cozy blankets, while an Aries-themed kit might feature high-energy toys and supplements for joint health.

4. Astrological Pet Events and Workshops

Astrology-themed pet events and workshops are gaining popularity, offering opportunities for dog owners to learn more about astrology and their pets. These events often include expert astrologers, interactive sessions on reading dog birth charts, and discussions on how astrological cycles affect dogs.

- **Astrological Pet Retreats:** Some pet care centers are hosting weekend retreats where dog owners can explore astrology while bonding with their pets. These retreats often include astrological readings, wellness activities, and educational sessions on how to integrate astrology into daily pet care.

- **Workshops on Dog Horoscopes:** Dog astrology workshops provide hands-on guidance on reading and interpreting dog horoscopes. Participants learn how to create and understand their dog's birth chart, and how to use astrological insights for training, behavior management, and emotional support.

Research and Science: Can Astrology Influence Canine Behavior?

While astrology remains a metaphysical practice rather than a science, there is increasing interest in how celestial movements may influence animal behavior. As more pet owners embrace astrology, researchers and experts in animal behavior are beginning to explore whether astrological patterns correlate with changes in dog behavior, health, or emotional states.

1. Exploring Lunar Phases and Dog Behavior

One of the most widely recognized astrological influences on behavior is the effect of lunar phases. Many dog owners report that their dogs become more active, restless, or anxious during full moons. While this observation is largely anecdotal, there is ongoing research into the potential link between lunar cycles and animal behavior.

- **Behavioral Changes During Full Moons:** Some studies suggest that lunar cycles may affect animal behavior, particularly during full moons. Researchers are exploring whether dogs are more prone to restlessness, heightened activity, or mood changes during certain lunar phases.

- **Moon Phases and Emotional Sensitivity:** In dog astrology, the moon is associated with emotions. Future research may delve into how lunar phases impact a dog's emotional responses, especially in more sensitive zodiac signs like Cancer, Scorpio, or Pisces.

2. Astrological Cycles and Canine Health

Astrology also raises questions about whether planetary movements might affect dogs' physical health. While scientific research in this area is still in its infancy, there is growing interest in exploring whether certain astrological cycles align with health patterns in dogs.

- **Retrogrades and Health Issues:** Some astrologers suggest that retrograde periods, especially Mercury retrograde, might impact communication, digestion, or coordination in dogs. Future research could investigate whether there are any statistical correlations between retrogrades and health incidents in pets.

- **Solar and Lunar Eclipses:** Eclipses are thought to bring intense energy shifts, and astrologers often advise humans to rest during these times. Anecdotal reports from dog owners suggest that some dogs may also experience heightened anxiety or agitation during eclipses, leading to potential research into how celestial events affect canine health and behavior.

3. Astrology as a Tool for Emotional Bonding

One of the most exciting areas for future research in dog astrology is the potential for astrology to deepen emotional bonding between dogs and their owners. Many dog owners report feeling a stronger connection to their pets after learning about their zodiac sign and tailoring their care accordingly.

- **Astrological Compatibility Between Dogs and Humans:** Some astrologers believe that certain zodiac signs are more compatible with others, both in dogs and humans. Future research could explore whether understanding astrological compatibility leads to stronger bonds, better communication, and more harmonious relationships between dogs and their human family members.

- **Behavioral Insights Through Astrology:** Just as astrology provides insights into human behavior, it may also offer a framework for understanding dog behavior patterns. Research could examine whether astrology-based training and care approaches result in improved behavior and emotional well-being in dogs.

Conclusion: The Future of Dog Astrology

The future of dog astrology is filled with exciting possibilities, from personalized dog horoscopes and AI-powered apps to research into the potential influence of celestial movements on canine behavior. As the field of dog astrology grows, more pet owners will have access to innovative tools, resources, and insights that allow them to understand and care for their dogs in new and meaningful ways.

Whether you're a long-time astrology enthusiast or a newcomer to the practice, the future of dog astrology promises to deepen the connection between you and your dog, offering a rich blend of ancient wisdom, modern technology, and emerging research. As we look ahead, one thing is clear: dog astrology is here to stay, and it's only getting more exciting.

Appendices

Appendix A: Glossary – Definitions of Key Astrological Terms and Concepts

Astrology is a rich and complex system with its own terminology, much of which can be unfamiliar to those new to the practice. In the context of dog astrology, many of these terms are adapted to better understand how celestial influences affect our canine companions. This glossary is designed to provide clear definitions and explanations of key astrological terms and concepts used throughout **AstroPaws**. Whether you're a seasoned astrology enthusiast or just beginning to explore its relationship to dogs, this glossary will help you navigate the language of the stars.

Ascendant (Rising Sign)

The zodiac sign that was rising on the eastern horizon at the exact moment of birth. In a dog's birth chart, the Ascendant represents their outward personality, how they present themselves to the world, and how they engage with their surroundings.

Aspect

The angular relationship between two or more planets in an astrological chart. Aspects can be harmonious or challenging, depending on the degree of separation between the planets. Common aspects include conjunctions, squares, trines, and oppositions. In dog astrology, aspects influence behavior patterns, emotional responses, and relationships.

Astrological Houses

The twelve divisions of the astrological chart, each representing different areas of life. In dog astrology, the houses provide insight into specific aspects of a dog's behavior, relationships, health, and daily routines. For example, the 6th house relates to health and wellness, while the 7th house focuses on relationships and partnerships.

Birth Chart (Natal Chart)

A map of the sky at the exact moment of birth, showing the positions of the Sun, Moon, planets, and other celestial bodies. A dog's birth chart provides a detailed snapshot of their personality, emotional tendencies, and life path based on the alignment of the planets.

Cardinal Signs

One of the three astrological qualities, which include cardinal, fixed, and mutable signs. Cardinal signs (Aries, Cancer, Libra, and Capricorn) are initiators and leaders, associated with new beginnings and active energy. In dogs, cardinal signs tend to be proactive, assertive, and eager to take the lead in activities.

Celestial Bodies

Planets, stars, moons, and other objects in space that have astrological significance. Each celestial body is believed to influence different aspects of behavior, personality, and emotions. For example, the Sun represents vitality and core identity, while the Moon governs emotions.

Conjunction

An astrological aspect that occurs when two planets are in the same zodiac sign and degree. Conjunctions amplify the energy of both planets, creating a powerful and concentrated influence. In dog astrology, conjunctions can indicate strong behavioral traits or emotional tendencies.

Cusp

The dividing line between two zodiac signs. A dog born on the cusp may exhibit traits from both adjacent signs. For example, a dog born on the cusp of Leo and Virgo might have Leo's confidence and Virgo's practicality.

Decan

Each zodiac sign is divided into three decans, or 10-degree sections, each ruled by a different planet. Decans add nuance to a dog's personality, providing a deeper understanding of how the traits of a zodiac sign manifest. For example, a first-decans Aries dog may exhibit stronger leadership qualities than a third-decans Aries.

Eclipse

A celestial event where the Sun or Moon is obscured, typically by the Earth's shadow or the Moon. Solar and lunar eclipses are significant in astrology, often signaling major changes or shifts in energy. In dog astrology, eclipses may affect a dog's mood, energy levels, and overall behavior.

Elements

The four basic qualities that divide the zodiac signs: fire, earth, air, and water. Each element is associated with specific traits:

- **Fire (Aries, Leo, Sagittarius):** Energetic, passionate, and action-oriented.
- **Earth (Taurus, Virgo, Capricorn):** Grounded, practical, and focused on stability.
- **Air (Gemini, Libra, Aquarius):** Intellectual, communicative, and social.
- **Water (Cancer, Scorpio, Pisces):** Emotional, intuitive, and nurturing.

Fixed Signs

The second of the three qualities (cardinal, fixed, mutable). Fixed signs (Taurus, Leo, Scorpio, Aquarius) are stable, reliable, and resistant to change. In dogs, fixed signs often exhibit strong loyalty and determination, thriving in consistent environments.

Full Moon

The phase of the Moon when it is fully illuminated by the Sun. In astrology, the full moon represents culmination, heightened emotions, and energy. Dogs may show increased activity or sensitivity during the full moon, reflecting its intense energy.

Grand Trine

An aspect formed when three planets are equally spaced (120 degrees apart), creating an equilateral triangle in the birth chart. A grand trine indicates harmony and ease in the areas of life associated with the planets involved. In dog astrology, this suggests a well-balanced, easygoing nature in your pet.

Lunar Phases

The eight distinct phases of the Moon, from the new moon to the full moon. Each phase carries different astrological energy:

- **New Moon:** Beginnings, fresh starts, and setting intentions.
- **Waxing Crescent:** Growth and development.
- **First Quarter:** Action and decision-making.
- **Waxing Gibbous:** Refinement and preparation for culmination.
- **Full Moon:** Peak energy and emotional intensity.
- **Waning Gibbous:** Reflection and gratitude.
- **Last Quarter:** Release and letting go.
- **Waning Crescent:** Rest and rejuvenation before the new cycle.

Mutable Signs

The final of the three qualities (cardinal, fixed, mutable). Mutable signs (Gemini, Virgo, Sagittarius, Pisces) are adaptable, flexible, and open to change. Dogs with mutable signs often display versatility and a willingness to adjust to new environments or routines.

Natal Planet

A planet's position in a birth chart. In dog astrology, each natal planet governs specific traits and behaviors:

- **Sun:** Core identity and vitality.
- **Moon:** Emotions and instinctive reactions.
- **Mercury:** Communication and intelligence.
- **Venus:** Affection and relationships.
- **Mars:** Energy and drive.
- **Jupiter:** Growth and expansion.
- **Saturn:** Discipline and responsibility.
- **Uranus:** Innovation and change.
- **Neptune:** Dreams and intuition.
- **Pluto:** Power and transformation.

Opposition

An aspect formed when two planets are directly opposite each other in the zodiac (180 degrees apart). Oppositions create tension but also opportunities for growth and balance. In dog astrology, oppositions may indicate internal conflicts, such as a struggle between independence and attachment.

Planetary Ruler

Each zodiac sign is ruled by a specific planet that influences the traits and behaviors of that sign. For example, Aries is ruled by Mars, which governs energy and drive, while Taurus is ruled by Venus, which influences love, beauty, and comfort.

Retrograde

A period when a planet appears to move backward in its orbit from Earth's perspective. Retrogrades are known for causing delays, miscommunication, or internal reflection. In dog astrology, retrogrades (especially Mercury retrograde) may impact communication, training, or routine changes for dogs.

Rising Sign (Ascendant)

The zodiac sign that was rising over the eastern horizon at the exact time of birth. The rising sign represents how a dog presents itself to the world, how it interacts with new situations, and how it is perceived by others.

Square

An aspect that occurs when two planets are 90 degrees apart, forming a challenging or tense relationship. Squares indicate areas of conflict or difficulty but also opportunities for growth and resolution. In dog astrology, squares may highlight behavioral challenges or emotional conflicts that need attention.

Stellium

A group of three or more planets located in the same zodiac sign or astrological house. A stellium intensifies the energy of the sign or house it occupies, amplifying its influence on personality, behavior, and life events.

Sun Sign

The zodiac sign the Sun was in at the time of birth. The Sun sign represents a dog's core personality, vitality, and overall character. It is one of the most important elements in understanding a dog's behavior and preferences.

Synastry

A technique used in astrology to compare two birth charts to determine compatibility. In dog astrology, synastry can be used to evaluate how well a dog gets along with other pets or human family members based on astrological factors.

T-Square

An aspect pattern formed when two planets in opposition both square a third planet, creating a challenging triangular shape in the birth chart. T-squares indicate tension and the need for balance between conflicting energies. In dogs, this may manifest as restlessness or behavioral challenges.

Trine

An aspect that occurs when two planets are 120 degrees apart, creating a harmonious and supportive relationship. Trines indicate ease and flow, where natural talents and positive behaviors are expressed effortlessly.

Zodiac

The 12 signs that form the astrological wheel, each occupying 30 degrees of the 360-degree chart. The zodiac signs are divided into four elements (fire, earth, air, water) and three qualities (cardinal, fixed, mutable), with each sign offering unique traits and influences.

Conclusion

This glossary provides foundational knowledge of key astrological terms and concepts, helping you better understand the language of astrology and its application to your dog. As you deepen your understanding of dog astrology, these terms will become essential tools for interpreting birth charts, reading horoscopes, and navigating the complex relationship between celestial movements and canine behavior.

Appendix B: Charts – Astrological Charts and Diagrams for Quick Reference

Astrology can be complex, but visual aids such as charts and diagrams make it easier to understand key concepts at a glance. This appendix is designed to provide you with quick-reference astrological charts related to dog astrology, including zodiac traits, planetary influences, moon phases, and astrological aspects. These charts serve as practical tools to deepen your understanding of how celestial bodies impact your dog's behavior, personality, and emotional needs.

1. The Zodiac Wheel

The zodiac wheel divides the sky into twelve 30-degree sections, each representing one of the zodiac signs. These signs are grouped by element and quality, influencing the core traits of each sign. This chart will help you understand the overall structure of the zodiac and how each sign fits into the larger astrological system.

Zodiac Sign	Symbol	Element	Quality	Ruling Planet	Dates
Aries	◈	Fire	Cardinal	Mars	March 21 - April 19
Taurus	◈	Earth	Fixed	Venus	April 20 - May 20
Gemini	◈	Air	Mutable	Mercury	May 21 - June 20

Zodiac Sign	Symbol	Element	Quality	Ruling Planet	Dates
Cancer	◇	Water	Cardinal	Moon	June 21 - July 22
Leo	◇	Fire	Fixed	Sun	July 23 - August 22
Virgo	◇	Earth	Mutable	Mercury	August 23 - September 22
Libra	◇	Air	Cardinal	Venus	September 23 - October 22
Scorpio	◇	Water	Fixed	Pluto	October 23 - November 21
Sagittarius	◇	Fire	Mutable	Jupiter	November 22 - December 21
Capricorn	◇	Earth	Cardinal	Saturn	December 22 - January 19

Zodiac Sign	Symbol	Element	Quality	Ruling Planet	Dates
Aquarius	♒	Air	Fixed	Uranus	January 20 - February 18
Pisces	♓	Water	Mutable	Neptune	February 19 - March 20

Quick Tips:

- **Cardinal Signs:** Aries, Cancer, Libra, Capricorn – Initiators of new energy.
- **Fixed Signs:** Taurus, Leo, Scorpio, Aquarius – Stable and determined.
- **Mutable Signs:** Gemini, Virgo, Sagittarius, Pisces – Adaptable and flexible.

2. Planetary Influence Chart

Each planet governs specific aspects of behavior, personality, and emotional needs. In this chart, you'll find an overview of the planets and their corresponding influences on your dog.

Planet	Astrological Influence	Key Traits for Dogs
Sun	Core identity, vitality, and energy	Self-confidence, leadership, personality
Moon	Emotions, instincts, and emotional responses	Sensitivity, nurturing tendencies
Mercury	Communication, intellect, and reasoning	Learning ability, curiosity, mental agility
Venus	Affection, love, and relationships	Social bonding, playfulness, and loyalty
Mars	Energy, drive, and physical activity	Enthusiasm, assertiveness, aggression
Jupiter	Growth, optimism, and expansion	Playfulness, optimism, curiosity
Saturn	Discipline, responsibility, and structure	Patience, obedience, persistence
Uranus	Innovation, freedom, and unpredictability	Independence, spontaneity, adaptability
Neptune	Intuition, dreams, and imagination	Sensitivity, empathy, creativity

Planet	Astrological Influence	Key Traits for Dogs
Pluto	Transformation, power, and depth	Intensity, focus, emotional depth

Quick Tips:

- **Sun and Moon:** Focus on core personality and emotions.
- **Mercury and Venus:** Influence communication and relationships with humans and other pets.
- **Mars and Saturn:** Govern physical energy, discipline, and structure.

3. Moon Phases and Their Influence on Dogs

The Moon's phases have a significant impact on dogs' moods and behaviors. Use this diagram to understand how different moon phases influence your dog's emotional and physical energy.

Moon Phase	Astrological Influence	Dog Behavior
New Moon	Beginnings, new opportunities	Calm, introspective, ready for new experiences
Waxing Crescent	Growth, forward movement	Increased focus, gradual energy build-up

Moon Phase	Astrological Influence	Dog Behavior
First Quarter	Action, challenges	Restlessness, problem-solving, increased activity
Waxing Gibbous	Refinement, progress	Motivated, determined, refining learned behaviors
Full Moon	Peak energy, heightened emotions	Hyperactive, emotionally sensitive, or restless
Waning Gibbous	Reflection, gratitude	Calmer, reflective, showing gratitude and bonding
Last Quarter	Release, letting go	Tired, ready for rest, letting go of accumulated stress
Waning Crescent	Rest, rejuvenation	Low energy, introspective, need for quiet and comfort

Quick Tips:

- **Full Moon:** Expect heightened energy and possible restlessness.
- **Waning Crescent:** Encourage rest and relaxation for recovery.

4. Aspects: Harmonious vs. Challenging

Astrological aspects represent the angles between planets and are crucial in understanding the interactions between different energies in your dog's chart.

Aspect	Degrees	Type	Effect
Conjunction	0°	Harmonious/Neutral	Amplifies the energy of both planets
Sextile	60°	Harmonious	Opportunity for cooperation, ease, and flow
Square	90°	Challenging	Tension, conflict, obstacles to overcome

Aspect	Degrees	Type	Effect
Trine	120°	Harmonious	Natural talents, effortless energy
Opposition	180°	Challenging	Polarized energy, need for balance, internal conflict

Quick Tips:

- **Harmonious Aspects (Sextile, Trine):** Encourage smooth behavior, ease in training, and harmonious relationships.
- **Challenging Aspects (Square, Opposition):** May indicate areas where your dog needs extra patience or training.

5. Dog Zodiac Traits at a Glance

Here's a quick reference chart summarizing the key traits of each zodiac sign as they apply to dogs, helping you quickly identify the behaviors and needs of your dog based on their sun sign.

Zodiac Sign	Key Traits	Best Environment
Aries	Energetic, bold, adventurous	Large spaces for exercise, outdoor activities
Taurus	Loyal, calm, comfort-seeking	Cozy, quiet home with plenty of rest areas
Gemini	Playful, curious, sociable	Dynamic environments with mental stimulation
Cancer	Emotional, nurturing, protective	Safe, stable home with close human bonding
Leo	Confident, attention-loving, bold	Social, active home where they can show off
Virgo	Practical, disciplined, focused	Tidy, well-organized environment with routines
Libra	Sociable, charming, peace-seeking	Aesthetically pleasing home, balanced lifestyle
Scorpio	Intense, loyal, protective	Quiet, secure spaces for privacy and bonding

Zodiac Sign	Key Traits	Best Environment
Sagittarius	Adventurous, independent, optimistic	Access to outdoor adventures and freedom
Capricorn	Disciplined, responsible, serious	Structured environment with clear roles/tasks
Aquarius	Independent, quirky, intellectual	Open spaces with freedom to explore and innovate
Pisces	Gentle, intuitive, emotionally sensitive	Calm, peaceful home with nurturing energy

Conclusion

This appendix offers quick and easy access to essential astrological charts and diagrams, allowing you to reference important astrological concepts as you deepen your understanding of how the zodiac influences your dog. Whether you're checking your dog's moon phase behaviors or looking at planetary influences in their birth chart, these charts serve as helpful tools for connecting astrological insights with practical pet care.

Appendix C: Recommended Reading – Books, Articles, and Online Resources for Further Study

For those who wish to dive deeper into the fascinating world of astrology and its connection to canine behavior, this appendix offers a curated list of books, articles, and online resources. Whether you're interested in further exploring dog astrology, understanding the broader principles of astrology, or delving into related fields such as pet psychology and holistic pet care, these resources provide a wealth of knowledge for further study.

Books on Dog Astrology and Pet Astrology

1. **"Star Signs for Pets: How Astrology Shapes Your Pet's Personality"** by Jackie Ford
   This book explores the impact of astrology on pets, including dogs, and provides detailed insights into how each zodiac sign influences their behavior, health, and relationships. It includes tips on how to use astrological knowledge to strengthen your bond with your pet.

2. **"Astrology for Dogs: Unlocking the Mysteries of the Canine Zodiac"** by Helena Kingsley
   A comprehensive guide specifically focused on understanding how zodiac signs shape a dog's personality. This book covers each sign in depth, with practical advice for training, care, and behavior management based on astrological traits.

3. **"The Pet Lover's Guide to Astrology"** by Marion D. March
   This book offers an overview of how astrology influences pets and their relationships with humans. While not exclusively focused

on dogs, it provides valuable insights into using astrology to understand and care for all types of pets.

4. **"The Stars and Your Pet: How Astrology Influences the Animals in Your Life"** by David Rae
   Covering both astrology and animal behavior, this book examines the connection between celestial movements and how they affect pets, particularly dogs. It's a practical resource for anyone looking to combine astrology with daily pet care.

5. **"Cosmic Pets: The Astrological Guide to Your Pet's Personality and Behavior"** by Jane Thompson
   A fun, easy-to-read book that delves into the astrology of pets. It provides entertaining and informative astrological profiles for each zodiac sign, helping owners understand their pet's needs, quirks, and preferences.

Books on General Astrology

1. **"The Only Astrology Book You'll Ever Need"** by Joanna Martine Woolfolk
   This is an essential resource for anyone new to astrology. It covers the fundamentals of astrology, including birth charts, planetary influences, and the meanings of each zodiac sign. While focused on human astrology, it's a foundational text that applies to pet astrology as well.

2. **"Astrology for the Soul"** by Jan Spiller
   A deeper exploration of astrology, focusing on the concept of "North Nodes," or the soul's purpose in life. While primarily for human astrology, understanding these deeper astrological concepts can help you explore the spiritual aspects of astrology that may influence animals.

3. **"Planets in Transit: Life Cycles for Living"** by Robert Hand
   This book explores how planetary transits affect life events and behaviors. It's a valuable resource for those looking to understand

how daily and yearly celestial movements may influence your dog's mood, health, or behavior patterns.

4. **"The Astrological Houses: The Spectrum of Individual Experience"** by Dane Rudhyar

   Rudhyar's book provides a detailed explanation of the twelve astrological houses, which are crucial for understanding the complexities of birth charts. This knowledge can be applied to reading your dog's birth chart for more detailed insights.

5. **"Parker's Astrology: The Definitive Guide to Using Astrology in Every Aspect of Your Life"** by Julia and Derek Parker

   A comprehensive guide to astrology, Parker's Astrology covers everything from birth charts to relationship compatibility. It's an excellent resource for learning the basics and advanced techniques of astrology, with applications to pet astrology.

Articles and Journals on Pet Astrology and Behavior

1. **"Zodiac Traits in Dogs: How Your Pet's Sign Shapes Their Behavior"** – PetMD

   An insightful article that breaks down the zodiac traits in dogs, this resource is helpful for understanding how astrology can influence a dog's behavior, personality, and training needs.

2. **"Astrology for Pets: How to Use the Stars to Understand Your Furry Friends"** – The Spruce Pets

   A general introduction to pet astrology, this article provides an overview of how to apply astrology to your dog's life, including tips on creating a birth chart and interpreting planetary movements.

3. **"The Lunar Influence on Pet Behavior: How the Phases of the Moon Affect Animals"** – Animal Wellness Magazine

   This article explores the connection between lunar phases and animal behavior, providing insights into how different moon phases may influence your dog's energy, mood, and emotions.

4. **"Planetary Movements and Pet Care: What Astrology Tells Us About Animal Health"** – Pet Astrology Journal
   Focused on how planetary transits impact pets' physical and emotional health, this article is a valuable resource for pet owners who want to understand how astrology can inform their pet's care and well-being.

5. **"Synastry for Pets and Owners: Astrological Compatibility Between You and Your Dog"** – The Astrology Hub
   This article explores the concept of synastry (relationship astrology) as it applies to pets and their owners. It provides practical advice on how to read compatibility between your zodiac sign and your dog's.

Online Resources for Dog Astrology Enthusiasts

1. **AstroPets.com**
   A comprehensive website dedicated to pet astrology, AstroPets provides daily horoscopes for pets, in-depth zodiac profiles, and insights into how to care for pets based on their astrological sign.

2. **StarryPaws.net**
   Specializing in astrological readings for dogs, StarryPaws offers personalized horoscopes, birth chart interpretations, and advice on how planetary transits affect your dog's mood and behavior.

3. **The Astrology Hub – Pets Section**
   The Astrology Hub is a popular astrology website with a section dedicated to pets. It includes articles, videos, and podcasts on how astrology affects animals, particularly dogs, and how to apply astrological insights to pet care.

4. **PetAstrologyBlog.com**
   A blog devoted to the intersection of pet care and astrology, this site covers everything from birth charts to lunar influences on pets. The blog is frequently updated with astrological forecasts for pets and advice for using astrology in training and care.

5. **AstroSeek.com – Pet Astrology Forum**
   AstroSeek is a popular astrology platform with an active forum for pet astrology discussions. Users can ask questions, share insights, and engage in conversations about how celestial events impact their pets.

Research Studies on Animals and Astrology

1. **"The Effect of Lunar Phases on Animal Behavior"** – Journal of Animal Behavior
   A research paper that explores whether lunar cycles have a measurable effect on animal behavior, including dogs. It provides scientific perspectives on the connection between lunar phases and changes in mood, activity, and restlessness in pets.
2. **"Planetary Influence on Animal Behavior: A Study of Dogs and Celestial Movements"** – International Journal of Astrology and Behavior Studies
   This study investigates the relationship between planetary transits and behavioral changes in animals, with a focus on how dogs respond to astrological influences such as Mercury retrograde and solar eclipses.
3. **"Astrological Synastry in Pets and Their Owners: The Role of Zodiac Compatibility in Pet-Owner Relationships"** – Astrological Research Journal
   Focused on the compatibility between pets and their human companions, this study examines how zodiac sign pairings influence the bond between dogs and their owners, and whether certain signs are more harmonious than others.

Conclusion

Whether you're looking for in-depth guides, scientific research, or engaging online communities, this appendix offers a wide array of resources to help you further your study of dog astrology. These books, articles, and websites provide valuable insights into how astrology shapes the lives of our canine companions, giving you the tools to strengthen your bond and provide personalized care for your dog based on the stars. Happy reading and exploring!

Message from the Author:

I hope you enjoyed this book, I love astrology and knew there was not a book such as this out on the shelf. I love metaphysical items as well. Please check out my other books:
   -Life of Government Benefits
   -My life of Hell
   -My life with Hydrocephalus
   -Red Sky
   -World Domination:Woman's rule
   -World Domination:Woman's Rule 2: The War
   -Life and Banishment of Apophis: book 1
   -The Kidney Friendly Diet
   -The Ultimate Hemp Cookbook
   -Creating a Dispensary(legally)
   -Cleanliness throughout life: the importance of showering from childhood to adulthood.
   -Strong Roots: The Risks of Overcoddling children
   -Hemp Horoscopes: Cosmic Insights and Earthly Healing
   - Celestial Hemp Navigating the Zodiac: Through the Green Cosmos
   -Astrological Hemp: Aligning The Stars with Earth's Ancient Herb
   -The Astrological Guide to Hemp: Stars, Signs, and Sacred Leaves
   -Green Growth: Innovative Marketing Strategies for your Hemp Products and Dispensary
   -Cosmic Cannabis
   -Astrological Munchies

-Henry The Hemp

-Zodiacal Roots: The Astrological Soul Of Hemp

- **Green Constellations: Intersection of Hemp and Zodiac**

-Hemp in The Houses: An astrological Adventure Through The Cannabis Galaxy

-Galactic Ganja Guide

Heavenly Hemp

Zodiac Leaves

Doctor Who Astrology

Cannastrology

Stellar Satvias and Cosmic Indicas

Celestial Cannabis: A Zodiac Journey

AstroHerbology: The Sky and The Soil: Volume 1

AstroHerbology:Celestial Cannabis:Volume 2

Cosmic Cannabis Cultivation

The Starry Guide to Herbal Harmony: Volume 1

The Starry Guide to Herbal Harmony: Cannabis Universe: Volume 2

Yugioh Astrology: Astrological Guide to Deck, Duels and more

Nightmare Mansion: Echoes of The Abyss

Nightmare Mansion 2: Legacy of Shadows

Nightmare Mansion 3: Shadows of the Forgotten

Nightmare Mansion 4: Echoes of the Damned

The Life and Banishment of Apophis: Book 2

Nightmare Mansion: Halls of Despair

Healing with Herb: Cannabis and Hydrocephalus

Planetary Pot: Aligning with Astrological Herbs: Volume 1

Fast Track to Freedom: 30 Days to Financial Independence Using AI, Assets, and Agile Hustles

Cosmic Hemp Pathways

How to Become Financially Free in 30 Days: 10,000 Paths to Prosperity

Zodiacal Herbage: Astrological Insights: Volume 1

Nightmare Mansion: Whispers in the Walls
The Daleks Invade Atlantis
Henry the hemp and Hydrocephalus

10X The Kidney Friendly Diet
Cannabis Universe: Adult coloring book
Hemp Astrology: The Healing Power of the Stars
Zodiacal Herbage: Astrological Insights: Cannabis Universe: Volume 2
<u>Planetary Pot: Aligning with Astrological Herbs: Cannabis Universes: Volume 2</u>
Doctor Who Meets the Replicators and SG-1: The Ultimate Battle for Survival
Nightmare Mansion: Curse of the Blood Moon
<u>The Celestial Stoner: A Guide to the Zodiac</u>
Cosmic Pleasures: Sex Toy Astrology for Every Sign
Hydrocephalus Astrology: Navigating the Stars and Healing Waters
Lapis and the Mischievous Chocolate Bar

Celestial Positions: Sexual Astrology for Every Sign
Apophis's Shadow Work Journal: **:** A Journey of Self-Discovery and Healing
Kinky Cosmos: Sexual Kink Astrology for Every Sign
Digital Cosmos: The Astrological Digimon Compendium
Stellar Seeds: The Cosmic Guide to Growing with Astrology
Apophis's Daily Gratitude Journal

Cat Astrology: Feline Mysteries of the Cosmos
The Cosmic Kama Sutra: An Astrological Guide to Sexual Positions
Unleash Your Potential: A Guided Journal Powered by AI Insights
Whispers of the Enchanted Grove

Cosmic Pleasures: An Astrological Guide to Sexual Kinks

369, 12 Manifestation Journal

Whisper of the nocturne journal(blank journal for writing or drawing)

If you want solar for your home go here: https://www.harborsolar.live/apophisenterprises/

get some solar here
Matthew Petchinsky

Get Some Tarot cards: https://www.makeplayingcards.com/sell/apophis-occult-shop

**get some tarot mats and tarot cards here
and other goodies**
Matthew Petchinsky

Get some shirts: https://www.bonfire.com/store/apophis-shirt-emporium/

get some shirts here
Matthew Petchinsky

Instagrams:
@apophis_enterprises,
@apophisbookemporium,
@apophisscardshop

Twitter: @apophisenterpr1

Tiktok:@apophisenterprise

Youtube: @sg1fan23477, @FiresideRetreatKingdom

Podcast: Apophis Chat Zone: https://open.spotify.com/show/
5zXbrCLEV2xzCp8ybrfHsk?si=fb4d4fdbdce44dec

Listen to my podcast here
Matthew Petchinsky

Newsletter: https://apophiss-newsletter-27c897.beehiiv.com/

sign up for my newsletter here
Matthew Petchinsky